FRED TRUEMAN'S CRICKET MASTERPIECES

FRED TRUEMAN'S CRICKET MASTERPIECES

Classic tales from the pavilion

Fred Trueman

with Peter Grosvenor

SIDGWICK & JACKSON

LONDON

**The publishers would like to thank
Roy Ullyett and the *Daily Express*
for kindly giving permission for us
to reproduce the cartoons in this book.**

Book design by Alan Chalk

First published in Great Britain in 1990 by
Sidgwick & Jackson Limited
Cavaye Place
London SW10 9PG

This edition published 1991 by Sidgwick & Jackson

ISBN 0 283 06112 X

Photoset and printed in Great Britain by
Butler & Tanner Limited, Frome, Somerset

Contents

Introduction

Cricket, greatest of games, has also produced the greatest literature, and this anthology attempts to capture some of it. Cricket is also a game of swings and roundabouts, thank God. If it hadn't been for our surprise revival against the West Indies in 1990 the national game would have been at a low ebb indeed. During the pathetic débâcle against Australia in 1989 there were times when I was ashamed to be an Englishman. We were shattered by two old men in cricketing terms – Alderman, then thirty-three, and Lawson, thirty-one, two ordinary seam bowlers which every county had in the old days, and most of whom never played for England. I was so disgusted on that final day of the First Test at Leeds that I had to leave the Radio Three commentary box because I was frightened what I might say. From the opening moments that morning, with Australia still batting, David Gower, instead of going on the attack, spread the field as if it were a one-day game with singles there for the taking. That, combined with sloppy bowling, gave away 72 runs in ten overs, thus letting Border, the Australian skipper, declare earlier than he need have done at 220 for 3, which set England an impossible 402. Then Australia bowled us out in under four hours on a wicket which was worth 600. As Gower himself said: 'We snatched defeat from the jaws of safety.' Too true.

Bobby Simpson said to me, 'What's the matter with this England side? They don't want to play.' Wally Grout, the late Australian wicket-keeper, used to say, when Ken Barrington or I walked out to play for England, that you could see the Union Jacks fluttering on our backs. That was what we lacked in 1989 and have now hopefully recovered. I think David Gower is a wonderful guy, but he's too laid back to be a good leader, too lenient with his troops. If Ian Botham is lying on the ground at Trent Bridge as I once saw him, while the rest of the team are going through their physical jerks, David is not the sort of man to give him a rocket. To be a good captain you've got to be a bit aloof, so that the lads take notice when you crack the whip.

But England's deficiencies weren't the whole story. The seeds of the great Australian victory were much the same as those of England's revival in the West Indies – planning and preparation. The left-handed opener Mark Taylor was the real revelation. From being a virtual unknown he finished the season challenging the great Don Bradman's aggregates for a series. He was aided by his own calm and determined temperament on the field and by four hard seasons in the New South Wales side having been blooded at a much younger age than we dare to contemplate in England. But there was more to it than that. Taylor had prepared himself for English conditions by playing for Green Mount in the Bolton League, where he established a league record of six centuries in a season, averaged 64.15 and just missed the aggregate record with 1,483 runs. 'Playing with ten amateurs taught me responsibility and tightened up my defence,' he said.

Then there was Dean Jones, a brilliant success at number five, who played for Nostell in the Leeds League. 'I learned more at Nostell about playing on difficult wickets where the ball does something than in a whole career in Australia,' he told me. In fact all the great successes in the Aussie team had benefited from their experiences of playing in England – Steve Waugh for Somerset, Alderman for Gloucester and Kent, Lawson for Lancashire, David Boon in league cricket in the Midlands, and Alan Border for Essex where he learned a lot playing under the experienced Essex skipper Keith Fletcher and still more about the weaknesses of his Essex team-mate Graham Gooch. English wickets after the faster Australian ones require adjustment, but they give you more time to play.

It could be that the Australians abused the overseas quota. They had Mark Waugh playing for Essex in 1989, getting paid and getting the experience of English conditions, who could have been pulled out of the Essex side at any time to play for Australia in the event of injuries. The Australians, led by their coach Bobby Simpson, had the whole thing as meticulously planned and ruthlessly mounted as Douglas Jardine had for England in the Bodyline Tour of Australia in 1932–3. There was team work and a togetherness which extended right into the practice sessions. And these sometimes took place after a hard day's play if there was something that needed to be worked on.

The Englishmen created many of their own difficulties, of course. I noticed that Gooch all too often finished a forcing shot to a straight ball with the leading edge of the bat facing the bowler, and the face of the bat pointing towards mid-wicket or mid-on. This suggests that only a quarter of the face of the bat was actually facing down the wicket at the moment of strike. No wonder poor Goochie turned Alderman, an ordinary medium-pace seamer who scarcely swings the ball but can keep it straight, into an unplayable demon bowler. Geoff Lawson is an unremarkable medium-fast bowler; Merv Hughes is more sound and fury than real pace. But we only managed to last a whole day on the square against them on one occasion. So many of our batsmen played around the front of the pad instead of down the line and they succumbed countless times to LBW decisions by ignoring the basic rule – either play forward as far as possible, which minimizes the chance of an LBW decision against you, or back as far as possible, which gives you more time. But the characteristic defensive shot of the Englishmen was the half-cock shuffle. The ball would hit the pad mere inches in front of the popping crease or even on it – a dead easy decision for the umpires. Attacking shots were often played with the feet close together and the bat away from the body. Given a little movement in the air, it was a birthday treat for the bowlers. However, once you get the feet in the right position, the pads also become a second line of defence. All the great batsmen I played with or against, Hutton, May, Compton, Cowdrey, Harvey, Weekes, Worrell, Walcott and Sobers had an almost unsurmountable defence. They were seldom clean bowled.

Then there is the baseball stance, bat held aloft, favoured by most of the English line-up in 1989 and apparently necessitated by the use of very heavy bats. The theory of the heavy bat is that even the half-shot or the miss-hit shot can be speeded to the boundary. But at what a cost. 'Standing with your bat in the air destroys rhythm and balance,' says Bobby Simpson. 'Our batters stand much easier at the crease. Our bats are also very much lighter than the Englishmen's and getting lighter all the time.'

Another common failing is moving before the ball is delivered. This gives the bowler an enormous advantage. The best thing is to make your play a fraction after the ball is released – Len Hutton was a master at that. You never saw people like Sobers, May, Compton or Graveney rushing around the crease. But today among English batsmen the people who keep still and don't move till exactly the right moment are the exceptions.

Mind you, there were some bad LBW decisions against the Englishmen. After the Pakistan débâcle, I do believe our own umpires, whom I consider to be the best in the world, bent over backwards to be fair to the opposition. Gooch got bad LBW decisions against him at Leeds and the Oval, Tim Robinson had another at Old Trafford. Even as an old bowler I am still of the firm opinion that batsmen should be given the benefit of the doubt. Conversely, Dean Jones looked plumb to me at Old Trafford and Steve Waugh should have been given out three times before he made 50 at Lords. He went on to make a match-winning 152 not out. Border survived an obvious catch by Botham at Old Trafford. The appealing by the Australian team in 1989 was diabolical and designed I think to intimidate the umpire into a decision. There were appeals from third man and cover for LBW, though it wasn't as bad as the Pakistanis in New Zealand the previous winter – they did a sort of war dance around the umpire to get a decision. If captains can't control the players then it is up to the umpires themselves, backed by the authorities, to take a stronger line – perhaps by restricting appeals for LBW and behind wicket catches to wicket-keeper, bowler and the slips. But I should hate to see the day when we have television re-runs to confirm or second guess the umpire's decision. Part of the great game is human error – by umpires as well as players. Our English umpires, if only because they stand in so many more games and have four times the experience, are still the best; but even here standards have slipped.

However, essentially England were beaten by a thoroughly professional approach. For years I have complained about the amateurishness which controls what is supposed to be a professional sport. Some of these men who never had to work hard at the game for a living cannot possibly know as much as the old pros who did it for bread and butter.

At least the disaster of 1989 had one good effect. The England team are now committed to a more professional approach. Having been defeated in 1989 by poor technique, all our batsmen, including the most experienced such as Gooch and Lamb, were prepared to look at themselves on the video camera and make alterations. Because a brilliant batsman like David Gower has made over 7,000 runs in Test cricket, it does not mean he has nothing to learn. World-class golfers like Sandy Lyle and Nick Faldo are forever studying themselves on video and taking professional advice, either because they had developed faults they did not know about or because not quite orthodox techniques that have been useful in the past now need to be replaced by something more reliable. Gower made many runs flashing outside the off stump, often with feet far from the ball. But now that technique of his has passed its sell-by date. He has been sussed too often by the opposition. He could have taken a leaf from the book of the England players who toured the West Indies. I am told that at Kingston, Jamaica, during England's first Test victory, there were players queuing up at the Sky TV room to see videos of their dismissals. In my day videos to sort out poor techniques were a rarity. Today they are added benefits. But they can't replace, only emphasize, the old-fashioned virtues: for batsmen to play down the line with the foot pointing to the ball; for the bowler to keep the ball well up and straight or just outside the offstump. 'There is no mystery about it,' said Alec Bedser. 'It's the way we played all the time. I have been telling England players for years, but they never listen.'

Now they are listening, and the other key to their success is physical fitness. I reckon I kept fit enough in a season by bowling over 1,000 overs and bowling fast. Only a handful of bowlers in an average English season bowl half that total today. The busiest bowler in 1989 was Somerset's Vic Marks with 843.5 overs of gentle offspin. Nowadays, particularly in the field, because of the influence of the one-day game, baseball standards of agility, running and catching are required. So no one should have a place in the England team without the highest standard of fitness. All the hard training sessions at the Lilleshall Centre before the England team left and the rigorous fitness sessions during and between games in the West Indies paid obvious dividends. Motivation and pride returned, rather than the almost cynical shoulder-shrugging resignation that attended previous humiliations in the West Indies. And if the tour to South Africa wasn't exactly a blessing in disguise, at least it enabled England to take a young team who weren't all shell-shocked and expecting the worst the moment they set foot in the West Indies.

I believe we should never have allowed the West Indies to dictate to us the nature and shape of Test cricket, contrary to the laws of the game. I have never seen so much short bowling as the West Indies served up after Clive Lloyd became captain in 1974. Thirty or forty years ago the West Indies bowlers would undoubtedly have been called for intimidation. Umpires must take a tougher line now. Significantly, the West Indies' sixteen-year period of dominance did not extend to the one-day game where persistent short-pitched intimidation is impossible because bouncers are called as wides. It is also a disgrace that the West Indies were allowed to drag the over rate down to twelve or thirteen an hour. It's easy to keep four fast bowlers fresh when each is bowling a maximum of six overs an hour. When Brian Statham and myself opened for England we rarely dropped below sixteen or seventeen overs per hour though we were just as fast and our run-ups were long. We gave the paying public value for money.

South Africa – Should we Play There?

Any decent person deplores apartheid – all the more reason therefore to encourage the development of multi-racial cricket in South Africa. Unlike many of South Africa's critics I have been to the country and seen the magnificent work being done in the townships by the South African Cricket Union to foster the game among black youngsters. The set-up in Alexandra township was better than anything I have seen in England. The kids were divided into three age groups: the five- to nine-year-olds, and the intermediate nine- to thirteen-year-olds began with a soft ball. Then for those aged over thirteen it was into the nets with the hard ball, using all-weather pitches which meant an even bounce. I saw a fast bowler who was the quickest I have seen for a fourteen-year-old, a left-arm spinner who bowled natural spin as well as Chinamen and googlies, and a fourteen-year-old all-rounder who looked like a black Botham in the making. All should be playing first-class cricket in three or four years. Graham Cross, the old Leicester player, was coaching, and he told me that if any blacks who came up through the system were good enough they would certainly play for their country, though South Africa would not pick someone as a token black if he wasn't good enough. I am sure Graham was right. The pressure for success is such at all levels these days that skin colour is irrelevant. As I looked at those lads in the townships I was only sorry that some of them weren't qualified to play for Yorkshire.

Along with Peter May, Ray Lindwall, Keith Miller, Neil Harvey and other internationals, I was in South Africa for the centenary celebrations of the South African Cricket Union and to commemorate the first game at Port Elizabeth played against an English team under the captaincy of C. Aubrey Smith, who later became a Hollywood actor. I felt very sad that the ban on South African cricket had meant we had never seen the real genius of a Graham Pollock or Barry Richards or Mike Procter at international level. I was also angry at the hypocrisy of it all. Rugby players and cricketers are singled out but not golfers. Over in England Imran Khan opened the bowling with South African Garth Le Roux for Sussex. Gordon Greenidge opened the batting for Hampshire with Barry Richards and with Andy Roberts to open the bowling. At Warwickshire Barbados-born Gladstone Small opened the bowling with the South African Allan Donald. Mostly the agitation over South African cricket, which has made every effort to be multi-racial, is the work of insignificant little politicians who use it as a world platform to get into the spotlight. A typical example was the ludicrous fuss over Robin Jackman in 1981. As a member of the England team, he was actually arrested and deported from Guyana because of his South African wife – and all this in a country where the black minority discriminates against the Indian majority. It was widely claimed that the government should have stopped Mike Gatting's tour of South Africa. Don't these people realize that we are a democracy, a state of development which has taken us centuries to achieve, and that in a democracy, provided you don't break the law, you are entitled to go when and where you please to earn your living? Now that such great changes have taken place in South Africa – and not just in cricket – it is time to take a sympathetic view.

What's Gone Wrong With Yorkshire Cricket?

The last time Yorkshire won the county championship was the season I hung up my boots in 1968 – and that completed a hat-trick of wins for the county that was once the most feared and respected in England. Since then we have been starved of success.

More than two decades have gone by without Yorkshire winning the championship, and this for a county which had won it thirty-three times over the previous century. In the 1930s Yorkshire were champions no less than seven times and in the 1960s we were champions six times. Since then nothing. Why? Geoffrey Boycott played a significant part in this. Magnificent though he may have been with the bat, though to my mind he was a good player rather than a great player as he always accumulated runs and never dominated the bowling, his failings were as a captain and a team influence. He lacked the ability to handle players and win their loyalty. He was not a team man. The brightest gleam in Geoffrey Boycott's eye was his batting average. Twice, in 1971 and 1979, he finished with an average of over 100 for the season, the only Englishman ever to do it. A remarkable feat, but Yorkshire were not so successful.

Since he was elected a committee member in 1984 while still a player, our unhappy cricketing county has been split from top to bottom. He was the only Yorkshireman to be sent home from a tour, after a golf playing episode in India when he was supposed to be too unfit to play cricket. Yet there is still a fervent Boycott camp.

To place the blame for Yorkshire's sorry plight on Boycott alone would be unfair, since for years as captain he had nothing much to play with. For some reason, or rather a variety of reasons, the conveyer belt of talent has dried up in Yorkshire. There used to be 2,000 games of league cricket played in Yorkshire on a Saturday afternoon. Now there are fewer but there are still a lot. Talented youngsters can enjoy themselves there; some may even go into first-class cricket, but only for a year or two. Then they see how hard the life is and they see the workload involved. When I was working in the mine at Maltby Main in South Yorkshire as an eighteen-year-old, to play for Yorkshire was *the* thing. Traditionally a Yorkshire cap was harder to win than an England cap and some, Brian Close, for instance, have played for their country before being capped for Yorkshire. In those days cricket was a way out if you were hard up. Like Len Hutton a generation before me, I walked into the Yorkshire dressing room with my mind full of legends about Wilfred Rhodes, George Hirst, Hedley Verity, Maurice Leyland and Bill Bowes. My dream was to be up with one of them. In those days the more poverty there was the more talent you could whistle up. Youngsters these days have it much easier. Some of them are thinking of their career structure and their pensions before they have even begun. Not for them the sheer hard work and hard slogging practice it takes to become a top first-class cricketer. The rewards at county level are not great, even with a tax-free benefit which netted me £10,000 in 1962 (not a great sum when set alongside the £100,000-plus of some of today's quite mediocre players).

Cricket offers no security and when I retired there was no pension. Not only that but careers are shorter than they used to be. Jack Hobbs scored more runs after forty than before. That couldn't happen today even with a great player like him: because of the one-day game where saving a single run can be vital, the standard of fielding makes it a young man's game. There is another reason for the shortage of home-grown talent: the game is being choked with far too many overseas' players, either here for the experience or the money or both. There is no comparable right for an English cricketer to go to the West Indies or India and there are fewer opportunities (because of fewer sides) in Australia and New Zealand, while the winter haven of

South Africa is currently blacklisted for those with international ambitions. So we should stop this one-way traffic. It's a ludicrous situation when out of a pool of 190 county players only about three-quarters are qualified to play for England. Never mind a limit of one overseas player per county. I say there should be none. For a start they are keeping out English nationals and weakening the pool from which our Test sides can be drawn. Secondly, the overseas players are getting all the practice they need in the county game so that they can go back to their national sides and beat the hell out of our Test teams. When there was a move for Yorkshire to drop its Yorkshire-born qualification for all players, I said I would quit my membership if that came about and I meant it. But as things stand, the absence of an overseas player, typically a West Indian fast bowler, puts Yorkshire at a unique disadvantage. Some people ask me why there has never been a black face playing for Yorkshire. Actually there has – the world's greatest all-rounder Sir Garfield Sobers. He once turned out for Yorkshire when the county was on a tour of Canada and Bermuda. We were short of a man so he played for us at Somerset in Bermuda. I met him for a drink the night before and retired to bed at about 1 a.m. So far as I know he never went to sleep at all that night, consumed a bottle of brandy, smoked about a hundred cigarettes, and then next morning opened the bowling for Yorkshire with me. He took four wickets before going on to score a century with the bat. There is only one Garry Sobers.

And he is the only black man so far to have played for Yorkshire. So why not one of our own Yorkshire-born blacks or Indians? I can assure you there is no colour prejudice. The country is desperate for success and we would play anyone who is good enough provided he was qualified. My own observation is that the coloured people in Yorkshire are rather cliquish, especially the Asians who tend to play among themselves. I've seen white kids on one side of the street playing football, while Asian kids on the other side are playing cricket. But it's still a mystery that more don't yearn to play for Yorkshire.

Forget the Four Day Game – Other Reforms are Needed

The one-day game has introduced bad habits among our cricketers. Batsmen have to play across the line of the ball throughout an innings and then finish off with a flurry of cow-shot slogs. Some of this has now carried across to the first-class game. As for bowlers, the one-day game has turned them into containment specialists; mediocre seamers bowl negatively because it is better to take no wickets for 20 runs than three or four wickets for 40 runs. This is bad preparation for any seamer faced with bowling a side out on a good wicket in a three-day or four-day game. One-day cricket has also proved to be the death of spin bowling as we knew it; Phil Edmonds, John Emburey, Nick Cook and others all got used to firing the ball in low and quick in one-day cricket. Gone are most of the traditional skills of flight and spin and, when it comes to Test matches, they find it difficult to reproduce those skills, even when wicket-taking rather than containment is the priority. Though the counties are so dependent on receipts from the one-day game, which often exceed receipts from six days of the county championship, we must find a solution.

One way is to make the three-day game more attractive. First off I'd abolish the bonus points system which is fiddly and harmful. Only a minority of people who watch three-day cricket – and that's a minority itself – can understand it. The batting side gets one point after the first 150 runs, a further point for over 200, a third point after 250 runs, a fourth and maximum point after 300 runs, provided they have been made within one hundred overs. The bowling side gets a point after the first three wickets, a second after five wickets, a third after seven wickets, a fourth after nine wickets. But far from encouraging aggressive batting or bowling, the effect has been containment, with the emphasis on keeping the score down rather than getting the side out. The old system of four points for a first innings lead and twelve points for a win (and this was the total points whether the side had or had not got the first innings' four points) was not only simpler but led to a much livelier contest for the first innings. Scoring was faster and there was generally much less need for a contrived result on the third day. But the powers that be, led by chairman of selectors Ted Dexter and England manager Micky Stewart, have decided that four-day cricket will cure most of our ills.

I go along with the argument that if we don't have healthy Test cricket most of the counties will go bankrupt because all are heavily subsidized by Test revenues and one-day internationals. I go along with the argument that we won't have healthy cricket if the counties cannot produce batsmen and bowlers of Test match calibre – batsmen who can build big innings, bowlers who can get the good batsmen out on good wickets. I know that Australia, India, Pakistan and the West Indies – all of whom have shorter days in summer – have domestic competitions played over four days. They also have far fewer first-class games. But I cannot see how four-day cricket, in any case now rejected by the counties, is going to revolutionize England's batting or bowling.

I seem to remember that Jack Hobbs, Walter Hammond, Dennis Compton and the Edriches (Bill and John) batted pretty well in Test matches as well as in three-day games (Hobbs even made a few in the two-day match season of 1919). Len Hutton played exclusively three-day county cricket. He could build a Test innings too. In 1938 at the Oval he spent thirteen hours and twenty minutes at the crease to score 364 runs against the Australians. Micky Stewart argues that the four-day game is necessary for bowlers. 'If you maintain the present domestic structure, fast bowlers will not be able to prepare properly. I don't suppose we have found ten genuinely quick bowlers at home since the war, given our existing programme. With seventy-two days' championship cricket under the three-day system you are asking far too much from them.' But under the four-day system you will still have sixty-four days of cricket. And today's fast bowlers are not exactly overworked. Not one of them in 1989 exceeded 800 overs. Top were medium-fast bowler Angus Fraser with 797.1 overs, Neil Foster with 713.2, Courtney Walsh with 627, Paul Jarvis with 617, Gladstone Small with 537, Malcolm Marshall with 428.3 and Devon Malcolm with 297.5. No one took 100 wickets, the leading taker being Fraser with 92. Any of that would have been a light workload for me. For four consecutive seasons from 1959 to

1962 I bowled over 1,000 overs, with 1,141.5 in 1962 when I was thirty-one and still bowling fast off a long run. Some of today's lads have never had it so good. If there is a shortage of fast bowlers I blame it on social conditions, because there are now many easier ways of earning a living. I would also blame the pitches. When any old seamer can take wickets on a bad pitch there is not much premium on bowling fast.

It's true that most county captains and, we are told, a majority of county players support the switch to four-day cricket. But the treasurers and secretaries are almost to a man against the idea. Festival weeks at Cheltenham or Bath, with all their opportunities for entertainment and sponsorship, in which counties like to cram in two or even three three-day games, plus two one-day games, would be badly hit. Although Graham Gooch, the England and Essex captain, backs the four-day game, Essex's chief executive Peter Edwards says: 'You can't guarantee that four-day cricket will provide a winning England side, but I can guarantee that five or six counties will go bankrupt if it goes ahead.'

Edwards is right. The priority is not to switch to four-day cricket. On present-day pitches, how many games will last four days anyway? The state of English pitches has been deplorable; on that just about all county players are agreed. That is the first problem to be tackled. We need hard true wickets with consistent bounce. What we get most of the time are dead wickets with low bounce, or fiery uneven wickets if the county has a nest of lively seamers. Some groundsmen are clever enough to produce a seamers' wicket at one end and a spinners' wicket at the other end to suit the needs of the home side attack. They should be clever enough to produce good wickets at both ends. Good wickets will produce all that four-day cricket is supposed to – batsmen who can play long innings, bowlers good enough to get batsmen out on shirtfront wickets. Hard true wickets would make the seam bowler pitch the ball up and bring back the art of the outswinger. We might even see the re-emergence of the genuine spinner bowling with plenty of loop and air, with all that will mean for speeding up the over rate – say 120 overs a day like they used to do in Test matches. That would please the spectators. And it can be achieved without crippling county finances. The improvement in 1990 showed what can be done.

In addition to better wickets I would like to see a return to uncovered wickets. Having once acquired a sound technique on true wickets, it can only advance a batsman's technique to learn to play well on a sticky wicket where the ball is really doing things. Hutton was the master player on all wickets in my time and he was very much the product of just the sort of pitches I would like to see the return of – hard true wickets which are also uncovered.

He also had the advantage of playing without the new LBW rule which has not made things easier for the batsmen. In the old days a ball pitching outside the off stump had to hit the pad on a line between the wickets to make an LBW decision possible if the batsman played no shot. But now the ball pitching outside the off stump which is padded away outside the line of the wicket can be given out LBW if it would have hit the wicket. So batsmen now feel obliged to play at a ball many inches outside the off stump. Bowlers, instead of getting close to the wicket, bowl wide and slant the ball in. The effect has been to curtail the genuine outswinger, to the detriment of bowling and batting techniques.

Some Lessons From Cricketing Life

Throughout my cricketing life professionals put up with all sorts of abuse from amateurs who often did not really know what they were talking about. The game is now too big to be left to the Oxbridge old-boy network. England team manager Micky Stewart is known to deplore the amateur way in which cricket has been run in this country. England's achievements in the West Indies were a welcome sign that planning and a more professional approach can pay off.

But have things changed a lot? It makes my blood boil to think that Ossie Wheatley (Cambridge University, Warwick and Glamorgan), a competent bowler in his playing days but the worst number eleven I ever bowled at, could as a selector exercise a veto against Mike Gatting as England captain in 1989 because of his shouting match with umpire Shakoor Rana over a year previously. Gatting had already captained England subsequent to that, so the incident, however regrettable, was not a bar to the captain's job. Yet Wheatley illogically decided it was. This may have cost England the Ashes, because Gatting is a doughty John Bull figure who does not roll over when the going gets tough. Wheatley's veto has certainly lost Gatting to English Test cricket for all time. Disgusted and frustrated at the neglect and lack of communication from the England selectors, he upped and went on the tour of South Africa. Interestingly, when Viv Richards had his celebrated shouting match with James Lawton of the *Daily Express* in which he threatened to whack him, and also failed to lead his team onto the field at the start of play at the Antigua Test, Glamorgan's chairman Tony Lewis said of Richards' 1990 contract with the county: 'Whatever action the West Indies authorities decide to take against Richards will have no effect upon us. If we went about banning people because of one outburst I can think of very few who would be let into Britain.' Yet Ossie Wheatley got Gatting the chop because of 'one outburst'.

I have never minded taking orders from people who know better than me – and believe it or not I thoroughly enjoyed my two years of discipline and square bashing in National Service in the RAF. But I could never stand taking orders from an amateur worse than me. The late Sir Gubby Allen, as England selector, more than once had a go at me. On one occasion in the nets at a time when I had taken over 200 Test wickets he asked, 'Why do you take such a long run-up? I took half the run-up and was as quick as you.'

I told him I'd studied Test match records and he didn't seem to figure much whereas my name was among the four fastest bowlers of the century.

'We can't tell you youngsters anything,' he said, quite upset.

I replied, 'That's not true, but *you* certainly can't tell me anything about fast bowling.'*

I was not the only one to have a run-in with Gubby Allen. On the ill-fated tour of the West Indies in 1947–48, when we sent out a second string side that was duly clobbered despite Len Hutton being flown out as a reinforcement, Allen had a

* Allen took 81 wickets in Test cricket, average 29.37, Trueman 307 Test wickets at 21.57.

blistering row with Joe Hardstaff of Nottingham. As Joe related the story to me it went like this.

Gubby said, 'You're the worst senior pro I have ever had the misfortune to travel with.'

Hardstaff: 'You're the worst f . . . . . g captain I've ever played with.'

Allen: 'You'll never play for England again Hardstaff.'

Hardstaff: 'I bet I do.'

Allen: 'If you do I'll give you £100.'

Hardstaff did, at Trent Bridge in 1948, and Gubby sent him a £100 cheque. Hardstaff tore the cheque into four pieces and posted it back.

All my cricketing life – and afterwards – I have spoken my mind. I reckon it probably cost me thirty Test matches and at least another hundred Test wickets.

The only man in my life I never dared answer back was my Dad, even when I was in my thirties. I was one of six children and in our household Alan Thomas Trueman was a stickler for discipline, a teetotaller and a God-fearing man who believed people should stand on their own feet and pay their own way. Despite his being a miner for many years, having started as a horse dealer, he never voted Labour. Nor have I. Apart from the aged and the infirm everyone should provide for themselves. He believed that. So do I.

Dad was cricket mad and played every Saturday for our village team, Stainton, where I was born on 6 February 1931, even then larger than life at 14 lb 1 oz. He was a good left-arm spin bowler and batsman and after watching him I could bowl out men on the village green when I was eight. Even then I had a natural outswing. But to be truthful I only played so much because of my father – not that I dared tell him that I was not as enthusiastic as he was. When I was only twelve I was hit in the groin by a fast ball. Like many boys I wore no protector. It was the worst injury of my life and stopped me playing for two whole seasons. In hospital doctors feared the worst. A huge lump formed in my groin and I could only limp along on a cane stick, unable to bat or bowl. Ten years later the same thing happened at Northampton when Frank Tyson got me with a full toss. This time I had a plastic protector, but the ball smashed it into splinters and pushed them into my body. My private parts shone like a rainbow, but happily my manhood remained intact. On neither occasion did I consider giving up the game.

At fifteen I played for a village side, Roche Abbey. In a knockout competition against a league side, in a different class altogether, we were put out for only 43. When they came to bat only three of them were in whites, the rest thinking they wouldn't be called on to bat. But my Dad told them: 'I've got a lad here who might cause a bit of trouble.' I did just that, taking six wickets for one run and they were all out for only 11.

That brought me to the notice of Cyril Turner, the former Yorkshire player, who was coach to Sheffield United Cricket Club. I know that Dad already believed I'd play for Yorkshire, but he never said a word. As for me, I wanted to be a bricklayer.

League cricket was heavily geared to supplying the Yorkshire county team and, when Cyril was asked what new talent there was, I was taken to the Headingley ground in Leeds – my first visit. I was stunned. The only field of that size I had ever seen before had been full of turnips.

I bowled eleven balls and hit the stumps three times, one of my victims being another youngster called Brian Close. George Hirst, the great Yorkshire left-arm bowler and the only man ever to perform the double of 200 wickets and 2,000 runs in a season, enquired anxiously if I was Yorkshire-born – which is still, thank God, an essential qualification to play for the county. I duly reassured him that I was. At seventeen I went on tour with the Yorkshire Federation side, which was for lads under eighteen, along with Close and another youngster who I felt very sorry for because he kept being sick on the coach. His name was Ray Illingworth. To this day he prefers to travel by train – especially if the alternative is to travel in Brian Close's car, and anyone who knows Brian's driving would readily appreciate that. That year, 1948, was a good year for me and when the legendary Herbert Sutcliffe said in a widely reported after-dinner speech that there was a young man called Freddie Trueman whom he predicted would be playing for Yorkshire before he was nineteen and for England before he was twenty-one, I knew I was on my way.

The first prediction turned out to be true – I was eighteen years and three months when I played for Yorkshire against Cambridge University in May 1949. The second prediction was not far out either. I was selected for a Test trial at nineteen, and I was twenty-one when I played my first Test against India in front of my home crowd at Headingley. I was in awe to find myself mixing with all the big names – Compton, Edrich and Hutton. In the first innings I took three wickets for 89, something short of a dream start, but the second innings was incredible. With my second ball I had Roy caught by Compton, then Bedser had Gaekwad in the gully and not a run had been scored. Next came Mantri, the wicket-keeper. I gave him the slower one which pitched on his middle stump and knocked his off stump out of the ground. Then I bowled Manjrekar with the next delivery. The score was none for four wickets, all in 14 balls. One evening paper asked its correspondent to confirm that the score hadn't been given the wrong way round, four for no wickets – and it took some reassuring that the score was indeed four wickets for no runs. We murdered India that summer and I ended up with 29 Test wickets, including 8 for 31 in the Third Test at Old Trafford, which has never been bettered. I collected more headlines than some cricketers earn in a lifetime – a lad of twenty-one from a working-class background was being hailed as the new white fast-bowling hope, someone to cheer after years of humiliation at the hands of fast bowlers like Lindwall and Miller. I was still doing my National Service in the RAF at the time and there was resentment from lots of the Erks and NCOs at my getting extra leave. One Member of Parliament even raised the issue in the house. He had had a letter of complaint from a mother because her boy had been refused extra leave to compete in the national banjo competition at the Albert Hall.

I was probably at my fastest then and, unusually for a fast bowler, I had a natural outswinger. 'Keep bowling the outswinger, Fred, and you'll be all right,' the great Maurice Leyland advised me one day in the nets. 'That's the one which gets the great players out.' Someone likened me to a Spanish fighting bull. My vital statistics were 5 feet 10 inches, 46 inches around chest and hips and 19 inches round the thighs.

Some people supposed I had built up my strength by manual labour in the pits. Wrong. My dad was working underground at Maltby Main and always declared no child of his would follow him. When I told him I wanted a job there he got me one in the tally office, which meant I didn't have to do rough work at the coal face like him. Sometimes I did go down to the seam where he was working, to help shovel coal on the belts so that he could have a rest. He was over fifty then. In fact I was blessed with a fast bowler's build from birth – strong thick legs (those are the first essentials for quick bowlers) plus big shoulders and hips. That's how I was able several times to bowl over 1,000 overs a season and kept bowling fast for twenty years. Even so, towards the end my legs ached so much after a hard day in the field it would keep me awake at night.

The real shock of my sudden rise to fame in 1952 was the total loss of my privacy. I found I couldn't go into a pub or restaurant without someone being provocative or badgering me for my autograph. If they didn't say please I would tell them to get lost – and so I acquired a reputation for rudeness. I *can* be blunt, but I've never said or done half the things attributed to me. Even today people seem to think I am a prodigious drinker. If I am speaking at a dinner someone will come up and say, 'You'll have a pint of bitter won't you, Fred, and there's nineteen more lined up where that one came from.' The truth is that I have never been a heavy drinker. My dad was a teetotaller and when I first joined the Yorkshire side I caused a laugh by ordering an orange juice. I might have taken two or three pints after a thirsty day in the field, but now I prefer a scotch or two spread over an hour or two. I can truthfully say I have never been drunk in my life. Needless to say, stories to the contrary have dogged me all my life. I was twenty-two and probably too young when I went on my first overseas tour of the West Indies in 1953–54 under the captaincy of Len Hutton, who was a marvellous tactician as a captain but not one to back his players off the field. I got myself into trouble with the locals when I bowled to the Jamaican idol George Hedley. 'King George, King George,' they chanted and I said to myself, 'If he is the bloody king, let's see if we can de-throne him.' I bowled him a bouncer which he hooked out of the ground, so a couple of overs later I tried him with another; he missed and broke a bone in his arm. The crowd went mad and I needed a police escort from the ground. For the rest of the tour I was Mr Bumper Man. A local songwriter wrote a verse to the tune of 'What Shall We Do With The Drunken Sailor?'

> What Shall We Do with Freddie Trueman/What Shall We Do with Freddie Trueman/
> What Shall We Do with Freddie Trueman/Now He's Bowling Bumpers.

> Head Down Up She Rises/Head Down Up She Rises/Head Down Up She Rises/
> He's a Bowling Bumpers/Four Hundred On The Scoreboard Rises/Four Hundred On The Scoreboard Rises/And Still He's Bowling BUMPERS.

The press printed lurid headlines like 'Terrible Trueman' and 'Maltby Mauler' and I became the victim of all kinds of rumour and innuendo. No, I never called one of the umpires a name in Georgetown, though Len gave me a terrible rollicking for doing so. When I met the umpire next morning at the top of the steps I asked him why he had told Len I'd called him a name. And he said, 'I didn't – I said it was one of the Yorkshiremen on the field but I know it wasn't you.' Len never apologized. In fact, I can tell you now, the guilty player was Johnny Wardle. Then I was blamed for throwing the ball onto the ground after the umpire gave a bad decision. It wasn't me but the gentlemanly Tom Graveney, finally sickened by some atrocious decisions. Word went round when we returned to England that Len couldn't control me and the big guns of the MCC like Freddie Brown and Gubby Allen, along with Brian Sellers, chairman of Yorkshire, decided to tame me.

When Len Hutton and the selectors announced the team to tour Australia the following winter I wasn't in it, even though I took 134 for under 16 runs apiece. I was set up as the untameable northern savage who ate broken glass and infant batsmen for breakfast. The men selected were Frank Tyson, 67 wickets, Brian Statham and Peter Loader, about 80 each, Trevor Bailey and Alec Bedser, just over 100 wickets each. I was never asked to play for England again under Len Hutton's captaincy. Once the Trueman legend was born the stories that began to circulate about me astounded and enraged me. I was supposed to be sitting at the top table at a dinner in honour of the 1952 Indian tourists given by their High Commissioner when I nudged a high-ranking Indian diplomat in the ribs and said, 'Hey, Gunga Din, passt' salt.' I did attend that dinner, but there was no incident and the flaw in the story is that, as England's most junior cap, I certainly wasn't placed on the top table.

Even after I had retired another daft legend was born. In 1974 at Worcester I met some of the Indian players and their manager, Colonel Adi Kari, for a chat. Two weeks later the story went round the dressing rooms that I had greeted the colonel with the words, 'How nice it is to see you've got your colour back.' A complete fabrication. But as Mark Twain said: 'A lie has gone halfway round the world before truth can put his boots on.'

The suggestion was made that I wasn't taken on the last tour to South Africa in 1964–65 because of my attitude to colour. I never knew I had one. But it is true that in the West Indies when I bowled one short in a minor match to a player who is now dead he called me a white English bastard. I told him if he said it again I would do him. He did – and I did – giving him a bouncer which broke his jaw. He asked for it, but I never really enjoyed hurting anyone. Another time at a private party in Melbourne during the 1962–63 tour I had a long and interesting chat about pace bowling with Bill Johnstone, the Aussie left-arm bowler. We got on very well, but a few days later he came to me most agitated saying that there was a story going the rounds that we had come to blows. I told him it was typical of the ridiculous stories that were ten a penny in England. I called it the curse of the Truemans. I can even feel sympathetic to Ian Botham, a man more sinned against than sinning, as I was. Much of the time I went to bed at nine o'clock absolutely knackered because that's the effect of bowling more than 1,000 overs a season, while my team mates were elsewhere having a drink. Yet it was assumed that I must be attending an even bigger orgy somewhere else. In some hotels chambermaids refused to bring breakfast to my room.

Often I was accused of a fracas when I wasn't even there. After the Yorkshire team had stayed at a Bristol hotel during a match against Gloucester, an official complaint was made about me to the Yorkshire Committee about 'Bad language and disgusting behaviour'. Hauled before the committee some time later, I explained to Sir William Worsley, the president, who was a real gentleman and one of the few on the committee who really liked me, that even the amazing Freddie Trueman couldn't play for Yorkshire at Bristol and for England at Lords on the same day. Sir William grabbed the fixture list, checked up and blew his top, demanding who was responsible for bringing me before the committee. He made the hotel withdraw its complaint and apologize. That was the only time I ever had words with Herbert Sutcliffe. He called me Trueman, which I have never been able to stand. It should be either Fred or Mr Trueman as far as I am concerned. I replied, 'Yes, Sutcliffe.' I thought Brian Sellers would burst a blood vessel.

Though I still consider Yorkshire to be the greatest cricket club in the world, it has not often been a happy club – the atmosphere was poisoned by jealousies among the players when I first joined and by the autocratic and begrudging behaviour of the committee. The tradition is a long one. When he was only seventeen in 1934 Len Hutton scored 196 (last man out) against Worcester, a remarkable feat. Reg Perks, the great Worcester pace bowler, was deeply impressed. When Worcester arrived back in Yorkshire for the return game he enquired where Hutton was. Back came the sour reply from one of the senior pros, 'Back in bloody second eleven getting feet back on ground.' I encountered that sort of thing too. Once when we played Notts at Sheffield the entire Trueman family and friends turned out to watch me and I did them and Yorkshire proud, taking 8 for 68 in the second innings. We won by an innings and the crowd cheered me all the way to the dressing room. There I found I had been dropped to the second team for the next game. Dicky Bird, now the most famous umpire in his white hat, once scored 181 not out against Glamorgan on a fearful Bradford wicket where everyone else including Test players like Gilbert Parkhouse had failed. When he returned to the pavilion Brian Sellers told him, 'Well played, Harold. You'll be playing in second team tomorrow.' Dicky was so disgusted he upped and left for Leicester.

When I was only twenty I almost did the same – both Lancashire and Surrey were after my services – because I kept being dropped after playing well. There was also a miserly refusal to award me my county cap, which I only got by threatening to leave. After a lean time in the 1950s Yorkshire finally won the championship in 1959. The committee gave us a bonus of £50, the same as that paid to the championship team of 1932 when the value of money was several times higher. The players were then reprimanded for insubordination for failing to thank the committee for its generosity.

Yorkshire kept me waiting for my benefit. I joined in 1949 but it wasn't until 1962 that I was awarded one – an unusually long time for a fast bowler who had sent down over 10,000 overs for them. It wasn't my last humiliation at Yorkshire's hands. When I was thirty-five, after seventeen years of service, I was accused of 'not trying' in a match in Sheffield against Lancashire, even though I had bowled solidly for an hour and taken six wickets. Sellers reckoned I was slow to field a ball. Back in the dressing room he called me a bastard in front of everyone. I kept my cool as the senior pro, though in the old days I might have thumped him. They even suspended me for a game without pay – though thanks to radio and TV interviews I made more money than my £22 match fee (from which we had to deduct our own travelling, food and hotel expenses). On top of match fees we got a monthly retainer of £24 plus a £2 bonus for a win.

The club's attitude was that of master to servant; you were expected to tug the forelock and be thankful for whatever crumbs fell from the master's table. Dissent deserved a rap on the knuckles as if you were a naughty schoolchild. What a pity they preferred to scold rather than advise. Encouragement means a lot to a player of any age. Yorkshire were always the last to give it. During the MCC tour of the West Indies in 1959–60 I lost a stone in weight taking 21 wickets, more than anyone else, which gave me a total of 149 Test wickets, beating Hedley Verity's total of 137. It had been a particularly arduous tour with a bottle-throwing riot at Trinidad when the teams had had to flee the pitch ('Don't worry Fred,' the crowd called as I ran for my life. 'We're not going to touch you. We want the umpires.')

Back at Yorkshire nobody bothered to congratulate me. When I mentioned it to a committee man he said, 'You are playing more Tests than Hedley Verity.' I pointed out he was wrong. Verity (one of my great heroes) had played in six more Tests than me at that stage. But he wouldn't have it that I could possibly be better than one of the old-timers.

Similarly, when I took my 250th Test wicket – then a world record in New Zealand in 1963 – I had congratulations from all over the world. The Duke of Norfolk, surprise choice as manager of the tour, was first on the field to shake my hand. Among all the messages and telegrams, including several from English first-class counties, there wasn't a word from Yorkshire. They eventually made the feeble excuse that there had been no telegram because Sir William Worsley, the president, was on holiday in Hong Kong at the time. As I commented in my autobiography *Ball of Fire*: 'I wonder what they did at Headingley when they wanted to go to the toilet and Sir William wasn't there to give his permission.'

In the end Brian Sellers' autocratic ways were to cost the county dear. We finished 1968 with a hat-trick of championship victories. I captained the Yorkshire side which beat the Australians by an innings that season. It was a triumph to relish, though the committee stopped our £5 win bonus because they said it wasn't a championship game.

Much of our success in the 1960s was due to the fearless captaincy of Brian Close who always led from the front, being prepared to stand at suicidal positions a few feet from the bat on the leg side. If Brian had a fault it was a reluctance to blood younger players, something that I was always on at him to change. Undeniably the team was long in the tooth but what happened next was inexcusable. Ray Illingworth, one of the finest all-rounders in the world and soon to prove himself as England's captain in Australia by regaining the Ashes, was allowed to leave for Leicester. All he wanted was a two- or three-year contract to provide security for himself and his family until he organized a new career when the time came for him to retire. But that was refused. Two years later Brian Close, who had put in twenty-three years dedicated work, was given half an hour to resign or be sacked – deprived of the captaincy and also thrown out of the club. He had been discarded as just so much rubbish, as had Johnny Wardle a decade previously.

I had the feeling there were those on the committee who would have enjoyed sacking me. So I decided not to give them the chance. I always kick myself for being so precipitate. For when I tendered my resignation in person to our president Sir William, by then father-in-law of the Duke of Kent, he told me the committee were planning to offer me the captaincy of Yorkshire – the supreme accolade for any Yorkshireman. But, alas, it was too late. I'd already announced my retirement in my column in *The People* and the first editions of several million copies had already rolled off the presses, too late to unroll them. I'll regret that for the rest of my life. Sellers affected a complete indifference to all these departures. 'They can all leave as far as I'm concerned. There's plenty in second team as good if not better.'

Twenty-two years on and we are still waiting to win another championship. Autocratic and amateur at the same time, Yorkshire wasted untold talent. Over the years English cricket suffered in much the same way. I am no great admirer of player power but I do want the men in charge to be real professionals.

Despite my beefing, cricket is still to me the greatest game and happy memories far outweigh the unpleasant ones. If the Yorkshire committee never gave me my due, at least I had the prime ministers of Great Britain and Australia on my side. When the team was in Antigua in the West Indies during the 1959–60 tour, R. W. Robins summoned Brian Statham and me and said, 'You've got the day off. You've been invited to lunch by a VIP.' Sir Anthony Eden, Lord Avon, by now retired from the premiership, had specially asked for Brian and me. We spent a wonderful day chatting about cricket. He told us the story of the Commonwealth Conference of 1956 which had been scheduled for March. Back came an irate message from Canberra: 'Don't you realize what year it is? In June England play Australia at Lords.' Eden told us: 'So that's how we altered the date of the conference – and started at seven in the morning so that we could get to the ground by 12.30 for lunch and cricket.' Cricket, it seems, could even change the destiny of an empire. During our conversations I broached the subject of Len Hutton's knighthood. 'Some of us were a bit surprised when he got it,' I said. Eden made it clear it was his recommendation.

Four years later Sir Robert Menzies entertained us cricketers at the Lodge at Canberra. During his speech he remarked, 'Today is a very special day.' I had no idea what he was talking about and couldn't have been more surprised when he went on, 'Today is February the 6th, Freddie Trueman's birthday.' Whereupon he presented me with a tankard suitably inscribed 'To Fred Trueman on his birthday from Robert Menzies, Prime Minister of Australia'. That is still one of my proudest possessions in my cabinet of trophies. Though I am no socialist I always got along splendidly with fellow Yorkshireman Harold Wilson. Brian Johnston let slip in one of his books that when Wilson was prime minister he wanted to give me a knighthood. Apparently it was all in the bag when they consulted the MCC who counselled that it was 'risky'.

As it was I was deeply proud in 1989 to go to Buckingham Palace with my wife Veronica to get the OBE from The Queen, who chatted to me about cricket and made me feel I'd known her one hundred years. I felt a million dollars.

Looking back I should like to have played two or three years more because I know I had it in me. John Arlott wrote in his biography of me, *Fred: Portrait of a Fast Bowler*: 'With years his pace did indeed deteriorate to fast–medium ... He was never content to be less than the fastest bowler he could be. So when at length the fact was borne in upon him that he was no longer fast he went away.' Not quite, John. Denis Lillee, Richard Hadlee and now Malcolm Marshall all discovered that there is life after fast bowling. In the early 1960s I had developed a shorter run which I used to bowl cutters. And I could still have made the batsmen hop about a bit. I'd also have earned another benefit and that extra £15,000 or so in the currency of those times would have helped towards retirement. That I didn't do so was due to my distrust of the Yorkshire committee who I thought, not without reason given their past record, were preparing to give me the chop. If only they could have given me a hint that they planned to make me captain before I made my retirement irrevocable!

I always had a good living from cricket and when I was only twenty-two I was the proud owner of a Rover car and my own house. On the domestic front my life was not all smoothness. The marriage to my first wife Enid, daughter of the one-time Mayor of Scarborough, broke up over a number of years and much of that was due to the stresses caused by cricket taking me away from home for long periods. Cricket got between us even when I was at home, with the phone ringing and people coming in to see me – and not her. So the rows started. For a long time my address was often The Car, Yorkshire Dales. We had three children. When we made the break for good I sat in hotels and friends' houses and cried like a kid. I was a genuine loner and basically still am. I vowed never to become deeply involved again – till I met a pretty redhead called Veronica at a charity soccer match at Keighley when I appeared for the Yorkshire all-stars. At first we were both still married, but eventually she became my wife. She rescued me because she gave me the warmth and comfort of a family life which I had missed. She organizes life for me, keeps my diary and is marvellous at making deals. We live in a wooded valley in the lovely Yorkshire Dales near Skipton. I didn't know what happiness was all about until I met her and I'm taking great pains to keep it that way.

These days I have a good time and a good living from my after-dinner speaking and cabaret act as comedian complete with topper, as well as from journalism and cricket commentating. I shall never be less than devoted to this great game of cricket which I have known and loved since my father first got me interested all those years ago in the village of Stainton. I am delighted that the standing and pay of the professional cricketer is so much higher than when I began. But I also have the greatest reverence for the old-timers and the great characters cricket has produced, some of whose achievements you will find commemorated in the pages of this anthology. If it gives the reader as much pleasure as it has given me and Peter Grosvenor to compile it, I shall be happy.

Fred Trueman's Record

1. All First-Class Matches

BOWLING SUMMARY

Season	Overs	Maidens	Runs	Wkts	Avge	5 wkts. Inns	10 wkts. Match
1949	243.3	49	719	31	23.19	1	–
1950	290.1	43	876	31	28.25	–	–
1951	737.4	166	1852	90	20.57	6	1
1952	282.4	58	841	61	13.78	5	–
1953	447.1	77	1411	44	32.06	2	1
1953–54 (WI)	320	81	909	27	33.66	1	–
1954	808.2	188	2085	134	15.55	10	–
1955	996.5	214	2454	153	16.03	8	3
1956	588.4	133	1383	59	23.44	2	–
1956–57 (I)	61	9	204	8	25.50	–	–
1957	842	184	2303	135	17.05	9	2
1958	637.5	176	1414	106	13.33	6	–
1958–59 (A)	265.1*	30	823	37	22.24	2	–
(NZ)	100.2	31	244	20	12.20	2	1
1959	1072.4	269	2730	140	19.50	6	–
1959–60 (WI)	342.3	86	883	37	23.86	2	–
1960	1068.4	275	2447	175	13.98	12	4
1960–61 (SA)	114.4	16	326	22	14.81	1	–
1961	1180.1	302	3000	155	19.35	11	4
1962	1141.5	273	2717	153	17.75	5	1
1962–63 (A)	229.3*	19	773	30	25.76	1	–
(NZ)	121.2	38	247	25	9.88	3	1
1963	844.3	207	1955	129	15.15	10	5
1963–64 (WI)	49	12	124	9	13.77	–	–
1964	834.1	171	2194	100	21.94	3	–
1964–65 (WI)	79.3	18	253	11	23.00	1	–
1965	754.4	180	1811	127	14.25	10	1
1966	859.1	203	2040	111	18.37	2	1
1967	595	135	1610	75	21.46	2	–

BOWLING SUMMARY

Season	Overs	Maidens	Runs	Wkts	Avge	5 wkts. Inns	10 wkts. Match
1967–68 (I)	18	2	58	1	58.00	–	–
1968	515	116	1375	66	20.83	3	–
1969	21	1	93	2	46.50	–	–
	15,968 and 494.4*	3,762	42,154	2,304	18.29	126	25

(* denotes 8-ball overs)

Hat-tricks (4)
Yorkshire v Nottinghamshire at Nottingham, 1951
Yorkshire v Nottinghamshire at Scarborough, 1955
Yorkshire v MCC at Lords, 1958
Yorkshire v Nottinghamshire at Bradford, 1963

How Trueman took his Wickets
Caught 1,115
Bowled 898
Lbw 274
Hit wicket 17
_____
Total 2,304

BATTING AND FIELDING SUMMARY

Season	Matches	Inns	NO	Runs	HS	Avge	100s	50s	Catches
1949	8	6	2	12	10	3.00	–	–	2
1950	14	15	9	23	4*	3.83	–	–	5
1951	30	24	7	114	25	6.70	–	–	21
1952	9	4	3	40	23*	40.00	–	–	5
1953	15	16	2	131	34	9.35	–	–	15
1953–54 (WI)	8	9	3	81	20	13.50	–	–	7
1954	33	35	5	270	50*	9.00	–	1	32
1955	31	38	8	391	74	13.03	–	1	26
1956	31	30	3	358	58	13.25	–	1	21
1956–57 (I)	2	4	2	96	46*	48.00	–	–	–
1957	32	41	14	405	63	15.00	–	1	36
1958	30	35	7	453	61	16.17	–	3	22
1958–59 (A/NZ)	17	21	2	312	53	16.42	–	1	16
1959	30	40	9	602	54	19.41	–	1	24
1959–60 (WI)	10	13	2	153	37	13.90	–	–	11
1960	32	40	5	577	69	16.48	–	3	22
1960–61 (SA)	4	5	1	139	59	34.75	–	1	2

BATTING AND FIELDING SUMMARY

Season	Matches	Inns	NO	Runs	HS	Avge	100s	50s	Catches
1961	34	48	6	809	80*	19.26	–	4	13
1962	33	42	4	840	63	22.10	–	1	24
1962–63 (A/NZ)	12	14	–	194	38	13.85	–	–	9
1963	27	41	6	783	104	22.37	2	2	15
1963–64 (WI)	2	2	–	28	28	14.00	–	–	2
1964	31	39	4	595	77	17.00	–	4	19
1964–65 (WI)	3	2	–	24	13	12.00	–	–	1
1965	30	39	2	636	101	17.18	1	2	17
1966	33	43	4	448	43	11.48	–	–	22
1967	31	33	5	342	34	12.21	–	–	31
1967–68 (I)	1	2	–	42	33	21.00	–	–	1
1968	29	30	5	296	45	11.84	–	–	16
1969	1	2	–	37	26	18.50	–	–	1
	603	713	120	9,231	104	15.56	3	26	438

(* denotes not out)

Hundreds
104 Yorkshire v Northamptonshire at Northampton, 1963
100* An England XI v Young England XI at Scarborough, 1963
101 Yorkshire v Middlesex at Scarborough, 1965

Most runs off one over (6-ball)
26 (440666) off D. Shackleton: Yorkshire v Hampshire at Middlesbrough, 1965.
(Yorkshire were dismissed for 23 – their lowest total in any first-class match –
in the second innings.)

2. Test Matches

BOWLING SUMMARY

Season	Opponents	Overs	Mdns	Runs	Wkts	Avge	5 wkts Inns	10 wkts Match
1952	I	119.4	25	386	29	13.31	2	–
1953	A	26.3	4	90	4	22.50	–	–
1953–54	WI	133.2	27	420	9	46.66	–	–
1955	SA	35	4	112	2	56.00	–	–
1956	A	75	13	184	9	20.44	1	–
1957	WI	173.3	34	455	22	20.68	1	–
1958	NZ	131.5	44	256	15	17.06	1	–
1958–59	A	87*	11	276	9	30.66	–	–
	NZ	44.5	17	105	5	21.00	–	–
1959	I	177.4	53	401	24	16.70	–	–

BOWLING SUMMARY

Season	Opponents	Overs	Mdns	Runs	Wkts	Avge	5 wkts Inns	10 wkts Match
1959–60	WI	220.3	62	549	21	26.14	1	–
1960	SA	180.3	31	508	25	20.32	1	–
1961	A	164.4	21	529	20	26.45	2	1
1962	P	164.5	37	439	22	19.95	1	–
1962–63	A	158.3*	9	521	20	26.05	1	–
	NZ	88	29	164	14	11.71	1	–
1963	WI	236.4	53	594	34	17.47	4	2
1964	A	133.3	25	399	17	23.47	1	–
1965	NZ	96.3	23	237	6	39.50	–	–
		2,203.3	522	6,625	307	21.57	17	3
	and	245.3*						

(*denotes 8-ball overs)

Seven or More Wickets in an Innings

O	M	R	W

8.4 – 2 – 31 – 8 v India at Manchester 1952
14.3 – 2 – 44 – 7 v West Indies at Birmingham 1963
30.2 – 9 – 75 – 7 v New Zealand at Christchurch 1962–63

Ten or More Wickets in a Test

12–119 (5–75 & 7–44) v West Indies at Birmingham 1963
11–88 (5–58 & 6–30) v Australia at Leeds 1961
11–152 (6–100 & 5–52) v West Indies at Lord's 1963

Balls per wicket: 49.4   Runs conceded per 100 balls: 43.6

Trueman's Record Against Each Country

Opponents	Tests	Overs	Mdns	Runs	Wkts	Avge	5 wkts Inns	10 wkts Match
Australia	19	399.4	83	1,999	79	25.30	5	1
	and	245.3*						
South Africa	6	215.3	35	620	27	22.96	1	–
West Indies	18	764	176	2,018	86	23.46	6	2
New Zealand	11	361.1	113	762	40	19.05	2	–
India	9	297.2	78	787	53	14.84	2	–
Pakistan	4	164.5	37	439	22	19.95	1	–
	67	2,202.3	522	6,625	307	21.57	17	3
	and	245.3*						

1
YORKSHIRE GRIT
My Father

Quite probably I would never have been an international cricketer but for the influence of my father. When I was a young lad he was keener on the game than I was – and I am sure one of my proudest cricket achievements, winning my Yorkshire cap, meant more to him than it did to me. Here is my tribute to him from the pages of my autobiography, *Ball of Fire*.

F.S.T.

By the middle of the 1951 season my patience was wearing thin with Yorkshire. I began to think I would never get anywhere. I would bowl well and get plenty of wickets in one match and get dropped for the next. There was no mention of being capped. Apart from the honour, which was considerable, a capped player was paid an extra £2 a match, plus a monthly retainer.

In the end I virtually had to ask for my cap. Both Lancashire and Surrey were making overtures and I came to the conclusion that to make any progress in cricket I would have to leave Yorkshire. So I went to Norman Yardley and told him I was going. That was midweek – and on the following Monday, 13 August, I got my cap. There was no warning and no ceremony. We were playing at Bradford when Norman Yardley told Bob Appleyard and myself to go to the office. When we got there he just handed over caps. I couldn't wait to get home, but in those days I had no car and was travelling by train and bus to the ground and back to save hotel bills, arriving home at ten o'clock at night. When I got into the house I saw my old Dad sitting in his chair. Now he was on the night shift in those days but, of course, the news had already reached Maltby via the newspapers and I knew what was up. I decided to have a bit of fun, saying, 'What's the matter, then? Last draw at the mine was 9.30 p.m. and here you are still at home at ten o'clock.' Well, his face puckered and I thought, 'Good God! He's going to cry.' Then he pulled himself together and said: 'On a night like this in a Yorkshireman's life, he doesn't go to work.' He looked me full in the face and said, 'Come on, where is it?' So I took my cap out and gave it to him.

I'll never be able to describe properly just what it meant to him, that cap. Only Yorkshiremen will understand. I never wore it again – it was his, and he'd worked for it. Mother was watching all this from the kitchen, so I turned to her and said, 'Don't worry, Mum, you can have my first England cap.' And she burst into tears. She got it too, but Dad never bothered about my England caps. They meant nothing to him. That Yorkshire cap was all he wanted and he still has it.

When he died it was placed in his coffin.

One of the great satisfactions of my life was that my father lived to see my entire career. He never changed one bit as long as I knew him, refused to move out of the old family home in Maltby even when I offered to arrange for him and my mother to live in a modern bungalow, and kept working at the pit until he retired. I knew he was terribly proud of me, although he never showed it, and so were my former workmates at Maltby Main. If ever I put away the wickets, they used to write my match figures on a board and put it in front of the cage so my father could see how I was doing the moment he came up from the coal face. He ended up training youngsters, but he hated mining from start to finish. He always said he would retire the day he was sixty-five and he did. It fell on a Thursday, and he came home and burnt all his pit clothes in the back yard.

My father remained a major influence in my life until he died. Many's the time I went back home to Maltby with problems and we would talk them out. He was a very sensible and knowledgeable person and there was nothing I wouldn't discuss with him. He worried for me when I was doing badly, and got angry for me when I was being wrongly accused or unfairly dropped. And his advice in the crisis time was generally: 'Bugger 'em, they'll want you before you'll want them, son.' He could also get angry with me if he thought I was being stupid, and I took several bollockings about my batting. It offended his cricketing principles to see me go in and swing the bat, take chances and throw my wicket away. I used to argue with him that I couldn't really be expected to bowl fast all day and then bat like an opener. He said I had a point, but he believed I could bat well and he advised me to get my head down and play properly because it would improve my chances for Test selection. He was right, of course.

During his retirement he did a bit of gardening and came regularly to watch me play. On the day I retired I went home to see him and said, 'That's it, Dad – I'm finished.' He was sitting in the same place where, twenty years earlier, I had given him my first Yorkshire cap and I could see he was deeply moved again. He thought for a bit, then looked at me and said, 'Well, I've been very fortunate. I was there to see you start playing cricket and I've lived to see you finish. I can die happy now. And I'll never watch Yorkshire play again.'

He never did. And he died two years later at the age of seventy-eight.

From *Ball of Fire* by Fred Trueman
(J.M. Dent, London, 1976).

Len Hutton's 364

I was only seven when I listened to my first cricket commentary on an old Cats Whisker set in 1938. What an occasion that was for all Englishmen, especially Yorkshiremen. Len Hutton, only twenty-two, made his world record test score of 364 against Australia at The Oval. I know Gary Sobers later broke that record against Pakistan. But with all due respect to Sir Garfield, whom I rate the greatest all-rounder of my time (and perhaps of all time), his 365 against a depleted Pakistan attack, with two of their front-line bowlers injured, cannot compare with Leonard's feat. His was the soundest technique I ever saw and the way he describes it in the piece which follows is an object lesson for batsmen today, including several of our Test players. This was a timeless Test, a play to the finish. So Hutton took no chances, but still averaged over 27 an hour, quick by today's Test standards. The rate at which runs are scored – and overs are bowled – in present-day Test cricket, with 'attrition' (an ugly word and an ugly sight) the order of the day, I can't see either individual score ever being beaten again in a Test match.

It had been a high-scoring series (except for the Third Test at Old Trafford when not a ball was bowled because of rain). In the First Test at Trent Bridge England made 658 for 8 declared with Hutton and Compton both making centuries on their first appearance against Australia; Charlie Barnett of Gloucester got a century off the first ball after lunch on the first day, and Eddie Paynter made 216 not out. When Australia replied, that great crisis player Stan McCabe came in at 111 for 2 and scored 232 off the 300 Australia added, an innings of such brilliance Bradman told his team, 'Watch this, you will not see the like of it again.' When Australia followed on, Bill Brown (133) and Bradman (144 not out) made the draw inevitable. At Lords in the Second Test, Hammond having made 240 for England, Brown 206 not out and Bradman 102 for Australia, there was another high-scoring draw. With Hutton and Leyland injured for the Fourth Test at Headingley, 'Tiger' Bill O'Reilly (10 for 122) and Fleetwood-Smith (7 for 107) wreaked havoc to give Australia a five-wicket victory. Bradman was the only century-maker in that game, though there were fourteen in all in the series, five batsmen getting to a double century and one to a treble century. And so to The Oval where England won the toss, determined to square the series and scored 903 for 7 declared. From his autobiography *Cricket is My Life*, Hutton tells here how he resumed on the second day of the game with Maurice Leyland.

Bradman neither forgot nor forgave that mammoth defeat in 1938. When in 1948 the all-conquering Australians returned to wallop the opposition everywhere they scored 721 in a day against Essex (at Southend, now currently a suspect pitch). Keith

Miller, waiting to bat, hated the merciless onslaught upon the hapless Essex bowlers: 'Why don't you declare, Don?' he said after he had gone cheaply. A whole decade and a World War had intervened, but Bradman replied, 'Remember The Oval in 1938?'

F.S.T.

A big crowd gave us a roaring send-off all the way to the crease, and straight away we broke the record of 323 for any partnership, held by Jack Hobbs and Wilfred Rhodes since the Melbourne Test of 1912.

We broke several other Test records before our partnership ended. At 411, the time being ten minutes past one, Maurice Leyland was run out. Hassett misfielded a ball near deep mid-off, and yet recovered promptly enough to help Bradman to throw the wicket down while we were trying for a second run. It was a misfortune and a regrettable end to a glorious innings and a second-wicket stand that had lasted six hours and twenty minutes. Maurice had scored an unwearingly patient, resolutely solid 187 out of 382, hitting seventeen fours. There was no real relief for the Australians in this adverse happening to us, however, because our captain Walter Hammond, another of the England batsmen in excellent form, was the newcomer: and at lunch we were 434 for two, my not-out figures being 191.

I have been often reminded about the stumping chance I gave and I heard a story later on that suggested I had escaped on another occasion as well. "'E's still in,' said one Pudsey lady to another, meeting after they had been listening at their homes to the running broadcast. 'Ay, 'e's still in,' was the reply, 'and when he 'it that one just over mid-on me 'eart fair popped out of me blouse!'

Hammond had told his batsmen at the opening of the England innings to keep in mind that this was a 'timeless' Test, and when he joined me he lived up to his injunction. Consequently the bowlers had not the ghost of a hope against us by then, and until a quarter to four the afternoon was all ours.

Bill O'Reilly seemed to me to bowl laboriously but with great heart. He had striven long and hard on that beautiful batsman's wicket, but he got no assistance from it. I place O'Reilly as the most interesting bowler I have ever faced. Every ball he sent down needed watching: he changed his pace with genius and was always attacking. He put everything into every ball that he had it in him to give. Maurice Leyland and I, recalling that game from time to time, have always found ourselves with a warm spot each for this tall Australian, than whom no more gallant trier has ever come to our shores.

Every time the Aussies turned to the scoreboard that Monday afternoon they must have had the shivers. The Hutton-Hammond partnership for the third wicket lasted until four o'clock: from 434 to 546 the England figures rose, and it began to look like a timeless Test in very truth!

A timeless Test! That meant defence and attack in right proportions, and I believed that we, one after another, were achieving it. Surely the tremendous advantage of possessing a rock-like defence was illustrated in the batting of Wally Hammond, let alone in mine! Heartbreak Hammond was his rightful title that afternoon!. ... As for myself, I had long since realized that no matter how brilliant a stroke-player one may be, there will be times when, in the best interests of his side, he is called on to defend his wicket at all costs.

Thirty thousand onlookers must have felt they were having the lesson of their lives as they watched the methods the England batsmen used to fit in with the play-to-a-finish idea. They saw how considerably the height of the back lift differs, according to the length and speed of the ball. If the batsman receives a half-volley outside the off-stump his back lift will be higher as he makes the logical cover-drive than if he played back or with a forward defensive stroke. And a good defensive batsman is always the one whose bat travels the shortest distance, which practically ensures a correct stroke.

Those onlookers must have noticed also that if the batsman's guard is leg-stump he lifts the bat up in line with the very same leg-stump, perfectly straight, although there are very few first-class players who actually do so consistently. To lift the bat straight may sound easy, but it isn't. It means a lot, though, because if it is lifted straight it is not likely to come down crooked!

Suppose, for instance, the bat is lifted in the direction of second slip, the position of it when the top of the lift is reached is a cross-bat position, and to make it possible to play down the flight of the ball a straightening of the bat is absolutely necessary. Otherwise the batsman plays across the line of flight – and that is fatal.

To watch Walter Hammond, as I watched him from the other crease at the Oval, was to be reminded once again that cricket is a game of timing and hair's breadth precision. An inch or two may mean a slip catch or a boundary, a second or two a fluke stroke or a complete miss. So that the time taken up in bringing the bat to the straight is of supreme value. The quicker a batsman's mind decides what shot is to be played, and the more economical his effort to shape for it successfully, the nearer greatness he is sure to be.

Hammond's greatness was plain. In backplay and forward-play alike. In attack as well as defence. He was thoroughly in agreement with the expert who declared that a ball pitched sufficiently far up to be played forward against is far enough up to be driven. The working principle of the attacking batsman is that a half-volley is a half-volley even if it is delivered by the greatest bowler in the world – even by an Australian in a timeless Test! And a footnote to the principle – no batsman of any sort can afford to overlook it – is that 'the bowler can only bowl one ball at a time!'

When my captain left me at a quarter past four, lbw to Fleetwood-Smith, the England total was 546 for three. Hammond scored 59, having spent eighty minutes gathering his last 21. My score had passed 250, and soon after the tea interval I beat R.E. Foster's one-time record for the highest individual score in England v Australia Tests – 287, a record that had stood for twenty-seven years, until Bradman broke it.

It can be imagined how moved I was to receive a telegram at the Oval from Mrs S. Foster, head of the famous Foster family, who, so they told me, was eighty-nine years of age. The message read:

'Cordial congratulations from the mother of R.E. Foster and all Aberdovey sportsmen.'

That telegram has been treasured among my happiest keepsakes ever since. Every time I turn it up I picture afresh that dear old lady, grateful that I had revived for others the memories she cherished of her 'boys', especially 'R.E.', who died in 1914. It is the sort of telegram my own Mother might have sent.

Meanwhile two more wickets had fallen – very cheaply. Eddie Paynter came and left for nothing, and Denis Compton came and left for just one run more than nothing. The encouragement derived from these happenings by the Australian bowlers and fieldsmen, however, was short-lived, for Joe Hardstaff joined me next, and at the close of the second day's play we were still together. Joe was 40 and I had reached exactly 300. The minute-long cheering that greeted me then still rings in my ears.

Some of the bowling figures when we went in were grotesque and almost incredible. Fleetwood-Smith, for example, had bowled seventy overs with only eight maidens, and one wicket for 235 runs! O'Reilly had two for 144 in sixty-six overs – nineteen maidens: and Waite had one for 121. I heard a humorist say as we left the ground: 'Old England seems well placed tonight!'

An understatement indeed. And yet it was as well that the timeless Test angle should not be hidden in that flood of runs. A lot of illustrious old-timers were present at the match, following it from hour to hour and day to day with far, far more than ordinary appreciation; there were not only Jack Hobbs and W.M. Woodfull, but J.N. Crawford, once an England and Surrey captain, and Cecil Parkin, also an England cricketer – from Lancashire. It was Cecil Parkin who asked a pointed question: 'How will our bowlers fare on this wicket? If the weather holds, I am afraid that Hammond will find himself in the same predicament as Bradman.'

In other words, the England score of 546 was only relatively a big one. There was no telling what the Australians would do in reply. Playing to a finish had a particular interpretation for them. . . . Our third-day purpose, therefore, must be to go on with the run-getting, and never mind the clock!

It was then that I listened to my team mates, my friends and the newspaper men who had been reminding me of the chance that was being offered me of beating Don Bradman's record score of 334, made at Leeds in 1930.

I needed only 35 to reach the highest ever compiled in a Test match anywhere: thirty-five runs, and remembering how swiftly a transformation can take place in cricket – and, moreover, remembering how the England scoreboard had changed from 545 for two to 555 for five that very afternoon, I realized that those runs would not necessarily be superfluous.

And as I thought all round the idea something reminded me that this was a once-in-a-lifetime opportunity, and it might never, never be mine again.

In that same season when I chatted with Don Bradman I had told him that eight years earlier as a youngster of fourteen I made the journey from Fulneck to Headingley with a bigger boy, Billy Bray of Pudsey – do you remember, Billy? – and there, sitting among the packed crowd on the popular side of the ring, I saw Don's world-highest innings, every ball bowled. Little did I think, that far-off day, that I would ever challenge his wonderful achievement: not even when I, a Test cricketer also, recalled it to him did it occur to me that I might ever be his rival in run-getting!

I slept hardly at all on the fateful night before the third day of the Test. I could not help picturing the culmination of my innings and it seemed as if the hardest part of it was still ahead – yes, even though I only needed a handful of runs! I began to believe that I was going to hit over the straight full toss as soon as I got to the crease or put the ball into silly mid-off's hands!

That night was an eternity of sleeplessness and introspection. Next morning my legs still ached and I was stiff all over. Joe Hardstaff, my partner, gave me his good wishes as we started out from the pavilion, and he spoke as if it was the most natural thing in the world that I should have a go for the Test record. Thus strengthened I faced a field which, being wholly defensive, made me aware that I would have to fight every inch of the way. I scored 10 in the first half-hour, and 10 in the second.

I was taking no chances. I tried to imagine myself playing an ordinary innings, and that I was just beginning it. . . .

At 328 Bradman stationed himself at silly mid-off, only a few yards from the bat. Bill O'Reilly bowled exactly as he had been doing for two days, keeping the immaculate length and direction that made him unique in his time. But my concentration never faltered for a single ball. . . . I took single runs and twos as they came . . . Nor did Fleetwood-Smith, going on at the Vauxhall end, exhaust my patience or tempt me unduly – and my score reached 331.

I had a feeling that Fleetwood-Smith – 'Chuck' to cricketers – might bowl me a bad ball sooner or later, one that I could safely hit to the boundary. The great crowd had clapped each of my scoring hits so far, but now a tremendous hush was on them, and the deep, collective sigh of relief and satisfaction that followed each of six deliveries from him, real beauties, requiring the utmost skill to counter – who can deny that I felt that sigh out there in the middle! Three hundred and thirty-one, and four runs wanted. . . .

It was exactly a quarter to one, after an hour and a quarter of the greatest intensity, that the ball I had been waiting for was bowled by Fleetwood-Smith – a short one inside the off-stump, and I cut it fiercely to the boundary.

Pandemonium broke out with such suddenness that I was staggered. The Oval crowd rose to me in a way I shall never forget, and a perfect blizzard of cheers and applause stopped play as effectively as violent rain can do. Hurrahs and cries of 'Well done,' victory shouts and a song, 'For He's a Jolly Good Fellow' – the latter accompanied by a cornet from somewhere near the gasometer – these were renewed again and again, and a Titanic roar of approval swept round the ground as Don Bradman, his wonder feat outdone, dashed up to me and shook hands, followed by Joe Hardstaff from the other crease, and the whole of the Australian team. . . . All except poor Bill O'Reilly, who saved his outwearied limbs the exertion of coming in from third man by flinging himself down on his back for a snatch of rest!

Celebration drinks were brought out while the thunderous noises went on flaming up everywhere, and such was the din that I could hardly hear what was being said to me. In fact the only thing quite clear amid the tumult was the scoreboard with its magical figures. When play was resumed they went on changing and changing until, at half past two, after I had batted thirteen hours and twenty minutes – longer than anybody else in a first-class innings – I was caught at cover-point by Lindsay Hassett off O'Reilly. My marathon total was 364, including thirty-five boundaries, and England were 770 for six wickets.

The warm-hearted cricket crowd were not too surfeited by their recent rejoicing to deny me, as I returned to the pavilion, a welcome home that in itself was memorable. Indeed, I found that the thunderclap as Don Bradman and Joe Hardstaff rushed up to me when I broke the record was really only the beginning of a storm of handshaking, back-patting, and all the other ways men have, good and not so good, of expressing their congratulations. The handshakes of my four Yorkshire colleagues in the England side, Maurice Leyland, Hedley Verity, Arthur Wood, and Bill Bowes, gave me the greatest pleasure of all. And of the fifteen hundred telegrams that came pouring in, the one I particularly remember was from a Yorkshire player in the county match at Trent Bridge. He expressed a 'sincere hope' that I would repeat my performance in the second innings!

While Joe Hardstaff was adding runs to the hundred he reached just before I got out – he finished up with 169 not out – and our own Arthur Wood was brightly knocking the depressed-looking attack for the fifteenth 50 of the match, I was promising Howard Marshall, the broadcaster, to say something over the air. I hardly appreciated what I was doing. I was in a sort of dream.... Altogether I gave three radio talks, eventually, about my achievement and other things in cricket, and Leslie Mitchell interviewed me in a televised programme. This was especially worth while to me, because it enabled me to see television at work for the first time.

In the broadcast soon after my innings ended I said: 'I must say that it was a very tiring and hard job. The Australian bowlers bowled very well, and they did not give any runs away at all. It was also difficult to get those last few runs and I was glad when it was all over.'

I did not bat again in that final Test, nor did any of the England side. For the few people who need to be told why, I will explain that our victory was overwhelming. We declared at 903 for seven, and in next to no time the bowling of Bill Bowes had made the Australian position hopeless. Bradman and Fingleton met with regrettable accidents and could not bat, so that with totals of 201 and 123 the defeat was by an innings and 579 runs. At the finish, because of Yorkshire's big share in the England victory, the thousands of cheering spectators who gathered in front of the pavilion joined in a community rendering of 'On Ilkla Moor Baht 'At'.*

From *Cricket Is My Life* by Len Hutton
(Hutchinson, London, 1949)

---

* England won by an innings and 579 runs and drew the series. England 903–7 (L. Hutton 364, M. Leyland 187, J. Hardstaff jun 169, W. R. Hammond 59, A. Wood 53), Australia 201 (W. A. Brown 69, W. E. Bowes 5–49) and 123 (K. Farnes 4–63).

Wilfred Rhodes and Herbert Sutcliffe

Neville Cardus

I used to listen to the great Wilfred Rhodes for hours at the cricket grounds. Though he had lost his eyesight in 1952, his brain and his tongue were as active as ever and he was ninety-five when he died in 1973. He was only twenty when he first bowled for Yorkshire in a match against MCC at Lords in 1898: thirty-two seasons later when he retired he had scored almost 40,000 runs and taken 4,184 wickets. In 1902 he went in last for England at The Oval joining George Hirst, when 15 runs were wanted to beat Australia. England won by one wicket, but Wilfred always denied, contrary to the popular story repeated here by Neville Cardus, that Hirst had said to him, 'Wilf, we'll get them in singles.'

In 1926 when he was nearly forty-nine he helped England win the Ashes back from Australia at The Oval. He reckoned Sidney Barnes was the greatest bowler of any kind he'd seen: 'The best of 'em today is half as good as Barnie.' He reckoned the best slow left-arm bowler was Colin Blythe of Kent and England, killed in action in 1917 at the age of thirty-eight, the same age at which Hedley Verity was killed in Italy in 1943. Wilfred was one of a succession of outstanding slow left-arm bowlers who played for Yorkshire, including Verity himself. Edmund Peate, who died when he was only forty-four ('It may fairly be said that he would have lasted longer if he had organized his life more carefully,' said Wisden) was succeeded by Bobby Peel, another who liked a drink.

Peel's great feats for Yorkshire and England included 8 for 53 when W.G. Grace led England to victory against Australia for the last time in 1896. But the following year when he was not yet forty Peel turned up at Bramall Lane much the worse for drink. Hirst and his other team-mates had tried to make him stay in the hotel and plead that he was unwell. but he insisted on turning up at the ground. He marked out his run and then proceeded to run towards the sight screen at his own end. Lord Hawke sent him off and he was never seen in the Yorkshire team again. This opened the way for Wilfred to come into the side and stopped him joining Warwickshire where he had been for trials. Peel's banishment was as abrupt as the dismissal of that other great left-arm bowler for Yorkshire, Johnny Wardle, after he'd written newspaper articles criticizing the new captain, Ronnie Burnet. As with Peel it was a shame for a player who had served Yorkshire so well to go out in public disgrace.

F.S.T.

Nobody scarcely heard Rhodes appealing except the umpires. He had a throaty voice and the quiddity of him was expressed by the brass stud he wore in his cricket shirt. He lived in the Golden Age; he was the greatest slow bowler in the world when he was a youth. He saw Trumper, Maclaren, Ranji. But he kept his head, in spite of them. In conversation with him, I once had occasion to deplore that in modern years the square-cut was seldom to be seen, much to the loss of the game's brilliance. He unhesitatingly answered 'Well, it never were a business stroke . . .'

He played against Australia at Kennington Oval in 1902, and had to go in last when fifteen were wanted for victory by England. He and George Hirst got them; and the story goes that Hirst met Rhodes on his way to the wicket and said, 'Wilfred, we'll get them in singles.' It was the most unnecessary caution ever given a Yorkshireman, young or old. And it was at Kennington Oval that Rhodes ended his Test match career, in August, 1926; and he played a big share in winning the rubber for us. As he grew older, he naturally lost some of his spin. But, as he informed me more than once: 'If batsman thinks ball's spinning', then it is spinnin'.'

Of Rhodes I wrote one of the best bits of prose of my life: it dates from my 'second period':

> 'Flight was his secret, flight and the curving line, now higher, now lower, tempting, inimical; every ball like every other ball, yet somehow unlike; each over in collusion with the others, part of a plot. Every ball a decoy, a spy sent out to get the lie of the land; some balls simple, some complex, some easy, some difficult; and one of them – ah, which? – the master ball.'

It is not known, and will now never be known, what Rhodes and Robinson in their hearts thought of Sutcliffe, who made his hair resplendent with brilliantine and wore immaculate flannels and on the whole comported with an elegance which in the Yorkshire XI was unique and apochryphal. He did not speak with the accent of Yorkshire but of Teddington. He would refer casually to the fact that he had yesterday 'mootered' down from Pudsey to London. Witnesses could be called to testify that at Lord's Sutcliffe has held up fast bowlers in the middle of their approaches to the wicket and with a wave of his bat has removed some obstruction to his vision in the pavilion, probably a peer of the realm, who has bent double and crawled away into invisibility while members have gone red in the face at him and said, 'Sit down, sir; sit down.'

Herbert Sutcliffe, so stylish and unruffled, raised the status of all professional crick-eters. He was also good to young players like myself – encouraging me with his interest and praise.

F.S.T.

Sutcliffe rose to the highest place amongst batsmen of his period, and rose there as much by self-esteem as by technique. He simply refused to bow before the best ball in the world. I have seen him beaten by five consecutive balls in a Test match and at the end of the over he has crossed his legs, reclined on his bat, and surveyed the scene with the air of one not to be touched by vicissitudes that affect common folk. In a Lancashire and Yorkshire match he was fielding close to the wicket on the leg-side. The batsman hit a ball straight at him and it struck him a cracking blow on the ankle. For a second he was compelled to forget himself; for a moment he hopped about, in undignified pain. But when one or two of his colleagues, including Emmott Robinson, came towards him to see how badly he was hurt, he recovered poise and waved them from him as though saying: 'Thank you, but we Sutcliffes do not have pain.' The county capable of containing a Rhodes, a Robinson, and a Sutcliffe is, I should say, capable of anything besides having as many acres as words in the Bible.

The advent into cricket, and into the Yorkshire XI of all places, of a Herbert Sutcliffe was a sign of the times; the old order was not changing, it was going; the pole was fall'n; young boys and girls level now with men; captains of cricket were henceforth called 'skipper' by all self-respecting professionals, never 'Sir.'

From *Autobiography* by Neville Cardus
(Hamish Hamilton, London, 1984).

'What is a Yorkshireman? A man born within the sound of Bill Bowes.'

Ted Dexter.

Hedley Verity

R.C. Robertson-Glasgow

When Captain Hedley Verity of the Green Howards died of wounds in Italy on 31 July 1943, Don Bradman said, 'He was one of the greatest if not *the* greatest left-hand bowler of all time. Most certainly he could lay just claim to that honour during the 1918–39 period. No doubt his Yorkshire environment was of great assistance, for left-hand bowling seems to be in the blood of Yorkshiremen. Although opposed to him in many Tests, I could never claim to have completely followed his strategy, for it was never static nor mechanical.'

In England alone in nine and a half seasons he took 1,558 wickets for an average of 13.71. No other bowler approached this economy – and that in an era when the bat generally reigned supreme. His last game was at Hove against Sussex on 1 September 1939 when, just hours after Hitler had invaded Poland and county cricket came to a full stop, he took seven Sussex wickets for just nine runs on a drying wicket. Sussex were all out for 33 runs and after the Yorkshire captain Brian Sellers had used the heavy roller, Yorkshire knocked off the 25 runs necessary for victory. As Verity walked off the field at Hove he said, 'I wonder if I shall ever bowl here again?'

Alas, he never did; a bigger game was afoot. After he was wounded an Italian doctor removed a bullet from his lung, but the wound became infected. He had three haemorrhages and died on the fourth day. It was not till 1 September, exactly four years after that last game at Hove, that the news of his death came through. Bill Bowes first heard the news in a prisoner of war camp. 'I walked out into the deserted roadway through the camp. The wind was cold but I did not notice it. Headley … dead. It was unbelievable. For a long time I walked up and down that road, time stilled, living again the many incidents and hours we shared together.' The achievements of this modest, quiet but tough and courageous man are well summed up in the Wisden obituary by the Somerset player and famous cricket writer R.C. Robertson-Glasgow.

F.S.T.

HEDLEY VERITY
Born May 18, 1905; died of wounds received in action, July 31, 1943

He received his wounds in the Eighth Army's first attack on the German positions at Catania, in Sicily. Eye-witnesses, who were a few yards from Verity when he was hit, have told the story. The objective was a ridge with strong points and pillboxes. Behind a creeping barrage Verity led his company forward 700 yd. When the barrage ceased, they went on another 300 yd and neared the ridge, in darkness. As the men advanced, through corn 2 ft high, tracer-bullets swept into them. Then they wriggled through the corn, Verity encouraging them with 'Keep going, keep going.' The moon was at their back, and the enemy used mortar-fire, Very lights and fire-bombs, setting the corn alight. The strongest point appeared to be a farmhouse, to the left of the ridge; so Verity sent one platoon round to take the farmhouse, while the other gave covering fire. The enemy fire increased, and, as they crept forward, Verity was hit in the chest. 'Keep going,' he said, 'and get them out of that farmhouse.' When it was decided to withdraw, they last saw Verity lying on the ground, in front of the burning corn, his head supported by his batman, Pte Thomas Reynoldson, of Bridlington. So, in the last grim game, Verity showed, as he was so sure to do, that rare courage which both calculates and inspires.

His Bowling Art

Judged by any standard, Verity was a great bowler. Merely to watch him was to know that. The balance of the run-up, the high ease of the left-handed action, the scrupulous length, the pensive variety, all proclaimed the master. He combined nature with art to a degree not equalled by any other English bowler of our time. He received a handsome legacy of skill and, by an application that verged on scientific research, turned it into a fortune. There have been bowlers who reached greatness without knowing, or, perhaps, caring to know just how or why; but Verity could analyse his own intentions without losing the joy of surprise and describe their effect without losing the company of a listener. He was the ever-learning professor, justly proud yet utterly humble.

In the matter of plain arithmetic, so often torn from its context to the confusion of judgment, Verity, by taking 1,956 wickets at 14.87 runs each in 10 years of first-class cricket, showed by far the best average during this century. In the recorded history of cricket the only bowlers of this class with lower averages are: Alfred Shaw, 2,072 wickets at 11.97 each; Tom Emmett, 1,595 wickets at 13.43 each; George Lohmann, 1,841 wickets at 13.73 each; James Southerton, 1,744 wickets at 14.30 each. It might be argued that during the period 1854 to 1898, covered by the careers of these cricketers, pitches tended to give more help to the bowler than they did during Verity's time. Verity, I know, for one, would not have pressed such a claim in his own favour. He never dwelt on decimals; and, while he enjoyed personal triumph as much as the next man, that which absorbed his deepest interest was the proper issue of a Test match with Australia or of an up-and-down bout with Lancashire; and if, in his country's or county's struggle towards victory, he brought off some recondite plot for the confounding, of Bradman or McCabe or Ernest Tyldesley or Edward Paynter, well, then he was happy beyond computing.

Notable Feats

Yet his bowling achievements, pressed into but overflowing the 10 years of his career, were so rich and various that they here demand some concentrated notice:

He played in 40 Test matches, taking 144 wickets at 24.37 runs each. He took 100 wickets in Test cricket in a shorter period than any other English bowler.

He is the only cricketer who has taken 14 wickets in a day in a Test match, this feat being performed against Australia at Lord's in the second Test, 1934. During this match, he took 15 wickets for 104 runs, thus sharing with Wilfred Rhodes, his Yorkshire predecessor, the honour of taking most wickets in an England v Australia match.

Twice he took all 10 wickets in an innings; in 1931, against Warwickshire at Headingley, Leeds, for 36 runs in 18.4 (6-ball) overs, six maidens; in 1932, on the same ground, against Nottinghamshire, for 10 runs in 19.4 (6-ball) overs, 16 maidens – a world record in first-class cricket for the fewest number of runs conceded by a bowler taking all 10 wickets in an innings, and it included the hat-trick.

Against Essex at Leyton, in 1933, he took 17 wickets in one day, a record shared only by C. Blythe and T.W. Goddard.

In each of his nine full English seasons he took at least 150 wickets, and he averaged 185 wickets a season; thrice consecutively (1935–36–37) he took over 200 wickets. His average ranged from 12.42 to 17.63. He headed the first-class English bowling averages in his first season (1930) and in his last (1939), and never came out lower than fifth.

How He Began

Verity was born at Headingley, but passed his 25th birthday before he played for Yorkshire, in 1930, the year that W. Rhodes retired. Some of his earlier seasons were spent in playing as an amateur for Rawdon in the Yorkshire Council; for Accrington in the Lancashire league; and for Middleton in the Central league. He was then, as always afterwards when allowed, an all-rounder. As a batsman, his height, reach, concentration and knowledge of what to avoid raised him distinctly from the ruck of mediocrity; but, whereas his bowling included grace, his batting had only style. The former was nature embellished by art; the latter was art improved by imitation.

As a bowler, Hedley Verity stands, and will stand, with his illustrious predecessors in the Yorkshire attack; Edmund Peate (1879–87), Robert Peel (1882–99), Wilfred Rhodes (1898–1930) – the dates indicate the time of their respective playing careers – but Verity was not a slow left-hander in the accepted sense, and he used to reject comparison with Rhodes so far as method was concerned, saying: 'Both of us are left-handed and like taking wickets; let's leave it at that.'

Verity's mean pace was what is called slow-medium; on fast pitches, often about medium; and he would send down an inswinging yorker of an abrupt virulence not unworthy of George Hirst.

Naturally, on wet or crumbled or sticky pitches, he reduced pace and tossed the leg-spinner higher, but even here his variety of pace and of angle of delivery was remarkable. He was a born schemer; tireless, but never wild, in experiment; as sensitive in observation as a good host, or as an instrumentalist who spots a rival on the beat; the scholar who does not only dream, the inventor who can make it work.

Comparison of Giants

Just how good a bowler was he? In relation to rivals in his own craft but of an earlier day, such a question is useless except to amuse an idle hour or to excite an idle quarrel. We can only say that, in his own short time, he was the best of his kind. In England, day in and day out, he may never have quite touched the greatness of Robert Peel, Colin Blythe or Wildred Rhodes. In Australia, neither in 1932–3 or 1936–7, did he perplex their batsmen quite as J.C. White perplexed them in 1928–9, but, as a workman-artist, he will take some beating. H.B. Cameron, that fine wicket-keeper-batsman of South Africa, playing against Yorkshire in 1935, hit him for three fours and three sixes in one over; but very rarely did a batsman survive a liberty taken with Verity. He had, besides, a wonderful skill in restoring the 'rabbits', early and with little inconvenience, to the hutch.

If a touchstone of Verity's greatness be needed, there is D.G. Bradman, the most inexorable scorer of runs that cricket has yet seen, whose Test match average against England stands at 91.42 in 46 innings. I think it was Verity who kept that average under 150. He was one of only three or four bowlers who came to the battle with Bradman on not unequal terms (*haud impar congressus*!); and Bradman was reported as saying: 'I think I know all about Clarrie (Grimmett), but with Hedley I am never sure. You see, there's no breaking-point with him.'

Beating the Best

Verity timed his blows. In the fifth Test match, at Sydney, early in 1933, Australia, 19 runs behind on the first innings, lost Victor Richardson for 0. Woodfull and Bradman added 115; Larwood, injured, had left the field – and that particular Larwood never came back – then Verity deceived Bradman in flight, bowled him for 71 and went on to take five for 33 in 19 overs and win the match. In the earlier Tests, amid the fast bowling and the clamour, not much had been heard of Verity, except as a rescuing batsman. But, when the last pinch came, there he was to relieve the weary line; very Yorkshire.

Verity never allowed the opinion that Bradman was less than a master on damaged pitches, refusing to stress the evidence of his own triumph at Lord's in 1934 (Bradman c and b Verity 36; c Ames b Verity 13) and referring to Bradman's two innings of 59 and 43 in 1938 against Yorkshire at Sheffield. 'It was a pig of a pitch,' he said, 'and he played me in the middle of the bat right through.' Maybe Verity's opinion of Bradman was heightened by a natural generosity in its giver, but on this matter I think that Verity had reason to know best.

As an all-round fielder, Verity was no more than sound, but to his own bowling, or at backward point, he sometimes touched brilliance; and there sticks in the memory the catch that he made at Lord's in 1938, when McCabe cut one from Farnes crack from the bat's middle.

Opened England Batting

As a batsman for Yorkshire, Verity was mostly kept close to the extras. His build and reach suggested power and freedom, but it remained a suggestion; and he was analogous to those burly golfers who prod the tee-shot down the middle to a prim 180 yd. A casual observer might have mistaken Verity for Sutcliffe a little out of form, for he seemed to have caught something of that master's style and gesture, and, like Sutcliffe, he could be clean bowled in a manner that somehow exonerated the batsman from all guilt. He never quite brought off 'the double', though in 1936 he took 216 wickets and scored 855 runs. But he had the sovereign gift of batting to an occasion. In the 1936–7 visit to Australia, G.O. Allen could find no opening pair to stay together, so he sent in Verity with C.J. Barnett in the fourth Test, at Adelaide, and they put up partnerships of 53 and 45. Not much, perhaps; but the best until then. In all Test matches, his batting average was close on 21; nearly three units higher than his average in all first-class cricket.

Verity had the look and carriage of a man likely to do supremely well something that would need time and trouble. His dignity was not assumed; it was the natural reflection of mind and body harmonized and controlled. He was solid, conscientious, disciplined; and something far more. In all that he did, until his most gallant end, he showed the vital fire, and warmed others in its flame. To the spectator in the field he may have seemed, perhaps, a little stiff and aloof; but among a known company he revealed geniality, wit, and an unaffected kindness that will not be forgotten.

There was no 'breaking-point' with Verity; and his last reported words: 'Keep going,' were but a text on his short and splendid life.

From *The Wisden Book of Obituaries 1892–1985*
compiled by Benny Green (Queen Anne Press, London, 1986).

Brian Close

Brian Johnston

For me Brian Close will always be remembered as the finest captain I ever played under. He led from the front with near-suicidal fielding positions; he was a tough disciplinarian who never accepted less than 100 per cent from his players; and it is not surprising that when he led Yorkshire from 1963 to 1970 we won the championship four times. When he left Yorkshire for Somerset in 1971 that county's fortunes immediately revived. And he knew how to handle the young Ian Botham too.

Closey has a high enough IQ to be a member of MENSA but he also has a very hot temper – especially on the golf course. Once, in a rage, he threw his golf clubs, bag and all into a lake, vowing he would never again play the bloody game and to hell with the clubs. Some time later his playing companions saw him wading into the lake. 'Thought you weren't going to play any more, Closey,' they said. A furious Close replied, 'I've left my car keys in the bag.'

He plays golf to a single figure handicap either right- or left-handed and he was once asked how he decided which way round he would play. 'When I wake up in the morning, if my wife is lying on her right side I play right-handed,' he is supposed to have said. 'If she is on her left I play left-handed.' 'But supposing she is lying on her back when you wake up?' he was asked. He retorted, 'I ring up the golf club to say that I shall be an hour late.'

In a car he is as fearless about fast driving as he was about fast bowling and many people, Illingworth among them, refused to ride with him. As an after-dinner speaker he will carry on for as long as Len Hutton batted at The Oval in 1938 – or would do if anyone let him. As an amateur magician he could have put Tommy Cooper out of business. None of his tricks ever work. It's hilarious.

But on the field he was deadly serious. In twenty-nine seasons he made nearly 35,000 runs batting left-handed and was a useful right-arm off-spinner taking over 1,100 wickets. But it was as a captain that he really excelled. Brian, like myself, was always outspoken and that cost him dear when he looked certain, after a very successful run as England's captain, to continue the job as skipper when England toured the West Indies in 1967–8. But then when Yorkshire played Warwickshire at Edgbaston in the August he adopted some time-wasting tactics, bowling only two overs in fifteen minutes, which left Warwick nine short of victory. He was seriously reprimanded and the selectors asked for an assurance that he would never employ such tactics in the West Indies. With a mixture of honesty and obstinacy Close felt he could not give the assurance, so the job went to Colin Cowdrey instead. My thoughts went back to this when I saw the cynical time-wasting employed by the West Indies in the third Test at Port of Spain in 1990 when England were denied victory by a West Indies over rate of less than nine overs an hour over a period of *two hours*. Fat chance of the West Indies selectors demanding a guarantee from the West Indian captain never to employ such disgraceful and unsporting tactics again! And why not a strong protest from our authorities? Are they men or mice who run British cricket these days?

F.S.T.

Once when Yorkshire were playing Gloucestershire, Brian Close was in his usual position at forward short leg, only a few feet away from the batsman, who was Martin Young. Ray Illingworth bowled a shortish ball which Martin pulled really hard. The ball hit Brian on the forehead over the right eye. From there it ricocheted to Phil Sharpe at first slip, who took an easy balloon catch. Blood poured from Brian's forehead, but except for the occasional dab with a handkershief he just carried on regardless, still only a few feet from the bat. At the interval as he walked up the pavilion steps, a member stopped him and said: 'Mr Close, I know you are very brave but you really must not stand so close to the bat. It's far too dangerous. Just think what might have happened if it had hit you in the *middle* of the forehead.' 'It would have been caught at cover,' was Brian's reply.

In 1963 at Lord's against the West Indies, he stepped down the pitch to play the fast bowling of Hall and Griffiths. If he missed the ball, he deliberately let it hit him on the body, and knowing him he would not have been wearing any protective clothing. I'm also pretty sure that he was batting bare-headed.

He made 70 before charging down the pitch once too often. When he got back to the dressing-room his body was a mass of purple bruises. I'm told he looked rather like a dalmatian dog – spotted all over. It was one of the most courageous innings I have ever seen, but he rivalled it thirteen(!) years later when he was recalled at the age of forty-five to the England side against the West Indies at Old Trafford. After Greenidge had made his second hundred of the Match Clive Lloyd declared just after tea on the Saturday, setting England a victory target of 552! Brian and John Edrich opened for England with a combined age of eighty-four, and had to face eighty minutes of the fastest and most hostile bowling I have ever seen. It was a travesty of what cricket is meant to be. Bouncer followed bouncer unchecked by the umpires. Both batsmen defended bravely and grimly, not attempting to score. Roberts and Holding were the chief culprits, backed up by Daniel. They were quite uncontrolled and even Lloyd had to admit afterwards that 'our fellows got carried away' (what is a captain for?). It finally took three bouncers in succession from Holding to Close before Bill Alley warned him. Both batsmen held on bravely until the close, by which time Brian had yet to get off the mark, but it was the most gallant nought I ever saw in a Test match.

From *It's Been a Piece of Cake* by Brian Johnston
(Methuen, London, 1989).

Surrey Grit: J.H. Edrich's 310

Colin Cowdrey

Grit isn't a monopoly of Yorkshiremen – not quite, anyway. I admired the fighting qualities of several Surrey players – Tony Lock who never knew when he was beaten, even when he had to remodel his bowling action in mid-career; battling Ken Barrington who, in Wally Grout's phrase, 'Always looked as if he had a Union Jack on his back whenever he went in'; and John Edrich, Surrey and England opener, one of only ten men to top 300 in a Test – a truly remarkable innings against New Zealand in 1965, as Colin Cowdrey here describes.

F.S.T.

An astonishing cricket episode in the mid-sixties period occurred at Leeds when John Edrich scored 310 not out against New Zealand. I have never witnessed a more remarkable innings, nor have I seen one which so accurately reflected the character and temperament of the man playing it.

The point here was that England batted first on a pitch so grassy, so classically a seam bowler's paradise, that it would not have surprised me had both teams been shot out for little more than 200 in each of their first innings. Furthermore, New Zealand, though hardly one of the dynamic cricketing powers of the period, were on this occasion ideally equipped to exploit the conditions. They had Motz, Collinge, Taylor and Congdon too, who could all move the ball off the seam with the expertise of an experienced English medium-pacer. This they proceeded to do with the early encouragement of Bob Barber's wicket.

At this point Ken Barrington joined Edrich and took the England score from 13 to 382. All the while I was padded up and perched on the edge of my seat, for never an over went by when it did not seem probable rather than possible that a wicket was going to fall. Barrington, calling on all his experience in these conditions, batted extremely well. But it was Edrich's innings that was truly remarkable. He either played and missed completely or thrashed the ball through the covers, over extra-cover, wide of mid-wicket or over mid-on. It was one of those innings which continually keep bowlers' hopes alive, whatever punishment they are taking, for sheer logic tells them that it cannot last. But in Edrich's case it did last, from start of play on the opening day until long into the next.

Eventually I got to the wicket with him and had a closer look at what was going on. From that range it just did not seem to add up. The ball was still seaming around, leaving a damp lush green mark every time it pitched, and Edrich continued to play and miss once or twice an over. Yet between errors he still pasted the New Zealand bowlers all over the ground with apparent ease.

The contrast was still more extreme because I could not settle in at all. New Zealand's bowlers held few terrors for me since I had scored 85 against them in the first Test and 119 in the second. But in the third at Leeds, with the ball veering about unpredictably, I played quite skilfully but could not keep the momentum of runs going. Eventually, I was out for 13 and left, bemused by it all. By the time I had taken my pads off Edrich was pounding his way to his third century and, as it transpired, the New Zealanders never did get him out. He scored 310 not out in England's total of 546 for four declared and I am convinced I shall never see another innings like it. It revealed the temperament of a man capable of divorcing from his mind a wild passing shot played only seconds ago, and concentrating on the next ball as a completely new challenge. It is an ability which the really great champion golfers have. Herbert Sutcliffe had this, I am told. Certainly Bill Lawry. It is a quality no coach can instil but Edrich has it in greater measure than any other batsman of his era and it is something for which England, on many occasions, have had reason to be duly thankful.

From *MCC – The Autobiography of a Cricketer* by Colin Cowdrey
(Hodder and Stoughton, London, 1976).

The Wit and Wisdom of F.S.T.

John Arlott

Big Spike, Big Hammer

Fred Trueman had, and still has, immensely strong legs which probably accounted, to a considerable extent, for his remarkable stamina and long career. He had also, as his measurements indicate, strong hips and, as a fast bowler needs to cushion the jolt of delivery, a wide stern. Jim Swanton, remarking on that fact as he passed Fred lying on the massage table, was halted by the instant retort 'A big spike needs a big hammer to drive it home'.

What A Bloody Stroke

The next week [July 1954] Yorkshire went to Northampton where, as one of the players said, 'It wasn't so much a match between Yorkshire and Northants as between Trueman and Tyson: you could tell the crowd felt it and the players did, too.' Tyson put out Lowson at once; then Billy Sutcliffe played a sound and brave innings of 105. Tyson, coming back in the afternoon, bowled Illingworth, which let in Wardle who was, in the words of Jim Sims 'not frightened, but somewhat apprehensive'. When Tyson eventually managed to get at him he gave him the Trueman treatment, first a bouncer and then a straight half-volley which bowled him on the retreat. Trueman was the next batsman, and as he passed Wardle on the way to the wicket he remarked acidly, 'What a bloody stroke'. Within a minute he too was on his way back – bowled Tyson 0 – and when he reached the dressing room, Wardle was waiting with 'What a bloody stroke'. 'Aye,' he said, 'I slipped on that heap of shit you dropped in the crease'. This piece of repartee was admired in the dressing-rooms for months. Tyson had four for 63.

From *Fred – Portrait of a Fast Bowler* by John Arlott
(Eyre and Spottiswoode, London, 1971).

LAST BALL

2

THREE SUPREME MASTERS
Sir Jack Hobbs

R. C. Robertson-Glasgow

No man will ever beat his aggregate of 61,237 runs (despite the loss of four war years), and his 197 centuries is 27 better than the next best. In his first first-class match at twenty-two he played at The Oval against the great W. G. Grace who stroked the beard and said, 'He is goin to be a good 'un.' According to Neville Cardus he never made a bad or hasty stroke – if he was out it was due to an error of judgment not of technique. Yorkshire's Herbert Sutcliffe, for years his opening partner for England, called him 'The best batsman of my generation on all types of wicket. On good wickets I do believe pride of place should be given to Sir Don Bradman.' His career overlapped with Bradman's and he was fifty-one when he hit his last century against Lancashire in his last season of 1934. Here the late R. C. Robertson-Glasgow, with the benefit of personal knowledge playing against him for Somerset, assesses Sir John Berry Hobbs.

F.S.T.

Hobbs was the greatest English batsman that I've seen and tried to remove. He was the most perfectly equipped by art and temperament for any style of innings on any sort of wicket against any quality of opposition. He was thirty-seven years of age when I first had the pleasure of bowling to him. Misleading suggestions are sometimes heard that a cricketer, after the age of thirty, is tottering on the brink of decline. This is humbug; not only in a Pickwickian sense. Tom Hayward was in his thirty-sixth year when, in 1906, he scored 3,518 runs in first-class cricket, which still stands as a record.*

The early Hobbs, before the last war, may have had all the brilliance and daring,

---

* Since, of course, superseded by Compton and Edrich in 1947.

but he would be a rash man who denied that his meridian of skill was shown about the years 1919–26. In the 1924–5 tour to Australia, under A. E. R. Gilligan, he and Herbert Sutcliffe formed an opening pair which many regard as the greatest the game has seen. Back in England for summer 1925, Hobbs scored 16 centuries. Of these, two were made in one match, against Somerset at Taunton. By them he equalled, then passed, Dr Grace's record of 126 centuries. In the next summer he and Sutcliffe made the memorable stand on a difficult wicket against Australia at the Oval in the Fifth Test, the first match of six running in which A. P. J. Chapman led England to victory. Sutcliffe made 161, Hobbs exactly 100; then had his bails flicked off by a beauty from J. M. Gregory. But, apart from the runs, Hobbs showed himself the master tactician. He foxed A. J. Richardson, who was bowling off-spinners, and the Australian captain into thinking he was in difficulties. He was not. So, while the pitch remained difficult, he contrived to keep on and, for the most part, to keep the strike against the spin bowler whom he least feared.

At Taunton, the year before, on a hot August Saturday, I saw him nervous for the only time that I can remember. There was a large crowd, as crowds go in the West; a news-reel cinematograph was perched on the reluctant roof of the little pavilion. The match was 'news'. For Hobbs had made his 125th century some time before, and had been followed round by ill-luck and most of the cricket correspondents. We batted first – more waiting! and fared poorly. Then the struggle began. He was anxious; the strokes were calculating, even stuffy; he was twice nearly lbw, once at each end. At about 30 he gave a chance to wide mid-on, which went wrong. But throughout these embarrassments his instinctive excellence of method saved him from those faults of execution which another man in the same circumstances would, fatally, have committed. At the close of play he was in the early 90s. Then – a Sunday, for more waiting. But nice for the Somerset gate.

On the Monday morning J. J. Bridges and I were the bowlers. I bowled a no-ball in the first over, which Hobbs hit to the square-leg boundary. Someone afterwards suggested that the no-ball was bowled on purpose! It wasn't. Hobbs never needed any presents at the wicket. In Bridges's second over Hobbs scored a single to leg that gave him what he has told me was the toughest century of the lot! His second hundred was a beauty, care-free and brilliant of stroke, and he began with a four past cover that I can still see.

I have seen Hobbs described as a frail man. Actually he had strength of thigh and forearm far above the average, a strength which was concealed in the art of method and grace of movement. His footwork was, as nearly as is humanly possible, perfect. In every stroke he moved into the line of the ball with so little effort that he could bat for hours without over-taxing energy of mind or body. I never saw him unbalanced in a forward stretch, or 'hopping' on a back-stroke. The interplay between judgment and execution was wonderful to see and baffling to attack. He covered his wicket much in defence. So did 'W.G.', according to one of his greatest admirers and opponents, S. M. J. Woods.

There was no one stroke of which you could say that it was less strong than another. You will hear someone remark – 'What a glorious square-cut Headley has!' or, 'Do you remember Hendren hooking?' You will not hear that of Hobbs. All his strokes, that is, all the strokes in the game, were equally strong and easy; they were of an even perfection. He would hook bumpers off his nose; and, as to leg-breakers, which can find out the faults of the best, he mastered them all in turn, from the South Africans on their matting, when he was young, to Mailey, Grimmett, and Freeman, when he was in early middle-age.

To crown all, he had the gift of smiling quietly at failure and triumph alike.

From *Crusoe on Cricket – The Cricket Writings of R. C. Robertson-Glasgow,*
introduction by Alan Ross
(Pavilion, London, 1985).

First-class Cricket at Fifty-four

John King, of Leicestershire, left-hand bat and bowler, went on playing for the county till he was fifty-four years old. In 1904, brought into the Player's side at Lord's as a substitute for J. T. Tyldesley, he scored a century in each innings. In his latter years he was a slowish mover between the wickets, and once, being run out at Leicester by many yards while facing the right way for the pavilion, he was told by umpire Reeves to 'keep on running, John, while your legs are loose'. John was very angry about this.

From *Crusoe on Cricket* by R. C. Robertson-Glasgow
(Pavilion, London, 1985).

A Memorable Test Match

Sir Donald Bradman

As much as anything else, Sir Donald Bradman was the master technician. He played in only 52 Tests and in 80 innings scored 6,996 runs for an average of 99.94. Another four and he would have averaged 100 in Test cricket, but an Eric Hollies googly got him for a duck second ball in his last test at The Oval in 1948. He reached three figures or more twenty-nine times in eighty Test innings – a century strike rate not approached by anyone else. Here he describes what was probably his most nearly perfect innings. It was at Lords in 1930 when he made only two false strokes – one was a thickish edge, and the second got him out for 254! Otherwise every ball went exactly where he intended it, as he now describes.

F.S.T.

My theme is the Second Test at Lord's between Australia and England in 1930. It was a magnificent match in which all the facets of the game were on display in a manner befitting the finest traditions of Test cricket.

Both sides had beautifully balanced selections. England's team was a captain's dream in that it contained a fast bowler to open one end (Allen) plus a medium-fast the other end (Tate), supported by a left-hand first-finger spinner (White) and a right-hand, leg-spin googly bowler (Robins). The reserve attack was another right-hand medium-pacer (Hammond) and a second left-hand first-finger spinner (Woolley).

Australia had a fast bowler (Wall) supported by two medium-pacers (Fairfax and McCabe), with the leg-spinner (Grimmett) and a left-hand first-finger spinner (Hornibrook) as the old ball brigade.

In batting, England had left- and right-hand openers (Hobbs and Woolley), plus a strong line-up to follow which included another left-hander (Chapman). Australia did not possess quite the same variety because she had no top line left-hand batsman.

The match was played in beautiful weather on a pitch which encouraged batsmen to play their shots freely. England won the toss and at the end of the first day had accumulated 405 for nine. As the match was limited to four days, some commentators believed Chapman could have closed at that figure, but he elected to bat on until the side was all out for 425.

The outstanding feature of England's batting was a glorious century by Duleep-sinhji, playing in his first Test. The young Indian played with a lissom grace that charmed friend and foe alike. His strokes were deceptively powerful. I had the job of fielding in the covers when Grimmett was bowling and my hands were sore from stopping his drives.

In the finish I caught him almost on the boundary at extra cover from a lofted drive. His total of 173 took four and three-quarter hours and must have pleased the great Ranji who, I understand, watched the whole innings. Rumour has it that Ranji gently rebuked him for getting out off a careless shot.

When Woodfull and Ponsford opened for Australia it was generally felt that Australia would be on the defensive, but these two solid openers put together a partnership of 162, of which Ponsford made exactly half. In accordance with accepted custom the players were presented to His Majesty the King around the time of the tea interval. Immediately following that break in the play Ponsford was caught at slip, causing some pressmen to say England's best bowler that afternoon was the King.

I was next in and recall clearly that my first delivery was from Jack White, a ball to which I jumped down the pitch and drove into the covers. Woodfull was eventually out ten minutes before close of play on the second day having made 155, and by a coincidence I was 155 not out at stumps.

On the Monday, Australia continued piling on the runs at great speed and finally Woodfull closed the innings at 729 for six wickets. There was temporary confusion when the scoreboard couldn't produce the requisite 7. My own innings ended when I was on 254. It was without doubt the most technically satisfying of my career. I batted altogether 330 minutes and in the whole of the innings only played two strokes which did not go precisely where I intended them to.

The first was a defensive stroke to which I got a thick edge towards second slip, and the second was a cover drive from which I was dismissed. Actually the latter went almost exactly where I intended it to go but I lofted the ball just enough for Percy Chapman to grab it in his outstretched right hand (he was a natural left-hander), inches from the ground. The ball was travelling like a rocket and I believe it was the finest catch ever to dismiss me in my whole career.

In England's second innings her outstanding batsman was Chapman, who played a breezy swashbuckling knock for 121 in which he really gave Clarrie Grimmett the stick. Percy took chances and led a charmed existence. Early on he skied a simple catch to cover but Ponsford and Richardson both left it to the other, only to see the catch fall harmlessly to earth.

Finally England totalled 375, thus leaving Australia a mere 72 to win. It looked a foregone conclusion as there was plenty of time, but amidst great tension and excitement Australia lost three wickets (including mine) for 22 runs. This time I was caught by Chapman, fielding in the gully, who picked up off his shoe laces a powerfully struck cut – another really wonderful piece of fielding. Suddenly England seemed to be in with a chance, but Woodfull and McCabe steered Australia safely home with about one and a half hours left for play.

The match produced magnificent batting by both sides, brilliant fielding, and even though the bowling figures suffered from the batting onslaught, there was much to admire and a great variety to savour. In ninety minutes less than the full four days allotted to the match no less than 1,601 runs had been scored, so that was a scoring rate of roughly 400 runs per day.

Australia bowled 244.8 overs, England 260.2, so that 505 overs were sent down at the rate of aproximately 132 per day; or close to 24 per hour. Looking at the quality and balance of the bowling sides, it makes a mockery of the funereal rates served up by most modern sides where there is undue reliance on fast and medium-pace bowlers who take run-ups out of all proportion to their speed.

I have seen more exciting, more intense struggles, but from an enjoyment point of view I think that wonderful Lord's Test produced everything spectators could ask for. It will always live in my memory.

From *Tales From Around the Wicket* by the Lords' Taverners
(A Graham Tarrant book by David and Charles, Newton Abbott, 1989)

Walter Hammond

Jack Fingleton

Wally Hammond began as an audacious stroke player – Oldfield of Australia called him 'The Perfect Batting Artist' and then he became, as Cardus put it, 'The Successor to Hobbs as the Monument and Foundation of the England Innings ... bringing into force the Jardinian theory of the Survival of the Most Durable.' In five tests against Australia in 1928–9 he scored 905 runs, averaging 113.12.

He was born in Kent in 1903. When his father was killed in World War I the family moved to Cirencester, and so he became the county's greatest player since W. G. Grace. In all first-class games he scored 50,493 runs for an average of 56.10 with 167 centuries. In Tests he made 7,249 runs for an average of 58.45. His last tour of Australia in 1946–47, at the age of forty-three, was an anti-climax. His form, crippled by lumbago, was poor. Nor was he the friendly outgoing ambassador of cricket that the Australians had a right to expect with the first MCC tour after the War.

He crossed swords with Sir Donald Bradman, his opposing captain. But when he died at the relatively early age of sixty-two, from an illness due in great part to severe injuries suffered in a motor accident five years earlier, the Don was generous in his praise: 'I have never seen a batsman so strong on the off side and as a fieldsman he ranked as one of the greatest. He was usually too busy scoring runs to worry about bowling, but he was a much better bowler than he was given credit for.'

F.S.T.

The Strand, from my fourth-floor eyrie in the Charing Cross Hotel, is always a fascinating sight by day and night. The commuters in the morning run helter-skelter in one direction. Another few hours and they are scurrying the other way. Yet again a few more hours, when all the lights are gleaming, and it is a hustle for the theatres. I never tired of watching the bustling throng and it was from high up, I recall, that I last saw Wally Hammond. He was unmistakeable as he weaved his way through the traffic and impulsively I called out 'Coo-ee, Wally'.

The pigeons slumbering or courting on the Cross below stampeded in flight. Several policemen looked up. So did some taxi-drivers. So also did Hammond, who waved. A piercing Australian bush call is an odd thing in the heart of London but that, on a July afternoon in 1948, I remember, was the last time I saw Wally Hammond, moving gracefully up the Strand as he once used to saunter from first slip to first slip.

Somebody once wrote that Hammond coming to bat was one of the sights of the cricket world – like a galleon moving along in full sail. Hammond was all grace. In moments of stress on a cantankerous turf, Bradman permitted his body some odd contortions. Once, on a wet Test pitch, he knocked his stumps over from behind against India. I used to think of Sobers as the very epitome of batting grace until one day at Port of Spain when his judgment forsook him against Sincock and his body, with legs plaited, became a convulsive question mark. I never saw anything like that happen to Hammond.

No action by him with bat, ball or in the field ever offended the eye. He was never caught off balance, or, if so, I never saw it and I saw a mighty lot of him in the middle. Once, in a Test, I snicked to slip. Ames had been injured and Paynter, standing back, was the substitute wicket-keeper. Paynter threw himself sprawling at the catch. He succeeded only in clouding Hammond's view, but, behind Paynter, Hammond took the catch inches from the ground, poised, unruffled, yet having only the merest glimmer of the ball.

Frank Woolley, who surely got out of bed on the wrong side at least this once, said in 1938 that there were thirty English batsmen as good as Hammond before the First World War. Maybe, as the politicians often say, Woolley was misquoted. O'Reilly says that Hammond was the best English batsman he bowled against – and they brought Woolley back in 1934 in England purely to negate O'Reilly, which he didn't do. O'Reilly scoffed at the suggestion that Hammond was weak on the leg stump. 'I never discovered it,' said O'Reilly, 'and I probed him there often.'

Hammond was at his commanding best in limitless Tests in Australia. In 1928–29 he made 251, 200, 177 and 119 not out. In Sydney, in 1936, he made 231 not out. No better innings by an Englishman has been played against Australia this century than his classical 240 at Lord's in 1938. It was a sunny Saturday, Lord's was crowded and Hammond, in all his majesty, made it a day of cherishable memory, even for us in the field. To field against Hammond, and especially in the covers as I did, was a rich adventure. No batsman hit the ball harder through the covers, off front and back foot, than Hammond. The ball stung the hands; it scorched the grass.

Yet it was as a killer of promising young Australian spin bowlers that Hammond excelled. He pummelled Fleetwood-Smith back four years in Melbourne although the same bowler won the Test for Australia in Adelaide in 1937 when he upset Hammond's stumps with one that whistled in from the off, so much spin did it possess. This was the ball, in the final analysis, that won that series for Australia after Allen's side had been two Tests up after two.

Hammond put young Chilvers and Campbell, both of New South Wales, out of English tours altogether, so high and hard did he hit them in Sydney games. In 1932–3, he bided his time in the final Test to hit Lee for two huge sixes on the off and so claim a special bonus for his team that was offered by an Australian firm.

Twice in Tests in Australia, when pitches were left open to the weather, he played memorable if small innings on nigh-impossible wet pitches that allowed the ball to rear and spit with spin. Such pitches, unfortunately, are no more in Australia. The critics and the cynics – the two are often synonymous – loved to see the great tested under such circumstances. Hammond had the mettle and the technique for them.

It was a pity he came once again to Australia, after the Second World War. His greatness had almost gone and he quickly fell out with Bradman, the opposing captain. This was when everybody stood aghast when umpire Borwick, who made some old blemishes in his time, ruled that Ikin had not caught Bradman at second slip.

'A fine bloody way to begin a series, I must say,' grumbled Hammond, when next he passed Bradman at the crease. The only time words passed between the two again on the tour was when Hammond called as Bradman tossed. It was sad that so many saw Hammond that tour for the first time. He was long past his best.

Hammond went to South Africa later and it was there he died. He suffered shocking head injuries once when his car rolled and his body was jammed in the door. Those injuries left their mark.

Hammond was truly great. There were days, and especially if he had failed with the bat, when his bowling was reminiscent of Tate. He was a superb first slip. One remembers a photograph of him batting in Sydney, making his famous cover drive. His black silk handkerchief peeped out of his trouser pocket, his muscles rippled under his billowing silk shirt. No more classical, no more correct stroke could ever have been played. It was faultless and the picture lives in the memory, so truly did it depict Hammond's grace, power and character.

From *Fingleton on Cricket* by Jack Fingleton
(Collins, London, 1972).

THAT MEANS WAR

Neville Cardus

Even if it never happened, Cardus made it seem so.

F.S.T.

A hundred times I have walked down the St John's Wood Road on a quiet morning – that's the proper way to enjoy Lord's: choose a match of no importance, for preference one for which the fixture card promises a 'band if possible'. I have gone a hundred times into the Long Room out of the hot sun and never have I not felt that this is a good place to be in, and if the English simply *had* to make cricket a national institution and a passion and a pride, this was the way to do it, in a handsome hall and pavilion, a resting-place for the game's history, with its constitution to be found as much in Debrett as in 'Wisden'. I have looked through the great windows on the field of play and seen the cricketers in the heat, moving like creatures in another element, the scene as though suspended in time; the crowd a painted canvas; the blue sky and the green of the trees at the nursery end; the lordly ones slumbering on the white seats of the pavilion, or quietly talking. On the Friday morning when Hitler invaded Poland, I chanced to be in this same Long Room at Lord's watching through windows for the last time for years. Though no spectators were present, a match was being continued; there was no legal way of stopping it. Balloon barrages hung over Lord's. As I watched the ghostly movements of the players outside, a beautifully preserved member of Lord's, spats and rolled umbrella, stood near me inspecting the game. We did not speak of course; we had not been introduced. Suddenly two workmen entered the Long Room in green aprons and carrying a bag. They took down the bust of W. G. Grace, put it into the bag, and departed with it. The noble lord at my side watched their every movement; then he turned to me. 'Did you see, sir?' he asked. I told him I had seen. 'That means war,' he said.

From *Autobiography* by Neville Cardus,
(Hamish Hamilton, London, 1984).

3

FAMOUS FOR FIFTEEN MINUTES

A Tale from the Golden Age – Alletson's Mighty Feat

Benny Green

No account of the evolution of cricket would be complete without acknowledging the fact that sometimes a cricketer may strive all his playing days for just one moment of true glory, knowing that one moment will be enough. When Botham was still in single figures at Millford Junior School, an old man crippled by arthritis and confined most of the time to a wheelchair, died at the age of 79 in a Nottinghamshire village. He was poor and obscure, but the incident of his death made him an interesting item in the obituary columns of one or two of the more literate newspapers. These death notices reminded readers of the one day in the old man's life when for an hour or two he took on the lineaments of a superman and then receded back into anonymity, leaving a few thousand spectators who had happened to be present on the right day in the right place, to marvel at what they had seen. Not long before the old man died, the cricket historian and commentator John Arlott had come to see him, to discuss the events of that one amazing day, and to put what he learned into the only book devoted to a single innings by one man.

On the morning of 20 May 1911 a young man hobbled over the shingle on Hove beach and strode into the surf. The sea front was almost deserted. It was the start of a summer whose heat was to become subtropical, but on that morning the weather gave no hint of the climax to come. Low clouds scudded across the sea's face, and a brisk breeze whipped the breakers into milky confusion. The young man was a perfect physical specimen, just over six feet tall, broad-shouldered and deep-chested, and although in the peak of condition, weighing over fifteen stone. As he cut a furrow through the green water, he seemed preoccupied with his right hand, which he kept flexing in mid-stroke. After a few minutes, he hobbled back across the beach, rubbed himself down, threw on his clothes and disappeared into the town. The name of the lone swimmer was Edwin Boaler Alletson, and although he could not possibly have suspected it, that swim was the prelude to the one sensational moment in a long and otherwise unremarkable life. He was to live on for another 52 years, but only on the day of his swim off a Sussex beach was he ever destined to accomplish something unique. Tomorrow his train would be clattering back to his native Nottingham, his hour of glory past.

Alletson was a professional cricketer, a nonentity in a sport enjoying a golden age crammed with dazzling figures who would hardly have spared Alletson a thought. English batting was dominated by the Aristotelean logic of C. B. Fry and the budding classicism of young Jack Hobbs. Sydney Barnes still looked like the greatest bowler of all time, and connoisseurs of slow spin, dismayed by the mysterious evolution of Wilfred Rhodes from a great bowler to a workmanlike batsman, consoled themselves with the curvilinear refinements of Colin Blythe. Compared to these men, Alletson was a bit player, a tail-end batsman who drifted in and out of the Notts county side in the years between his debut in 1906 and his retirement eight years later. There were many professionals like him, honest artisans who appeared on the county grounds of England for a few seasons, gradually faded away and were never heard of again until the death notices, which often ended with a phrase like '. . . in his last years he fell into unfortunate circumstances'. It seemed almost certain that Alletson would be numbered among this anonymous army, for at 27 he was already past the age when any dramatic improvement in his technique might be wrought. Indeed, it was already five years since Alletson had made one last attempt to turn himself into a cricketer of real distinction. The attempt failed.

Alletson was not the first young man, nor would he be the last, to dream of that succulent slice of cricketing pie in the sky, the fast leg-break, a ball which would turn from leg with the venom of wrist-spin and yet at a fast-medium pace. But because the leg-break has to be delivered out of the back of the hand, real pace is almost impossible to achieve. Well aware of this, Alletson began in 1906 to pursue the unattainable. His father worked up on the Duke of Portland's estates in Welbeck, and now, using his father as his wicket-keeper, Alletson spent the winter of 1906–7 practising his new ball in the Duke's orchards. Progress was slow, but Alletson found that by turning his body at the moment of delivery and swinging his powerful shoulders through a wide arc, he was occasionally able to produce a fast-medium ball which turned from leg. But five years later, on the morning of the swim at Hove, he still lacked the consistency demanded in a match of any consequence. Notice it was as a bowler that Alletson aspired to power, not as a batsman, which makes his story doubly remarkable. Reports of the period describe his batting as 'orthodox', in the sense that he could play a straight bat in defence. But although his immense shoulders and a freakish armspan of 78 inches made him a powerful hitter when he happened to connect, his batting could never be effective against bowling of any quality because of his inability to use his feet. He never moved to the pitch of the ball, but stayed rooted to the crease, driving from there when the chance came. Most bowlers could therefore subdue him quite easily by pitching a shade short or a shade wide. Alletson was also a good deep field with a safe pair of hands and a strong accurate throw. And that was all. It was not much on which to base a professional career.

A summary of his ability would see him as a tail-end batsman who occasionally hit a spectacular drive, a mediocre bowler in a side already packed with good bowling, and a reliable deep fielder. It is no surprise that in his years with the county he never established a regular place in the side.

Three days before his dip in the sea, the Notts side had arrived at Hove for the annual championship match with Sussex. Doubts about fitness had complicated the process of team selection, so that not eleven but twelve men had travelled down, two of them nursing minor injuries. One was a bowler called Wass, the other Alletson himself, suffering from a sprained wrist. At the last moment Wass was declared unfit to play and Alletson found himself drafted into a side which had been alternatively picking and dropping him for the past six seasons. Notts, a powerful side, champions in 1907 and boasting at least four England batsmen, won the toss on a genial wicket and started well. Then the Sussex bowler Killick took five wickets for 14 runs and Notts were all out for 238. Sussex now piled up 414 in their first innings and took control of the game. By the end of the second day Notts were drifting to certain defeat, and it was clear that the issue would be decided long before the end of the allotted three days. One local newspaper, which had been following the fixture in detail, ended its comments on the eve of the final day with 'Tomorrow's play promises to be most interesting', evidently without believing anything of the kind. It sent no observer to the Hove ground on 20 May, and no further mention of the match appeared in its columns. The only press representatives to witness the closing formalities were from *The Sussex Daily News, The Nottinghamshire Guardian, Cricket* and of course the inevitable man from Wisden.

On that last morning Alletson was still troubled by his injured wrist, and thought that perhaps contact with sea water might ease the sprain. But he was careful not to prolong his swim. Half the Notts second innings was already over, and he might be required to bat at any moment. When play commenced on the last morning, all went as the experts predicted. Notts wickets fell at regular intervals. When the seventh man was out with nearly an hour still to go to lunch, and with Notts only seven runs ahead, it looked very much as though the players would have the afternoon to themselves. In the Notts dressing-room the mood was one of cheerful acceptance of defeat. Nothing short of a thunderstorm could save them now, and already the sun was out and the weather steadily improving. The Notts captain, Arthur Jones, having realized the game was lost, no longer bothered to brief his batsmen. Before he went out to bat Alletson asked him: 'Mr Jones, does it matter what I do?', to which Jones replied: 'No, Alletson, I don't think it matters what you do'. Alletson's reply to this innocent remark was the first hint that a thunderstorm was actually coming, although not quite the conventional kind. 'Oh', said Alletson, 'then I'm not half going to give Tom Killick some stick,' with which he emerged from the Hove pavilion and marched to the wicket carrying a bat weighing only two pounds three ounces, an absurdly flimsy weapon for so huge a man.

Alletson started to bat in a manner which he later described as 'normal', scoring 47 runs in the fifty minutes before lunch, including two sixes. During this session, however, two more Notts wickets fell and Alletson was himself dropped twice. When the teams went in for lunch, Notts had only one wicket left standing and had extended their slender lead to 84.

The game was still lost, and only a handful of spectators bothered to wait for the afternoon session. What is a little more surprising is that three of the four reporters departed, leaving only one official observer to witness the most extraordinary batting episode in the history of cricket.

At this point an exasperating veil falls over events on the Hove ground. The details of play have since been documented, examined, analysed, and discussed with relentless attention to every incident, but as to what, if anything, went on in the pavilion during the lunch interval nobody could be found who remembered. This fact is fundamental to the story of Alletson's great day, because he re-emerged from the pavilion after lunch like a man transformed. No record has survived of what the players were given for lunch, but in view of what was about to happen, nectar and ambrosia seems as good a guess as any. Three minutes after the resumption Alletson drove the four which gave him his half-century, and from this point he did not so much assault the Sussex bowling as enter a mood of inspired dementia.

In no time the game had drifted out of reality into the realms of pure moonshine. Five times Alletson drove Killick's bowling into the middle distance. One of his hammer blows flew right out of the arena, hurtling into the pavilion bar like a shell from a cannon, sending broken glass and cascading whisky all over the premises with Jessopian exuberance. Another straight drive disappeared out of the ground, soaring over the entrance gates into the street, where it was picked up by a small boy, who was later found playing with it down on the beach. A third shot was despatched over the South stand, coming to rest on the roof of a nearby skating rink, a carry of at least 160 yards. Only thirteen minutes after reaching his fifty, Alletson had completed the first century of his career, by which time the proceedings on the field no longer resembled a cricket match at all.

Play was repeatedly brought to a halt because there was no ball for the players to play with, Alletson having struck five of them out of the ground. Bemused officials wandered about the precincts of the pavilion searching for one or another of these lost balls. In the meantime a subtle change had also come over the fielding side. By now the Sussex players had forgotten about winning the match, or even losing it, and could only stand by, witnesses to something they could not believe. Poor Killick, the conqueror of the first innings, had abandoned all hope of getting Alletson out or even stopping him scoring at so phenomenal a rate. All Killick asked was to be allowed to get out of the ground alive. John Gunn, one of the Notts batsmen watching this crazy display, said: 'Killick was almost frightened to bowl. I don't think he minded his bowling being hit so much as he was worried Ted might hit one back at him.' Neither were the fielders much inclined to lend a hand. John Gunn's brother George, himself a batsman of wayward genius, remembered calling out to Vine, the Sussex deep fielder, 'Look out, he'll hit you any minute now,' to which Vine replied, 'Bugger him. I don't want it.' Gunn goes on: 'The ball fizzed through the fielders as if they had been ghosts. I have never seen another innings like it. One of those drives would have smashed a man's hand if he had tried to stop it.'

Having arrived at his hundred, Alletson got down to business in earnest. It was now just half-past two, and as he thrashed the bowling the ball could literally be heard humming past the Sussex outfielders. No person or place on the Hove ground was safe. H. P. Chaplin, the Sussex captain but a spectator that day, described it as 'the most amazing innings ever. Once he just lay back on his heels and pushed and the ball went through the pavilion clockface.' Relf another of the Sussex fieldsmen, observed, 'He stood up and hit like a giant. I don't think any man could have played two innings like that and lived.' Years later Relf was asked to recall his impressions of Alletson's exhibition. He said, 'My chief memory is that shower of cricket balls going over the boundary and the crowd mad with delight. It cost us a match we were winning, but I don't think anyone minded about that. It was such an experience to watch it.'

Understandably, the more impressionable members of the audience went slightly hysterical, and could no longer make sense of what their eyes were showing them. A gentleman called C. P. Foley later dedicated part of his autobiography to a lurid description of the innings and, as he strove to give an accurate impression, drifted from factual reportage on to the higher planes of literary invention: 'Time was wasted in trying to prise the ball out of the new stand into whose soft wood Alletson had driven it, no chisel being available.' Perhaps closer to the truth is Foley's observation, 'The fieldsmen and umpires had a very anxious half-hour, but by skilful agility managed to avoid contact with the ball, and nobody was killed, or indeed seriously injured.'

By 2.55 Alletson had amassed 189 runs and there seemed to be no known way of getting him out. A Notts rout had been transformed into a Sussex Massacre. But then Alletson connected with yet another prodigious drive which the fielder C. Smith caught with one foot over the boundary line and his head resting against the grandstand. The rules of cricket define this as an illegal catch, and Alletson knew this well. But he knew also that time was running short and that Notts still had an outside chance of winning the game, so he acknowledged the catch and ran back to the pavilion. When George Gunn ran after him to tell him he was legally not out, he is said to have replied, 'It's all reet'. Gunn later remarked, 'He had had enough.'

In 90 minutes Alletson had scored 189, the last 142 of them in only forty minutes. Nothing like it had ever been seen or would be again. Alletson became the most notorious athlete in England. For a brief spell he was what he had always wanted to be, a great cricketer. And yet, if the hysterical Mr Foley is to be believed, what followed was even more outlandish. According to Foley, who saw the whole business as an epic of Attic proportions, Jones, the Notts captain, told Alletson that from now on his place in the side was assured indefinitely on condition that he went out to hit in every match. 'But', said Foley, 'after hitting a ball over the clock at Lord's later in the season he retired into his shell and absolutely refused to hit.' The facts are rather less dramatic. In his very next innings Alletson again smashed the ball all over the place, scoring 60 in half an hour against Gloucestershire. But then a change of attitude seemed to set in, and gradually his approach to cricket subsided back to the norm.

But for the moment the entire cricket world was in ferment. A fortnight after the record-breaking innings, Alletson, this obscure bottom-of-the-order batsman unable to command a place in the county side, was invited to play in the official Test trial at Sheffield. He failed, scoring 15 in the first innings and only eight in the second. It was the only time in his entire cricketing life when he appeared in a first-class match for any other side than Notts.

There are many possible explanations for his return to mediocrity, and the most persuasive is that he was still preoccupied with his potential as the bowler of the elusive fast leg-break. Two years later, in 1913, he was ready at last to try his new delivery in a county game, at which point fate, which had been so lavish in its prizes that day at Hove, turned sour on him. At first everything went splendidly. Against Kent he won the match with six wickets for 43, and followed up with four for 17 against Derbyshire. The long hours in the orchard at Welbeck were paying dividends at last. And then, in the next match, against Gloucestershire, he bowled only two overs before the umpire, in Alletson's own words, 'told me to stop bowling'. Rumours began to circulate that his bowling action was not within the letter of the law. He bowled no more that season.

In 1914, against Derbyshire, his captain asked him to bowl again, and once more he was taken off because of the alleged illegality of his action. He never appeared in a first-class match again. At the time of the Derbyshire match he was just 30 years old. In the Great War he served in the Royal Garrison artillery, and later went to live at Worksop to work at the Manton colliery. In 1950, crippled by arthritis, he retired reluctantly to a wheelchair. A visitor described him at this time as 'still tall, dark and huge, his voice deep, his relish for cricket immense, and his humour good'.

As to his one day of glory, it was never completely forgotten, and remains in the record books to this day as the fastest big innings ever played. The only point left unanswered, the one mystery which Alletson was too inarticulate to explain, is the most vital one of all. What got into him that afternoon? The only explanation he ever offered on the subject was that 'after lunch, A. O. Jones told me to have a go, and I did. Runs kept coming and I cast care aside and hit harder'. There is a nice poetic flourish to that last phrase, but it still seems possible that something is missing from the equation. What happened to Edwin Boaler Alletson over lunch in the Hove pavilion on 20 May 1911? Probably nothing at all, but it is irresistibly tempting to speculate whether someone slipped a double brandy into his glass of ale, or whether a wink from the groundsman's daughter had something to do with it. Perhaps a metabolic change in his body, brought about by agencies unknown, and whose effects lasted for only a few hours? A metamorphosis caused by something he ate or drank or saw or heard or thought? Absurd to entertain such romantic notions, and yet why not? When an ordinary man suddenly turns into a giant, no merely rational explanation will do. It is a subject worthy of Joseph Wells' son Bertie.

It is an odd and endearing fact about human nature in its relation to cricket that, as Nyren and Cardus well knew, the backward look is always with us. As Botham observed, 'Too many people live in the past.' There is no question that even as Botham was destroying the Australians in 1981, there were those who sighed for the lost felicities of Denis Compton. And just as sure that when Compton was rewriting the record books, the older generation was wondering whatever happened to Ranji and Jessop. And perhaps also Alletson. The Golden Age is behind us. But then it always was.

From *A History of Cricket* by Benny Green
(Barrie and Jenkins, London, 1988).

Big hitters are the game's greatest excitement, none more so than the late Colin Milburn.

Wedlock One, Wickets None

Neville Cardus

There are many things about cricket, apart from the skill and the score. There is, first of all, the leisure to do something else. Cricket, like music, has its slow movements, especially when my native county of Lancashire is batting. I married the good companion who is my wife during a Lancashire innings. The event occurred in June, 1921; I went as usual to Old Trafford, stayed for a while and saw Hallows and Makepeace come forth to bat. As usual they opened with care. Then I had to leave, had to take a taxi to Manchester, there to be joined in wedlock at a registry office. Then I – that is, we – returned to Old Trafford. While I had been away from the match and had committed the most responsible and irrevocable act in mortal man's life, Lancashire had increased their total by exactly seventeen – Makepeace 5, Hallows 11, and one leg-bye.

From *Autobiography* by Neville Cardus
(Hamish Hamilton, London, 1984).

The Wisdom of Fred

Late to Bed, Late to Rise ...

Is the ideal preparation for the eve of a Test.

Once I was taken by a friend for a night club party on the eve of a Test match against New Zealand, and next morning there was an enormous headline about me living it up at one o'clock in the morning. When I arrived at Lord's I was carpeted with a vengeance, which made me boil when I thought about the things the golden boys had got away with time and again. There was only one way to answer the charges, and I did it – I took six wickets and helped to put New Zealand out just after lunch.

By this time I had changed my sleeping habits. I found that getting up at half past five or six o'clock in the morning, which I had done ever since I'd been a newspaper delivery boy, was no use. By the time a match started at 11.30 a.m. I was half knackered, so I found it a positive advantage to go to bed late and get up late. Being up at one o'clock in the morning just before a match wasn't really unusual.

My Easiest Test Wicket

In one Test in the 1958–9 series in Australia the umpires stuffed us out of sight. We just couldn't get favourable decisions. When Colin Macdonald was run out by at least five yards the umpire had gone to the wrong side of the wicket and turned down the appeal. Even the Aussies were so embarrassed by this time that Colin Macdonald came up to me and said: 'For Christ's sake, Fred, bowl me one straight. I'm fed up with this.' So I bowled one straight, he just had a swing at it and his stumps were flattened. That must be the easiest Test wicket I've ever taken!

4
FAST MEN

Is there a fast bowlers' trade union? You wouldn't have thought so when Yorkshire played Northampton in the fifties. People said it was more a match between Trueman and Tyson. I know I used to will myself to bowl faster to show everyone who was boss. I also remember when Frank took the new ball and hit me with a very fast full toss straight in the groin, shattering my protector. It hurt like hell and I thought I'd finish up a eunuch if this happened often. But I never bowled a bouncer at a tail-ender whether he could take retaliation or not – not unless he had hit me first.

In that great Test against the Australians at The Oval in 1953 when we retained the Ashes for the first time in twenty years, I got a very sore shoulder because Lindwall let me have a bouncer which hit me on the shoulder. It was very painful, like someone had plunged a knife in it. I didn't show it – just made a mental note to pay him back. I had to wait more than five years for the second Test at Melbourne in 1958–9 before I gave him one which reared up, struck his bat handle, clouted him between the eyes and flew up to give a simple catch. Ray complained after the match, so I told him I hadn't squealed when he'd hit me at The Oval. He was surprised that I remembered, but we finished up having a drink.

Keith Miller also bounced me – twice – and I paid him back in the end. But off the field we were firm friends. We don't guard our secrets – fast bowlers share them. Lindwall taught me a lot when I was still only twenty-one. When we played India in 1952 he was in the Lancashire League and came into the dressing room. He helped, showing me different grips, and advised me not to bowl too quick all the time. 'Bowl within yourself.' And he later warned his fellow Aussies: 'He'll cause us trouble.' I did my best to do so.

Years later in 1975 when Dennis Lillee was playing here he sought me out. 'Fred, I'm in trouble – can you help?' He may have been an Aussie and a natural enemy but he was also a leading member of our trades union. It took me a quarter of an hour to sort him out. He was setting off on his run-up too quickly and his left arm and left shoulder were dropping too early. Next day he went out and got everything right against England and when he bowled John Edrich with a beauty, as he came back to his run-up he gave me the thumbs up. People complained – what the hell was I doing helping an Australian? But I've always been ready to coach anybody because I know I owe the game of cricket a great deal and I'm always anxious to put something back.

Fast bowling brings out the worst in people – think of the Bodyline tour or the crowds baying for my blood in the West Indies. Fast bowling is the equivalent of the heavyweight division in boxing – there's the drama, the danger, always the chance of serious injury. In the long-standing debate about who is the fastest bowler of all time there can be no sure answer. Harold Larwood in his heyday was once timed at 96 mph, though no one can be sure how accurate the method then was. Godfrey Evans reckons Frank Tyson was faster than me. He was very quick, no denying that, but he only lasted at the top for about three years. I only know I bowled faster over a longer period than anybody else. In 1960 when I was nearly thirty and three years past my peak a scientific apparatus was assembled which came up with these readings:

– Wesley Hall registered 93 mph through the air, and 92 off the wicket.
– Trueman, 92 mph through the air, 93 off the wicket.
– Statham (my senior by eight months) and Peter Loader came into the 80s.
– Alan Davidson of Australia was in the 70s.
I like to think that if I had been filmed when I was twenty-five I would have topped the ton.

Here is my pecking order (overall talent rather than pace) of the greatest fast bowlers since my time:
1. Dennis Lillee: intelligent as well as very fast and could move the ball both ways.
2. Michael Holding: superbly athletic, silk-like approach to wicket, could have been an Olympic runner.
3. Michael Marshall: Hadlee, Imran Khan and Kapil Dev pale by comparison.
4. Joel Garner: that enormous height made his high bouncing deliveries all but unbearable.
5. Andy Roberts: varied his pace – a very clever bowler, though there was the suspicion of a throw in his quicker delivery and bouncer.
6. John Snow: best English fast man of the last two decades.
7. Jeff Thomson: quicker than Lillee. He had the biggest arc with his right arm of any bowler I have ever seen, that right hand almost touching the ground in the moment before delivery.
8. Bob Willis: for sheer heart and guts, to come back after two knee operations and make himself England's main strike bowler, I'd put Bob at the top. He may not have had Snow's fire, but he could make it bounce.

F.S.T.

Harold Larwood

Jack Fingleton and Bill Bowes

Harold Larwood in his prime was the hero of many, including a number of up-and-coming would-be fast bowlers. When he was a lad Lindwall saw Larwood and tried to copy him. Yet with the exception of the 33 wickets he took at an average of 19.51 in the Bodyline series, Larwood's Test figures of 78 wickets for 28.41 runs were not all that outstanding. But in that 1932–3 series he was devastating. Sixteen of his victims were clean bowled. Having been tickled up by 'Rib Ball' they backed off and fell victim to the fast Yorker. And for once Bradman 'failed'. He made *only* 396 runs for an average of 56.57, skipping to leg to hit the ball into a largely unguarded off-side field.

But from England's point of view it was vastly better than the 974 Bradman scored in seven Test innings when Australia came to England in 1930. Of course the short-pitched bowling could be countered as Stan McCabe showed in the first Test at Sydney with a withering display of pulling and hooking for 187 not out. Country-born Stan did it with a good sense of fun, too. He told his father, 'If I happen to get hit out there, Dad, keep Mum from jumping the fence and laying into these Pommy bowlers.'

England won easily at Sydney as they did in four of the five Tests. But it was the end of Larwood's Test career. Asked by MCC to apologize for his tactics, which had been ordered by his Captain, Jardine, he proudly and rightly refused to do so. Like myself, Harold Larwood was born in a mining village. He was a pony-boy in the Nottinghamshire pits at fourteen and he was only 5 feet 4 inches when he had his first trial for Notts at the age of eighteen. But by the time he played for the first team he had grown to 5 feet 9 inches, an express bowler who instilled fear into opponents, even good players like Jack Fingleton. He also had the unstinted respect of team-mates like my old Yorkshire friend Bill Bowes.

F.S.T.

I will never see a greater fast bowler than Larwood. I am sure of that, and at this moment pay a tribute to him as a truly magnificent bowler. His genius in 1932–3 with the ball was of the same mould as Bradman's with the bat in 1930.

I saw so much of other fast bowlers from all other lands that I do not hesitate in placing him on the highest pinnacle by himself (I never saw E. A. Macdonald). One could tell his art by his run to the wickets. It was a poem of athletic grace, as each muscle gave over to the other with perfect balance and the utmost power. He began his long run slowly, this splendidly proportioned athlete, like a sprinter unleashed for a hundred yards dash. His legs and arms pistoned up his speed, and as he neared the wickets he was in very truth like the Flying Scotsman thundering through an east coast station. He was full of fire, power and fury – or so he looked at the batting end just before he delivered the ball at you at an estimated speed of 90 miles an hour.

I had this interesting experience from batting against Larwood. The first dorsal interosseous muscle, between the thumb and the index finger, ached for a week after batting against Larwood, so severe was the concussion of the ball hitting the bat. I experienced this against no other fast bowler.

Jack Fingleton

... *I* say this purely and simply as a bowler judging another – Larwood was magnificent. He had a spot-on accuracy in direction. He could switch easily from off-stump to leg-stump attack ... and at what a terrific pace!

Larwood seemed to skim off the hard Bulli soil surfaces of Australia like a pebble skimming off water and with a bounce equally unpredictable. He had such pace that any delivery pitching more than halfway down the pitch was good length. He had the additional great asset (which he said he noticed on his first trip to Australia) that whereas most deliveries would go flashing through at less than stump height, one out of every three or four deliveries would skim off the surface to be chest height at the batsman. He did not have to dig the ball in deliberately. It happened naturally. If Voce, Allen or myself wanted to make the ball get chest height at the batsmen we had to dig it in, and it bounced like a tennis ball and with all the speed taken out of it.

Bill Bowes

Both pieces are from *In Celebration of Cricket,* compiled by Kenneth Gregory (Granada, London, 1978).

Brief Encounters of a Terrifying Kind – A Minute with Larwood

Bill Andrews

Larwood was lethal on the county circuit. More than one tail-ender would play and miss and start walking out. 'You're not out,' the wicket-keeper would say. 'Just the same I'm going,' the batsman would reply. On one occasion, bowling against Hampshire, Larwood received a telegram on the field. He read it, pocketed it and proceeded to work up a blistering pace which had the Hampshire men ducking and weaving. One of them enquired at the end of the session what in the telegram had so inspired Larwood. 'His wife has just given birth to a daughter,' replied the Hampshire batsman. 'Thank God it wasn't twins.' Here the old Somerset all-rounder Bill Andrews recalls the fears of lesser batsmen.

F.S.T.

Somerset's meeting with Notts and Larwood at Trent Bridge in 1935 was one to remember. Notts had made 459 with centuries from their Nos 8 and 9, George Heane and Harry Winrow. My analysis: 32-4-112-3. Towards the end of the innings I bowled a short one to Larwood which hit him in the 'box'. It meant he couldn't open the bowling next day and as such probably saved the game for us.

All the second day, Harold lay on the masseur's table. Messages kept arriving from the good-natured Notts boys. 'He's after Bill and is going to give him all he's got when he comes on to bowl again.'

I believed it. On the third day they said Larwood, fastest bowler in the world, was fit to have a go at the tail-enders. The new ball hadn't been taken so far. Dickie Burrough, one of our amateurs, faced Larwood – with his tail up and with the new ball. The fourth delivery flew up off a length straight at the batsman's head. Somehow Burrough managed to protect his face with his batting gloves. But he was in great pain.

Apprehensively, I rushed down from the other end. Blood was spurting on to the wicket. The batsman's thumb which should have been upright was lying the other way and was clearly broken. Burrough retired and in came Wally Luckes, looking pale and intent on getting a quick touch for a catch behind the wicket.

In all my career I have never seen such bowling. Larwood would make the ball swing into the batsman and then when it hit the pitch, it would hurtle away at a speed of ninety miles an hour. Luckes looked as though he was fishing the way he unhappily waved his bat. He got a 'bite' and was taken behind the stumps. Hazell, the best No 11 in the business, came in to join me and dryly hummed 'Nearer my God to Thee' during our mid-wicket consultation. When I did face Larwood, I immediately went the same way as Luckes. And I had no complaints about that.

In another match at Trent Bridge, when the wicket was lively and a little wet on top, I found myself high in the batting order. I watched the first few overs bowled by Larwood and Voce and that was enough for me. I had pains in my stomach. So I retired to the lavatory.

'Hey, Bill, you're in!' Wellard's shout reached me.

'Who's out?'

'Frank Lee. They're bringing him back on a stretcher.'

I was really in a state and it took some time to adjust my clothing. At last I went down the stairs and on to the ground. As I passed the umpire, I said – hopefully – that I must have broken the two-minute rule.

It was a nightmare for an ordinary batsman to face Larwood and Voce in their prime. I had always had the impression that their skipper, Arthur Carr, fielding in the gully, liked to see opposing batsmen hit on the body. In a strange way, I didn't mind receiving a blow early on in my knock. I used to think to myself that the next one couldn't be any worse!

Once I made 50 against Larwood at Taunton, hardly seeing the ball once. Earlier, in my career, going in last man, I had edged slightly away from a fast bowler and been bowled. Jack White quite rightly lectured me and told me that if I ever did it again I should be out of the side. So when I hit a half-century off Larwood I made sure I was behind the ball – in fact, *too far* behind. I left my leg stump exposed deliberately hoping that the great bowler would aim at it, probably, and knock it over. Oddly, it put me in the right position for the hook, a shot I was never good at.

Harold Larwood and Bill Voce were great chaps and I counted Larwood, even in my early days, as a real friend.

From *The Hand That Bowled Bradman* by Bill Andrews
(Macdonald, London, 1973)

Herbert Sutcliffe was absolutely right when he said that some batsmen can play fast bowling and some cannot, but if they all told the truth none of them like it.

F.S.T.

Brian Statham

Michael Parkinson

When I worked in harness with Brian Statham, he was not only very quick but the most accurate fast bowler I have ever known. He had really only the two types of ball – the one a bit short of a length nipping back, and the bouncer. He couldn't intentionally swing the ball. Like Frank Tyson he was just very quick and straight, but there's no denying his greatness.

Brian – or George as everyone called him – was an easy-going guy. We got on well – despite rumours to the contrary – and still do. When I heard my old mate had a chronic bone disease I set up a fund for him. Off the field we shared rooms and spent a lot of time socially.

But as the following piece by Michael Parkinson shows, we couldn't have been more different in temperament. He was not one to be dropped for speaking his mind. Brian could drink and smoke far more than me and still be a blue-eyed boy. If he had a fault it was his lack of aggression. He never won a championship for Lancashire. Had Brian been more like me – an arrogant bastard on the field – then I am sure Lancashire would have done better. But there was no more honest craftsman in the hardest trade that cricket has to offer than Brian Statham.

F.S.T.

I first saw him in those distant days when people used to queue to see a cricket match. We were standing outside Old Trafford in the inevitable gloom waiting to see the Roses game and this slender youth walked by carrying a cricket bag.

'Who's yon?' said the old man.

'Our new fast bowler,' said the Lancashire supporter standing in front of us.

'Fast bowler,' exclaimed the old man. 'He's not big enough. He'll fall down before he reaches t'wicket.'

The Lancashire supporter looked sheepish and stared hard at the locked gates. There was nothing he could say because the youth who passed us by was certainly the unlikeliest looking fast bowler imaginable.

The old man wasn't letting it drop there. He sensed an opportunity to put the old enemy to shame.

'What's his name then?' he asked.

'Statham,' said the Lancashire supporter.

'He'll get some stick today,' said the old man.

Two hours later we were sitting behind the bowler's arm as the new boy, spindly and pale, prepared to bowl against the might of Yorkshire. As he measured out his run the old man said, 'He's not strong enough to run that far. Somebody ought to tell him.'

An hour later and we were a couple of very depressed Yorkshiremen. Statham had taken the first three wickets for next to nothing and we knew in our sinking hearts we had seen a great fast bowler in action.

Going back to Yorkshire the old man said, 'Tha' knows he's going to bother us that Statham.'

That was seventeen years ago [1950] and in that time John Brian Statham has done everything to prove the old man right. I have never forgotten my first sight of him all those years ago and have never forgone the chance to see him in action since. Watching him through the years has been a constant pleasure. In a changing world he has remained aloof from fashion's whims, unscathed by the advance of time. Even now, at the age of thirty-seven, the figure is as lean and as pliable as in his sapling years. There's the odd fleck of grey in the hair but the eyes are bright and youthful. I sought him out at Old Trafford to discover how many more seasons I might have the pleasure of watching him.

'About three more I reckon. I'd like to complete twenty years with Lancashire,' he said.

What then? 'Probably league cricket. Back to where I started,' he said with a smile.

In the seventeen years since he left the leagues to play for Lancashire, Brian Statham has established himself as one of the truly great fast bowlers. He hasn't got the subtlety of a Lindwall, the flair of Trueman or the blasting speed of Hall. His success is based on the two classic precepts of the bowler's art, length and direction. He is the most honest of bowlers. His avowed intention is to knock all three stumps down and he never disguises the fact. In a game slowly being strangled to death by the niggardly defensive tactics of a legion of second-class seam bowlers he stands out like a bold knight at the head of a peasant army.

The nearest this gentle cautious man gets to anger is when he talks about the modern-day seam bowler. 'Little phantoms' he calls them.

'They come on to bowl and they've no intention of getting a wicket. They just plop away all day, preventing the batsman from scoring, boring the crowd to death. It's wrong, terribly wrong,' he said.

He shakes his head and looks out of the dressing-room window across the sunlit green of Old Trafford. The years rest lightly on him and yet one feels that perhaps Brian Statham has not reaped their full harvest. The comparison with the fortunes of Fred Trueman is inevitable if only because of their great partnership. Trueman the businessman, Trueman the journalist, Trueman in the gossip columns, on the telly, Trueman in the gravy.

Brian Statham says: 'I'm happy. It's a question of what you want really. Fred's different to me. He likes the limelight. I think people should be what they are. I wouldn't go on television and talk about things I knew nothing about because that's not my job. Similarly you wouldn't ask Eamonn Andrews to captain Lancashire would you?'

Statham is content to remain just a very good cricketer taking only what the game offers him and not expecting more. This and his exemplary conduct on the field and off made him the ideal man to rebuild the pride and faith in Lancashire cricket. It is a daunting task. The club has bled internally in the past from dissent among the players and the committee. It has been snubbed by the cricket lovers who see no reason to accept second best after many seasons of rich and splendid diet. At an age when, if there were any justice, he ought to be grazing in the outfield, Brian Statham is required to accomplish the most important task ever given to a Lancashire cricketer. He doesn't make any predictions. He simply says: 'We'll be all right. Just wait and see.'

In the three years we have left to us we ought to savour Brian Statham. The present legion of 'little phantoms' who are boring us all to death should be made to watch him for a full season and then given the choice of either emulating him or retiring. Those who mourn McDonald and the Ancients should seek solace in the sight of one of the few English cricketers still playing who can stand any comparison, and those of us who write about the game should always use him as the yardstick of our judgments. In any period of the game, no matter how enriched, Statham would be a treasure. Today, even in his twilight, he is simply priceless.

From *Cricket Mad* by Michael Parkinson
(Stanley Paul, London, 1969).

Frank Tyson – The Glad Animal Action

David Frith

Frank Tyson was quick, no doubt about that. I do not rate him as a great fast bowler because I reserve the word great only for those who stay at the top for ten years or so. Frank's career at the top spanned only three years. But such is the unique power of pace that he frightened the Aussies clean out of the Ashes in our 1954–5 tour (the tour I missed because of the nonsense in the West Indies). The team with his pace on its side had to win, and after losing the First Test England won the next three, with the last a drawn game because of rain. Here David Frith pays his tribute.

F.S.T.

'To bowl quick,' Frank Tyson wrote in his autobiography (*A Typhoon Called Tyson*), 'is to revel in the glad animal action; to thrill in physical prowess and to enjoy a certain sneaking feeling of superiority over the other mortals who play the game. No batsman likes quick bowling, and this knowledge gives one a sense of omnipotence.'

He could not recall a time when he did not want to bowl as fast as humanly possible, and by the time he had shortened his excessive run and found his rhythm for the second Test match of the 1954–5 tour of Australia few onlookers could recall a cricket ball bowled faster. The delivery was no more – or less – than a flash, a blur. The ball hardly deviated. As with Kortright, it really had no need to at that speed. Tyson and Statham were timed in Wellington in 1955 at slightly under 90 mph, but it is certain that, flat out, Tyson was appreciably faster.

He announced himself to the 1953 Australians with several snorters at the early batsmen, and word went round, as it does, that here was someone out of the ordinary. In Australia he made no impression to start with, and at Brisbane, in the first Test, when Australia ran up 601 for 8 and won by an innings, he took 1 for 160. At Sydney, however, he bowled off a reduced run, but at the same hot pace on a rather more sympathetic pitch, and took 4 for 59. When he batted, a bouncer from Lindwell, in retaliation for one from Tyson, had him turning his head, ostrich-like, to be hit squarely on the back of the skull with a smack that echoed all round the ground. Carried off with a lump visible from over a hundred yards, he later continued his innings and went on to bowl like a man possessed when Australia set about scoring 223 for victory. With 6 for 85, including Lindwall's wicket, bowled as the batsman left a lot of air between himself and the stumps, Tyson swept England to a dramatic

38-run win to level the series. With Statham's great-hearted support from the other end, he blew holes in Australia's batting line-up with yorkers and fliers, bringing out Neil Harvey's true greatness as the little left-hander parried, glanced and cut his way to an undefeated 92. Classic fast bowling parenthesizing classic batsmanship.

There was better to come. At Melbourne, on a poor pitch, after Miller had taken 3 for 5 off nine overs before lunch on the first day, Statham's 5 for 60 had prevented Australia from taking too long a lead, and when England managed 279 in their second innings Australia needed 240. They made 111, Tyson taking 7 for 27 (6 for 16 off his last 51 balls). The brilliant leg-side catch with which Godfrey Evans dismissed Harvey was the turning point.

Thus Tyson was the name on everyone's lips. This broad-shouldered, balding, scholarly-looking man had shot Australia out before lunch on a day when 60,000 people at the Melbourne Cricket Ground expected to see a long, tense struggle. The batsmen had been no match. England's discovery, with his shuffling launch, giant, raking steps, and spring-steel spine-action, had, with his laser-beam bowling, given his side a victory weapon. Both sides had batsmen, bowlers and all-rounders of established reputation, but the side with a bowler of 'Typhoon's' pace – so long as he remained fit – had to win.

And win they did, though the match at Adelaide was not over until Miller's last-day flames had been extinguished by injury. England's five-wicket victory (Tyson 6 for 132) gave them a three-one lead, and the fifth Test was barely a contest since the first three days were rained off. Even then there was something of interest when Tyson bowled: wishing to rush through the over in an outside bid for victory, Hutton asked him to bowl off just half-a-dozen paces. He still propelled the ball with sufficient vigour to knock the bat from Miller's hands. Throughout the series wicketkeeper Evans had waited in the far distance, taking the ball airborne or leaping sideways.

Tyson inflicted physical damage all along the way. Bill Edrich spilt blood at Lord's when hit on the cheekbone, and his cousin John, just as fearless, had a knuckle smashed first by Trueman and later Tyson, and had to have the bone junction surgically rebuilt. Not surprisingly, a whole army of batsmen winded, bruised, and nursing split fingers, could have been collected. Tyson himself was not free from disability. The strain on his ankles told, and he missed Test matches at the stage when he might have been expected to continue with his Australian carnage. Certainly in 1955, against South Africa, he turned on a shattering display at Trent Bridge, taking 6 for 28 – 5 for 5 off 45 balls. But injury and lost form rendered his England appearances intermittent thereafter, and by the time he toured Australia a second time, in 1958–59, he was unexceptional. Bowling at Northampton was not the most uplifting experience for a fast bowler, but he had loyally resisted a suggestion that he attempt to transfer to Old Trafford, and he had always been aware that the life of an express bowler was the shortest of all.

Like Larwood before him, he moved to Australia, whose test team he had once dismembered, and took up a teaching appointment in Melbourne, continuing to give something to the game with his perceptive radio and television commentaries and writing. To return to his book, he wrote with unnecessary modesty: 'Oh yes, there have been better fast bowlers.' (His opponents would not be convinced.) 'But I doubt whether there has been one who derived more pleasure from bowling fast. One of its greatest attractions for me is its straightforwardness. It is an honest pursuit whose rewards are gained by the sweat of the brow, and not by any underhand or surreptitious methods.'

From *The Fast Men* by David Frith
(Van Nostrand, Wokingham, 1975).

John Snow – The Rebel

Brian Johnston

Most of the great fast bowlers had a touch of the rebel about them – the kind of arrogance that translates itself into action on the field. Dennis Lillee was a typical case – some even said I was myself! – and the same applied to John Snow. Like many great pacemen he could drive crowds to extremes of reaction, including that controversial incident at Sydney in 1970–71 when Illingworth led the team off after trouble and beer-can throwing from the crowd.

Snow was a bit square-on, which meant he was basically an in-swing bowler, but I rate him England's best paceman of the late sixties and seventies. In this piece my old Test Match Special colleague Brian Johnston gives his assessment of 'Snowy' and also of that unpleasant incident at Sydney which he personally witnessed.

F.S.T.

I don't know whether 'Snowy' ever did any acting when he was a schoolboy at Christ's Hospital, but he would have made a perfect Hamlet. He was moody and temperamental, and normally went round with a fierce dead-pan expression on his face. It was only when you knew him that he broke into a friendly smile. I suspect he put on this façade to promote fear in the hearts of batsmen, although it's true to say that he was genuinely anti-establishment and against any sort of authority. Quite why this should be I don't know, because his father was a Church of England vicar, but throughout his career he had brushes with committees, his captains and occasionally the press.

He was undoubtedly one of England's best fast bowlers, filling in between the Statham–Trueman era and Bob Willis. In 49 Tests he took 202 wickets, and it's interesting to compare this with Bedser's 236 in 51 Tests, Statham's 252 in 70, Trueman's 307 in 67 and Willis's 325 in 90. He was one of those fast bowlers whom it was a pleasure to watch, if not to play. He was wiry and slim and had a relaxed, loping, rhythmic run-up. At the wicket he was not completely sideways on, but near enough. He was not anywhere near as square-on as Bob Willis. He was probably not as regularly fast as Trueman, Statham and Willis, but could send down some quick and vicious deliveries. He had a good bouncer, but didn't over-use it. He was basically in-swing, though with movement off the pitch from leg to off. When in the mood he could be lethal, and here comes the crunch: there were too many occasions – even for

England – when he didn't appear to be putting everything into it.

One cannot expect a fast bowler in between Tests to give his maximum the whole time for his county – although look at Trueman's figures for Yorkshire – but it is surprising that Snowy only took 100 wickets in a season twice, although on the Hove pitch he could prove devastating. It needed a Mike Brearley to make a study of him to find the best way of handling him. Ray Illingworth succeeded on his MCC tour in Australia in 1970–1. Prior to the first Test at Brisbane, Snowy didn't seem too interested in the State games. Perhaps he was keeping himself for the Tests, and he also had some skin trouble with his toes, but Ray decided to have a chat and made it quite plain that if Snowy didn't buck up, he would be dropped and possibly even sent home.

It worked like magic. Snowy proceeded to take 6 for 114, and 2 for 48 at Brisbane with bowling which *Wisden* said 'filled the Australians with apprehension'. He went on to take 31 wickets in the series, which would surely have been more had he not broken a finger at the start of Australia's second innings in the final Test at Sydney. This was the match when Illingworth led the England team off the field, and as I was commentating at the time I think it is worth repeating how I saw the incident.

England made 184 in their first innings, and just after tea on the second day Illingworth took the new ball with Greg Chappell and Terry Jenner together and the score 180 for 7. The first two overs with the new ball were bowled by Snow and Lever with no suspicion of a bouncer. With the seventh ball of the third over Snow, however, did bowl a bouncer at Jenner who ducked into it, was hit on the back of the head, collapsed, and had to be carried off. The crowd naturally enough booed and shouted, roaring their disapproval of Snow. While the new batsman Lillee was on his way out to the wicket, Lou Rowan, the umpire at Snow's end, told Snow that he should not have bowled a bouncer at a low-order batsman like Jenner. Snow became incensed at this and asked Rowan in not too polite a way whose side he thought he was on. Umpire Rowan then seemed to lose his temper and in what appeared to be an emotional decision, promptly warned Snow under Law 46, Note 4 (IV) for persistent bowling of short-pitched balls. Then it was Illingworth's turn to protest at what he considered a wrong interpretation of the law. How could one bouncer come under the heading of persistent?

Unfortunately, in the heat of the moment, Illingworth also became annoyed and was seen by thousands on the ground and tens of thousands on television to wag his finger at Lou Rowan. What in fact he was trying to indicate was that Snow had only bowled 'one' bouncer. He was not trying to admonish the umpire. Amid a storm of booing – I've seldom heard such a noise on the cricket ground – Snow completed his over by bowling one ball at Lillee. He then turned to go off to his position at long leg. When he had got halfway there some beer cans were thrown in his direction from the small Paddington Hill to the left of the Noble Stand. Snow turned back and returned to the square, where Illingworth told the umpires that he would not go on playing until the field was cleared of the cans. The team sat down while this was being done by the ground staff. After a few minutes the ground was clear and Snow set off again for long leg.

I remember saying on the air at the time that I thought the whole incident was going to end happily, as members in the Noble Stand and people on the hill started to applaud Snow and a man stretched out over the railings to shake hands with Snow. Snow went up and shook hands, but a tough-looking spectator who had obviously 'had a few' then grabbed hold of Snow's shirt and started to shake him. This was the signal for more cans and bottles to come hurtling on to the field, narrowly missing Snow. Willis ran up and shouted something to the crowd. Then Illingworth came up, saw the bottles flying and promptly signalled to his team to leave the field. The two batsmen and two umpires stayed on the square. Then the two umpires made their way to the pavilion – the first time they had left the square since the trouble started. Rowan made it plain to Illingworth that if he did not continue he would forfeit the match and an announcement was made that play would be resumed as soon as the ground had been cleared, not only of the cans and bottles but also of a number of spectators who had clambered over the fence. This, in fact, took only ten minutes and Illingworth led his men back thirteen minutes after leading them off. In the remaining forty minutes the England side somewhat naturally seemed to have lost their zest, and Chappell and Lillee added 45 runs so that Australia finished the day 235 for 7 – a lead of 51.

I said at the time, and I still believe, that Illingworth was right to lead the side off. Not only was it becoming dangerous with bottles flying around, but this action so stunned the crowd that the throwing stopped immediately and play was very soon restarted. In other similar circumstances in the West Indies, the fielding side had stayed on the field and play had to be abandoned for the day. There was, of course, no excuse for Illingworth to argue in such a demonstrative manner with the umpire. He has since publicly said he was sorry he acted as he did, and also concedes that he should have gone back to the square and warned the umpires that he was taking his team off, but he had to make a quick decision and it is surprising that neither umpire left the square at any time to go to deal with the incident at the trouble spot. Snow was criticized for going up to the fence and accepting the proffered handshake. Who can say what the reaction would have been if he hadn't? An unhappy incident, and now you must judge for yourselves.

It was in Australia's second innings, after Snow had bowled Eastwood for 0, that going for a high catch at long leg off Lever he somehow caught a finger in the boundary fence and broke it. He went off with the bone showing through the broken skin, and couldn't bowl again that Test.

Snowy enjoyed batting and in fact first went to Sussex as a batsman who could bowl, occasionally opening for them in one-day games. He played some useful innings for England and perhaps most enjoyed his last-wicket stand with Ken Higgs at the Oval against the West Indies in 1966. They both made their maiden first-class fifties and put on 128 for the last wicket, only 2 runs short of the world-record last-wicket stand of 130, made for England by R. E. Foster and W. Rhodes at Sydney in 1903–4. Snowy's share was 59 not out, and as the West Indies attack included Wes Hall, Charlie Griffith, Gary Sobers and Lance Gibbs he had every reason to be pleased.

This was not his highest Test score. That came in 1971 at Lord's against India, when he was top scorer for England with 73, but the match finished unfortunately for him. In India's second innings Gavaskar was going for a short single, and Snowy, following through, seemed deliberately to block his way and knock him over. In spite of an apology at the lunch interval, Snowy was dropped from the next Test as a disciplinary measure.

When trying he could be a fine fielder with a strong arm, but he did tend to lose interest in a game as he stood down at long leg. This is not just me being critical. He himself confirmed many of the criticisms against him by entitling his autobiography *Cricket Rebel,* but to soften this rather macho image, he also published two volumes of poems. One was about a butterfly and my son, Barry, tried to put it to music, but I'm afraid nothing came of it. Snowy was one of the first to sign for Kerry Packer, thus virtually ending his first-class career in this country. I still see him, and the smile always breaks through. So it should. He is happily married with two young daughters and has become a successful travel agent, concentrating especially on cricket tours.

From *It's Been A Piece of Cake* by Brian Johnston
(Methuen, London, 1989).

My old mate Johnners has been a bit restrained about the Sydney crowd on the Hill, which an Australian columnist described as 'Drunk. Smashed. Orry-Eyed ... There were more howling dangerous drunks on the Hill than I've seen before and it was madness to stir them up ... Snow hadn't been intimidating Jenner.' England duly won the series 2–0, including both games at Sydney, with four drawn.

F.S.T.

Bumper War – England Versus Thomson and Lillee

Keith Fletcher

Not for the first time fast bowling had won a series for England in 1970–71, but in 1974–5 it was Australia's chance to turn the table with the formidable duo of Dennis Lillee and Jeff Thomson. They took 58 wickets between them in the six Tests – 33 to Thomson for an average of only 17.94. England captain Mike Denness dropped himself after three Tests, having scored only 65 in six innings. John Edrich, his successor, then got his ribs broken by Lillee. Australia won the Fourth Test and thus the Ashes. Here Keith Fletcher describes the travails of the England batsmen, including a forty-one-year-old Colin Cowdrey, recalled to Test cricket from virtual retirement.

F.S.T.

None of us enjoyed going out to bat. I thought of it as my job to get in line, play straight and try to build an innings as naturally as possible. But the knowledge that one needed to move very fast to keep one's body intact was not a pleasant way to spend a day in the sunshine, and there were times for all of us when a few weeks in frozen England seemed quite a palatable alternative to yet another session of ducking the stream of short balls.

At least half a dozen times, I flicked my head out of the way through sheer instinct as balls I had not seen at all whipped past the end of my nose. Some missed me by only fractions of an inch and I am sure that someone unused to quick bowling, or simply someone older with slower reactions, would have been hit on the head.

In the midst of all this, enter Colin Cowdrey. A man whose Test career seemed to have been ended by the previous tour of Australia under Illingworth, was now answering an English SOS following a couple of injuries. He was approaching his 42nd birthday, also close to retirement from the first-class game. Yet he could not resist the final challenge. He was thrown straight into the Test side at Perth, on a fast, bouncy wicket and against an ogre, in Thomson, he had never set eyes upon. What is more, he even opened the second innings, Luckhurst having joined the casualties.

I have no idea how he survived. More than once, I watched him go to hook either Lillee or Thomson, only for Marsh to be holding the ball above his head before Cowdrey was even half-way through with the shot. Sensibly, he scrubbed the stroke off the menu, but the fact remained that he needed more time than the rest of us to adjust. His defensive technique was as sound as ever, though; he got into line and played the ball on its merit, often being struck on the body but never flinching from the job. He made 22 and 40 in that match, as courageous a performance as I have seen in a Test.

From *Captain's Innings* by Keith Fletcher
(Stanley Paul, London, 1983).

Before I arrived, opening batsmen were having it easy, able to play off their front foot without a care in the world. Now, if a batsman started playing forward to me before I'd even delivered the ball there was every chance he would find it whistling round his ears. They didn't like it. I wasn't trying to hurt them – just forcing them to go on their back foot and play a little – but inevitably one or two got hit. I was sorry when this happened but I never allowed myself to show it. Batsmen were my natural enemy.

F.S.T.

Bumpers, Screams and Blood

David Frith

The so-called Bumper War of 1974–5 began as a war of words when Jeff Thomson was quoted in a magazine article in June 1974 as saying, 'I enjoy hitting a batsman more than getting him out. It doesn't worry me in the least to see a batsman hurt, rolling around screaming and blood on the pitch.'

Later he dismissed these words as 'Garbage – the greatest joke ever'. But, as David Frith describes here, both Thommo and Lillee were fiery characters and all the more fearsome when operating in tandem.

F.S.T.

'Thommo' had been known to lose his temper. In 1972 he broke a soccer referee's nose with a straight left after disagreeing with a free-kick decision. He was banned for life 'for a while'. He loved his soccer, but there were other things in life, and he is never happier than when surfing or water-skiing. He took to rugby, and planned to take up baseball. At school he had been a javelin champion. A section of the Press, after he became a Test match star, concentrated on his love-life. And shortly after the 1975 World Cup, in which his form had been disappointing, it was suggested that homesickness and the temporary loss of the joys of Australian outdoor life were affecting him. Whatever the case, England's batsmen could never be persuaded to forget the mauling they had sustained from him the previous winter.

Jeff Thomson was born in Bankstown, near Sydney, on August 16, 1950, and grew up to bowl with a similar action to his father's, the right foot briefly passing behind the left in the delivery stride, the bowling arm cocking a long way behind the backside, the left leg kicking parallel to the ground. Thomson's broad shoulders take much of the strain as he catapults the ball, tumbling through to a short follow-through, long hair flying in a cock's comb. The young 6 ft, 13 stone Australian was timed in Melbourne at 88 mph, but claimed he was 'not flat out'.

He had played once before for Australia – in 1972–3, his first season in first-class cricket, when his figures of none for 110 against Pakistan at Melbourne were seen in perspective when it was revealed that he had been carrying a broken bone in the left foot. He had concealed the injury as he felt this could be his one chance of an Australian cap, with so many rival fast bowlers around. He need not have worried. From the first Test in Brisbane in 1974 he became an indispensable part of Australia's attack.

When Colin Cowdrey was flown out as a replacement batsman to the injury-stricken England side, Thomson is supposed to have said that 'he'll cop it too'. Though there was more of him to aim at, Cowdrey withstood the withering Australian fast attack, and was the first to hook the 'unhookable' Thomson – even though it was as late as the third Test match, and he had taken his share of knocks, including one on exactly that part of his left forearm broken by Wes Hall a dozen years before.

The other man who has made Australian wicketkeeper Rod Marsh's life so uncomfortable is Dennis Lillee, whose philosophy appeared unretractably in 1974 in print in his autobiography: 'I try to hit a batsman in the rib-cage when I bowl a purposeful bouncer, and I want it to hurt so much that the batsman doesn't want to face me any more. I don't want to hit a batsman on the head because I appreciate what damage that can do.' He claims, with some justification, that he is expressing what most fast bowlers have been afraid to reveal.

He was born in Perth on July 18, 1949, and found early inspiration in Wes Hall's athleticism. Lillee's name first attracted attention when he took 5 for 84 in his Test debut at Adelaide against England. He cemented his place with an astonishing 8 for 29 next season against a World XI on the lightning-fast Perth wicket. He had felt off colour after a few overs, but captain Ian Chappell persuaded him to have another over, and then another, and in fifteen balls he took a further six wickets for no runs. He had bowled every ball as fast as he could, and learned that life could be short if he stuck to this principle. A thoughtful man, he never stopped learning that season or the next, when he toured England.

Later in the World XI series he widened his education further by bowling to Sobers as he put together a magnificent 254 at Melbourne, straight-driving Lillee's yorkers – and some deliveries 'on the up' – back past the tumbling bowler to the sightscreen.

In England, when he had spent a season in the Lancashire League, Lillee, now with a Mephistophelean moustache, was consistently threatening, and finished with a record 31 wickets in the five Tests, including a proud ten in the last, won by Australia to level the series. What was not generally appreciated was that he had nagging back pains from a seriously damaged spine. He bowled gallantly against Pakistan in the following home season, and went with Australia to the West Indies. There the back gave way completely, and it was left to Max Walker ('Tangles', the very tall Tasmanian with the odd action) and Jeff Hammond, the young South Australian tearaway, to carry the side's fast attack – a task they carried out heroically.

With four stress fractures at the base of his spine, there were few willing to bet that Lillee would play Test cricket again. They took no account of his burning desire to overcome the near-crippling disability. He spent six weeks in a plaster cast, resumed light training, and built up to a state of fitness where he could play as a batsman. Eventually he tried bowling – at medium pace – and there were no twinges. His training was intensified – hours upon countless hours of dedication away from the public glare. The season of 1973–4 saw him as simply a club cricketer.

Then came the important 1974–5 season, with England landing for a six-Test series in defence of the Ashes. Lillee pronounced himself fully fit, and the moment of fulfilment came as he took the field at Brisbane in the first Test with his relatively unknown new partner Jeff Thomson. By the end of the rubber – in fact after two

Tests – their names had become synonymous with pain or victory, depending on one's nationality.

Lillee took two wickets in each of England's first eight innings in the series, and then increased his output to four in each innings of the fifth Test, at Adelaide. In the sixth Test he was forced to withdraw after six overs with a bruised foot, but he had in that brief spell inflicted on Dennis Amiss his third consecutive Test duck, having had him caught twice at Adelaide. Lillee's mark, embellished by a relationship with the crowds worthy of a prizefighter's and by some red-hot verbal exchanges and gesticulations to and from his opponents in the middle, had been made strong and clear on the series. He was back, with beautifully-controlled nineteen-pace approach, almost as fast as the pre-breakdown model and considerably cleverer.

From *The Fast Men* by David Frith
(Van Nostrand Reinhold, Wokingham, 1975).

When Tony Greig Fired Us Up

Dennis Lillee

In his autobiography, Lillee recalls his return from back injury – and says the Bumper War was inspired by some riling tactics from Tony Greig.

F.S.T.

It was like starting my career all over again. After all those heart-breaking experiences with the back injury, the long periods of not knowing what was wrong, the weeks encased in plaster and then wearing a harness, and finally the long period of rebuilding my strength and fitness, there I was back in the Test team.

A couple of happenings early in the game helped to take my mind off my back. We batted first and when I went in at the fall of the eighth wicket we were a shaky 229. Peter Lever was bowling and very soon I heard Tony Greig encouraging him to bang them in short at me. But 'Plank' was a bit tired and just couldn't get them up. I was playing him fairly comfortably, which seemed to really upset Greigy. 'Give me the ball . . . I'll show you how to do it,' he said. Then he took the ball and slipped a couple of bouncers in at me straight away. I tried to hook the second one out of the ground, but took it on the glove and was caught behind. As I walked past him on the way back to the pavilion I said, 'I hope you can handle what you've got coming.' He just laughed.

I wasn't the only one in our tail who got the short-pitched treatment and, on reflection, these were rather foolish tactics. I don't think Greigy quite realized the implications – there's no way he and his team-mates could have known that Thommo was going to be such a force to contend with during the series. Also, the only time they'd seen me bowl was in Adelaide at the start of the season when I'd bowled only fast-medium at best. So they probably thought Thommo wasn't what the Press had cracked him up to be and that I was finished as an express bowler.

As it was, those bouncers from Greigy really fired us up and we decided then and there that, 'Okay, it's good enough for them to be firing in bouncers at our tail . . . let's see how well their tail can handle some of the same medicine.' That's where the so-called 'Bumper War' started.

I don't think anybody could blame us for bowling bouncers at their top-order batsmen, but a few of their tail-enders did start to squeal a bit towards the end of the tour when we were bowling much quicker bouncers at them than they were able to bowl at our tail. Our bowlers didn't really want to be part of the carry-on that followed that first innings up in Brisbane, but we felt we had to answer fire with fire.

Out of it all, in some ironical way, Greigy emerged as something of a winner himself. There's no doubting that his antics and behaviour on the field got us riled right from the start and we probably played into his hands. We got a bit carried away with bowling short to him when perhaps we should have realized that it's awfully hard to bowl good bouncers to a man of his height. His answer was to stand back and slash at the ball and time after time it flew over the in-field to the boundary. There were some good shots, but a lot went flying over slips off the edge. Greigy also displayed a lot of arrogance, signalling boundaries himself and really carrying on out there. I became quite irritated by him. It's obvious now that it was his idea to break my concentration.

That first Test in Brisbane was really the beginning of the 'Lillee and Thomson' partnership which was to prove so fruitful for both of us and for Australia.

England had their one moment of joy for the tour in the final Test, which Thommo missed because of his injury and in which I bowled just six overs before breaking down with a bruised foot. The England batsmen came out of the woodwork, with Mike Denness and Keith Fletcher each making centuries, and we ended up losing by an innings and 4 runs. Such a comprehensive defeat did little, if anything, to take the gloss off our four-one win over England in the series. It had been a rough and tough series, with many tense moments as the 'bumper war' raged pretty well throughout. But at the end of it all there was great satisfaction.

From *My Life In Cricket* by Dennis Lillee
(Methuen, London, 1982).

Good On Yer 'Oz

I was warned at the start of my first trip Down Under that my aggressive nature would get me into trouble with Aussie spectators, but I found a lot in common with the Australians, players and spectators alike. I liked their basic attitude. The players were good shouters, perhaps a bit too cocky when they were winning. But you had to watch them when they were losing – they hated losing. I found that the only way to deal with an Aussie cricketer was to get stuck in – like they always did with us – and then you found that underneath all the noise was a good bloke. Their supporters had exactly the same frame of mind. They respected and admired a man who would give as much as he took without squealing.

F.S.T.

Malcolm Marshall

Brian Johnston

When you put Malcolm Marshall alongside the greatest fast bowlers of other countries today, like Imran Khan of Pakistan, Hadlee of New Zealand or Kapil Dev of India, he seems in a different class. When MCC played Rest of the World at Lord's in MCC's bicentenary match in 1987 there was a chance to make a direct comparison – same pitch, same conditions. I noticed Marshall was the only bowler who consistently beat the bat. Even with a broken arm the man was a menace to England, as Brian Johnston describes.

F.S.T.

Have you ever thought what it would be like to stand in the path of an express train approaching at 90 m.p.h.? I don't expect that anyone has ever done such a crazy thing, except possibly in films, but any batsman who has ever faced Malcolm Marshall at his fastest knows what it would feel like. He must be a terrifying sight as he sprints in at a tremendous pace off a twenty-yard run. He takes tiny steps and is going so fast by the time he reaches the stumps that there is no chance of an orthodox bowling action. He is more square than sideways on, and there is practically no swivel of his body. He simply brings his right arm over like a whiplash, and the ball hurtles towards the batsman at about 90 m.p.h.

Unlike most of the West Indian bowlers, he does not bring the ball down from a great height. He is only five feet eleven inches tall, and most of them are anything from six foot three to six foot seven. The result is that the ball tends to skid through at chest or throat height rather than bounce over the batsman's head. He has been called lethal and destructive, and when he is bowling at his fastest he is certainly both.

You can check with Andy Lloyd of Warwickshire, who in his first – and only – Test at Edgbaston in 1984 was struck on the helmet from a short rising ball. He retired hurt, suffered from blurred vision and did not play again in 1984. And that was *through a helmet!*

By now Malcolm has joined the band of great fast bowlers – Lindwall, Trueman, Lillee, Holding and Hadlee. He varies his pace from very quick to fast-medium, often off a shortened run. His main ball is the one which leaves the batsman, but he has also perfected the one which swings *in* unexpectedly. This gets him many lbw decisions, and among his eleven lbw victims in the 1988 series against England were Gooch and Lamb twice and Gatting once, padding up without playing a stroke.

He has always been a fitness fanatic and is said to do fifty to sixty press-ups a day –

or sit-ups, as I think they are now called. During his ten years of Test cricket he has kept remarkably free from injury. He has boundless energy, and when not playing cricket plays tennis and golf. Since 1981 he has led a double cricketing life, playing for Hampshire in our summer, and for the West Indies during the rest of the year. He has worked wonders for Hampshire, and between 1981 and 1986 he was always one of the three top wicket-takers in the County Championship. In 1982 he took 134 wickets in the twenty-two match Championship, and this is still a record. Unlike so many of our modern Test bowlers, he has always given of his best for his county, and tried as hard as he does when playing for the West Indies.

I was in Barbados in February 1988 when there were rumours of him having knee and ankle trouble. Certainly, when I saw him bowl for Barbados against Guyana he only seemed to be at three-quarter pace, but in fact he started to bowl genuine leg-breaks and promptly took three wickets. I asked him afterwards whether this was going to be his secret weapon against England in the summer, but he said no. He was captain and thought the Bridgetown pitch might take spin. He had, he explained to me, begun his bowling life as a leg-spinner, and only took up fast bowling later.

After missing the first Test against Pakistan soon afterwards he regained almost full fitness, though he was troubled by a rib injury during the summer tour of England. Indeed, in the first Test at Trent Bridge he was forced to retire hurt in England's second innings. It is perhaps worth noting that this was the only Test out of five which the West Indies failed to win.

It was unusual for him, as he has tremendous guts and loathes giving up. This is what makes him such a great competitor. At Headingley in 1984 he suffered a double fracture of his left thumb, stopping a ball from Chris Broad in the gully, but this did not prevent him from going in to bat so that Larry Gomes could reach his hundred. He had to bat one-handed, and even so managed to hit a four. Better still – although his thumb was encased in plaster, making it difficult to use his left arm, he proceeded to take 7 for 53, including a two-handed caught-and-bowled to dismiss Graeme Fowler.

As a batsman he has improved so much that he very nearly qualifies as a genuine all-rounder. His method and style are correct and he hits the ball very hard. He has a top test score of 92 (against India) and has also scored four hundreds for Hampshire.

It took him about four years to become a regular member of the West Indies fast quartet, and since then has been reckoned the fastest bowler in the world. His record is phenomenal.

As a person he is reserved and not easy to get to know, but he is an immense enthusiast and trier. So long as he keeps fit and maintains his present form I would back him at least to pass 350 before he finally decides to retire. And it could so easily be 400!

From *It's Been A Piece of Cake* by Brian Johnston
(Methuen, London, 1989).

The Ethics of the Bouncer – Never at a Tail-Ender

F. S. Trueman

Of course I was aggressive on the field and I suppose I looked it. But I reasoned that you can't act like a pansy and be respected as a fast bowler, and batsmen were there to be got out as soon as possible. If the odd bouncer helped to break their concentration – and that is what I was trying to break, not their skulls – then I considered it a fair weapon. In my prime I could have hit anybody I wanted. Those I did, apart from the three exceptions, happened either accidentally or in the heat of the moment – such as that occasion when that West Indian batsman persisted in calling me a white English bastard. And whenever I did injure someone, I knew there would be a reckoning – and I don't mean in the dressing room or pavilion, which I could cope with. It happened when I had to face the only man I suppose I was ever afraid of. My father. He would be waiting for me when I got back home with the words, 'You've been at it again, have you!' He certainly gave me some stick about clobbering people, did Dad. I would try and protest that it had been an accident, but he would point out that I risked damaging my career permanently. He was also worried that I might seriously injure a fellow professional with a wife and family to support.

One thing I never did was bowl bouncers at tail-enders. And it was nothing to do with the 'fast bowlers union'. I considered it beneath any fast bowler of Test status to use aggressive tactics with men who clearly had little or no skill with the bat, whether they were pace or spin bowlers. Many times I was asked to let a tail-ender have one round the ears because he was pushing steadily down the line and trying to bat out time, but I always refused, whatever the circumstances.

From *Ball of Fire – an Autobiography* by Fred Trueman
(J. M. Dent, London, 1976).

Above: Fred in 1964 – the year he took his
300th Test wicket. (*Syndication
International*). *Right*: Len Hutton scores
his marathon 364 – it took 13 hours,
20 minutes – against Australia at the Oval
in 1938. (*Syndication International*).

Wilfred Rhodes – the greatest in a great tradition of
Yorkshire left-arm bowlers. (*Sport and General*).

Jack Hobbs, the great stylist. His technique
was so sound he scored more runs after the
age of 40 than before. (*Syndication
International*).

Above: Yorkshire grit – a helmetless Brian Close at Old Trafford in 1976 suffers the worst bumper barrage in Test cricket history from the West Indies. (*Patrick Eagar*). *Below*: From the great Don Bradman a rare miscue and Leslie Ames, the wicket-keeper prepares to catch him at Lord's in 1934 – the last time England beat the Aussies at cricket's H.Q. (*Syndication International*).

Left: Harold Larwood never played for England after the controversial Bodyline tour of 1933. Many rated him fastest of all time. (*Syndication International*). *Below*: Walter Hammond's cover drive was classic and unforgettable. (*Sport and General*).

Above: Brian Statham in 1962. With Trueman he formed England's most successful post-war opening attack. (*Sport and General*). *Below*: John Snow of Sussex and England hunting them down in 1975. (*Sport and General*).

Above: Frank Tyson – the 'Typhoon' who blasted Australia out of the Ashes in 1954-5. (*Syndication International*).

Left: Keith Miller in characteristic swashbuckling form as he hits Jim Laker for 6 at Lords in 1948. Laker was not yet the scourge of the Aussies. (*Syndication International*).

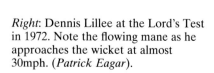

Right: Dennis Lillee at the Lord's Test in 1972. Note the flowing mane as he approaches the wicket at almost 30mph. (*Patrick Eagar*).

Above: Gary Sobers, greatest all-rounder of all time, on his way to scoring 150 not out on his last appearance at Lord's in 1973 – even though he'd never been to bed the night before! (*Patrick Eagar*). *Right*: Jeff Thomson demonstrates the wide arc of his very fast deliveries on the tour of England in 1975. (*Patrick Eagar*).

Ian Botham with characteristic ferocity straight drives Australia's Matthews for 6 at Old Trafford in 1985 (Texaco Trophy). (*Patrick Eagar*).

5

THE GREATEST ALL-ROUNDERS
365 Not Out

Sir Garfield Sobers

For me there is no question about the greatest all-rounder in cricket history – Sir Garfield Sobers. Sir Donald Bradman is just as emphatic: 'There were many contenders for the title, men like Hammond, Botham, Miller, Benaud and Davidson, but I unhesitatingly rated Garry Sobers as the greatest all-rounder I ever saw.' He excluded Grace, Rhodes and Woolley, having never really had the chance to evaluate them and making the point that in every sport where there is a meaningful yardstick for comparison, the modern athlete is way ahead of the champion of yesteryear. Even if you include today's greats, Richard Hadlee, first to take 400 test wickets, or Imran Khan or Kapil Dev, Garry still takes the top spot.

Figures don't tell the whole story, though 8,032 Test runs at an average of 57.78 and 235 wickets (at 34.03) is remarkable enough. It was the manner of his play – Calypso cricket at its best, especially the 254 he made for a world eleven against Australia when he confronted Dennis Lillee at his peak and smashed him back over his head at a time when his side faced apparent defeat. 'The best innings I have ever seen on Australian soil and I believe the best ever played in this country,' opined Sir Donald Bradman.

Garry was also a brilliant close-in fielder and three bowlers in one – a good swing bowler with a new ball, an orthodox left-arm spinner, and a wrist spinner with chinamen and googlies. A mighty hitter in 1968, he hit Glamorgan's Malcolm Nash for 6 sixes in an over at Swansea. Here in his own words from his autobiography Garry describes two other highlights in his life: in 1958 at Sabina Park, Jamaica as a twenty-one-year-old, beating Len Hutton's Test record of 364, never having scored a Test century before (though admittedly against a Pakistan attack depleted by three injuries); and finally a remarkable test innings at Lords in 1973 when he hadn't had a wink of sleep the night before.

F.S.T.

When play ended on the third day, I was 228 not out and Conrad was 242. As it was a six-day Test, there was time for one of us, or maybe both, to set a new individual Test record. Normally I sleep well when I eventually go to bed, admittedly later than most people, but on this occasion I had a restless night. Perhaps because of the talk of records and the possibilities the next day, I found myself lying awake. This was before the days when the team doctor gave players sleeping tablets!

I was not concerned about records. I never was at any time in my career. I felt I could bat on and on, and that no one could get me out. If this happened, I would be sure to beat the record – providing my captain, Gerry Alexander, did not declare.

When Conrad Hunte was run out at 266 – a tragedy because he could have got many more – our stand was worth 446.

Everton Weekes was next man in. What a man to come in at 533–2! He had been sitting with his pads on for many hours but he showed no sign of stiffness as he started to play his shots from the outset.

He hadn't been in long when he whipped a delivery from Khan out to mid-wicket and I set off on a run. I was horrified to see that Everton had not left his crease. Fortunately the fielder, Waqar Hussain, one of the two substitutes, threw to the wrong end! That was the only time I could have been out in my innings. It was a chanceless innings.

I celebrated my escape by passing 250 in 421 minutes, and soon the total of 576 had bettered the previous highest by the West Indies on the ground. The gates were shut, and the crowd was talking excitely of the next record once I passed George Headley's 270, the previous highest by a West Indian. On the radio, Roy Lawrence was reminding hundreds of thousands of listeners that Hutton's record was in danger.

Everton went at 602–3, caught by Hanif Mohammad at slip for 39 off Fazal Mahmoud. When Clyde Walcott came in, he told me that Gerry Alexander was thinking of declaring. As the West Indies were almost 300 ahead that made sense. 'Don't worry about it,' said Clyde. 'Settle down. Take it easy. The runs will come, and I will give you as much of the strike as I can.'

Clyde started with a two and a six off Fazal Mahmoud and then struck Karder, bowling with a broken finger, for one of the biggest sixes ever seen at Sabina Park. The taking of the new ball accelerated the scoring, as usually happens when two batsmen are set. A single off Fazal took me to 300. I was the first West Indian to reach that figure in Tests. I had tried not to think of the figure 365, but it was now impossible not to do so. The way I approached it was that I didn't really have 300 on the board but was new to the crease and needed 64 to win the match.

I did not feel tired. My restless night had not affected me. The excitement had stimulated me. The runs kept coming. I felt good. The noise from the spectators, many in trees and on pylons, was incredible. They cheered the 100 stand, posted in 90 minutes. At tea the total was 730 for 3, with me on 336 and Walcott 58.

Two runs later I passed Hanif's 337, and he ran up from cover to shake my hand. I was told later that most people in Barbados were listening on their radios.

When I was on 363, Kardar asked Hanif to bowl for the first time. Hanif was not a bowler of note! Walcott took a single off his second delivery, and I faced him with the spectators shouting and baying. I needed to refrain from taking chances. I stroked the ball out to long off, and we ran a single. I was level with Hutton.

When I faced Hanif again, he asked the umpire if he could bowl left-handed. 'You can bowl with both hands if you like,' I said. I pushed his first ball into the covers. Clyde called, and off I went. Sabina Park was in a state of bedlam. There were no high fences then, and hundreds of spectators ran on to engulf me. I was overjoyed. It was something unique, something that may never happen again.

Before order was restored, the bell sounded signifying that the innings had been declared closed at 790–3. My innings had taken 10 hours 8 minutes against Hutton's 13 hours 20 minutes. *Wisden* said I hit 38 fours and did not mention any sixes. I cannot remember if I hit any sixes. I find that rather strange! I hit many balls out of the ground at Sabina Park in my time.

That innings didn't change me as a person but it changed my life. From that moment on, I was instantly recognized throughout the Caribbean and the cricketing world. It did not alter my bank balance. There were no bonuses in those days. We won the match by an innings and 174 runs early on the final morning.

One person who congratulated me, one of many hundreds, was Len Hutton. He said he was pleased for me and hoped I would break more records.

He was a few months older than me, twenty-two, when he set the record. I had seen him score 205 against us in Kingston four years earlier and knew from my own experience what a great player he was, even though he was past his best. I was proud to have beaten his record.

From *Sobers – Twenty Years at the Top* by Sir Garfield Sobers and Brian Scovell (Macmillan, London, 1988).

A Late Night at Lord's

Sir Garfield Sobers

At the age of thirty-seven Garry was still a lad at heart.

F.S.T.

One of my most satisfying innings was the 150 not out in my final Test appearance at Lord's in 1973. But what most of the 25,000 crowd didn't know was that I failed to go to bed on the Friday night. It was well known in cricket that I liked a drink after play. I rarely went to bed at a normal time because I am one of those people who can have four or five hours' sleep and still wake up fresh.

Instead of lying in bed thinking over what had happened on the field of play, I preferred to go out with friends to restaurants and clubs. My philosophy was, and still is, that life is for living. I played hard and drink reasonably hard on occasions without making a fool of myself.

I enjoyed the social side of cricket so much that it was to become my motivation to do well. If I were to have a bad run with the bat, people would start asking questions and might come up with the answer that my failure was due to too many late nights. I had to make sure those late nights could continue by maintaining a consistently high level of performance.

Many cricketers liked a night out during matches. It was a traditional part of the game, particularly when Australians were involved. Not that all Australian cricketers were like that. Some, like Brian Booth, Ken 'Slasher' Mackay and Neil Harvey, didn't drink at all, although I believe Ken and Neil did when they retired. Nowadays, with cricket becoming much more competitive and the rewards for success greater, there are fewer opportunities for players to enjoy themselves after hours. Most teams have curfews, and anyone staying out will soon find himself in trouble.

My 'live for today' approach was really fostered by the late Sir Frank Worrell. He liked to enjoy himself after matches, and I remember many nights when we sat up together in hotels talking and drinking. There was a curfew for the team, but he used to say to me: 'That's not for you. I know you well enough.'

What he meant was that he recognized we had a lot in common. He knew that if I went to bed early I wouldn't sleep. My view about sleep is that you go to bed when you are tired. If you still have plenty of energy to burn, you burn it.

After close of play on the Friday of the Lord's Test, I met an old friend of mine now living in London, Reg Scarlett, the former Jamaican and West Indian off-spin bowler. Reg was a useful player and should have played more than the three Tests he was picked for against England in 1959. We were out until 5 a.m. and then went back to the hotel where we never managed to get any sleep!

Reg drove me to the ground in the morning, and I resumed my innings. The West Indies were in a very strong position. Skipper Rohan Kanhai, timing the ball superbly, made 157, and Bernard Julien helped me add 231 for the seventh wicket on one of the best Lord's batting pitches I ever encountered.

Wisden records that 'there was a quiet period at the start when Sobers played within himself'. That was probably because I wasn't seeing the ball too clearly! Bob Willis, then twenty-four and bowling at his fastest, beat me several times, and I remember saying to myself: Just play straight.

I managed to overcome the crisis, and when I was in the seventies felt churning pains in the stomach. They were so bad that I thought about going off. But I rejected that option because I felt it would break my concentration. I needed that twenty-sixth Test hundred to prove to the selectors who had left me out of the previous series against the Australians that I was still a good player!

When I eventually passed my hundred, the discomfort was such that I said to umpire Charlie Elliott: 'I'm not feeling well. Can I go off?' Charlie sounded a little perplexed. 'You're not injured,' he said, 'What can I put it down to?'

'I can't stay,' I said. 'I've got to go.' So off I went and in came Keith Boyce to join Julien.

Around this time the authorities were still letting spectators sit on the grass at Lord's. There had been pitch invasions at the Oval, and they were followed by more at Lord's. So many people came on that it became tiresome, and the MCC finally decided to ban sitting on the grass. When Julien reached his hundred off 127 balls, on came several hundred fans, and umpire Dickie Bird was most upset but powerless to act.

This was also the Test where a bomb scare held up play on the Saturday. All these matters were far from my mind as I slumped on a chair in the dressing-room and Rohan Kanhai asked me what was wrong.

'Captain, I had to come off,' I said. 'My stomach is giving me trouble.' Even after he had taken over from me, Rohan always called me 'Captain' and, turning to the twelfth man, said: 'Bring the captain a brandy and port to settle his stomach.' The drink was quickly produced, and I drank it. Rohan knew that a brandy and port usually worked with me. As I downed it, Rohan said: 'Bring the captain another brandy and port.' So I had another one!

Boyce was eventually out for 36 at 604–7, and to my surprise Rohan asked me to resume my innings. I believe John Arlott was commentating at the time. 'Goodness me,' he said. 'West Indies 604 for 7 and here comes Sobers.' I will never forget the expression of sheer disbelief on the face of England captain Ray Illingworth when I walked out of the pavilion.

Rohan declared when I reached 150 with the total at 652–8. England, thoroughly demoralized, were bowled out for 233 and 193, and we won by an innings and 226.

It was Illingworth's last Test as captain. Mike Denness, captain of Kent, took over for the tour to the West Indies later that year.

Earlier in my career I did not drink a lot. But then occured an event in my life that changed that and for a time forced me to seek comfort from drink: the death of my great friend Collie Smith in a car crash in 1959.

Collie shared a room with me in England and also in Pakistan. On the night of 6 September I picked him and Tom Dewdney up to travel through the night to a charity match the next day in London. We left it late because of the heavy traffic. Tom was a big Jamaican medium-fast bowler who played 9 Tests between 1955 and 1958.

I do not remember much about the accident. But at the inquest on Collie a few weeks later it was said that I was driving on the A34 near Stone in Staffordshire when my vehicle ran into a ten-ton cattle-truck driven by a Mr Andrew Saunders. The time of the collision was 4.45 a.m.

I remember being blinded by headlights as I approached a bend and was sure my car was on the right side of the road. The impact left us stunned, but none of us lost consciousness. Collie did not appear to be in too bad shape. 'Don't worry about me. Look after the big fellow,' he said, referring to Tom Dewdney.

We were taken to a hospital in Stone. I had a cut eye and a severed nerve in a finger on my left hand which took some time to mend. I was also suffering from shock. When I asked about Collie, the kind nurses and doctors said: 'Don't worry, he's coming along fine.' I learned that his spinal cord was damaged. Tom was recovering.

Three days later Collie died. I was stunned. He was such a wonderful person, such a good friend. He had the ability to become a better all-rounder than me. His off-spin bowling was in the Test class.

Collie provided the stabilizing influence in my life up to then. He was not puritanical. He loved enjoying himself as much as I did, but if I showed signs of going too far he would say: 'That's enough for tonight. Let's go home.'

Around that time, with plenty of time to spare between weekend matches, I became increasingly interested in gambling on horses. It was something to do. Now, with Collie gone, I had no restraints. I drank heavily, I had the capacity to down a lot of liquor without it having any harmful effects on me.

Later I was charged with driving without due care and attention and was fined £10. It was the saddest episode of my life and it has been on my conscience ever since.

From *Sobers – Twenty Years at the Top* by Sir Garfield Sobers with Brian Scovell
(Macmillan, London, 1988).

Keith Miller

Neville Cardus

I never believed that Keith Miller played to his full potential. He was a brilliant fielder and a fine batsman – 2,958 Test runs at an average of 36.97. He took 170 wickets at an average of 22.97, and there might have been more, but he was unpredictable. Loose-limbed and athletic, he was as fast as Lindwall, sometimes off a run of only a few paces; but he also did the Rt Rev. David Sheppard at Lords with an irreverent googly. Len Hutton told me he had more trouble facing Miller than he did facing Lindwall. Like Botham, Miller had the ability to change the entire course of a match in a few overs – whether batting or bowling. Here Neville Cardus, once a neighbour of Miller in the same block of flats at Sydney's King's Cross, captures perfectly the spirit and personality of the man.

F.S.T.

Keith Miller, nearly six foot tall, knows the almost forgotten secret these days of *panache*. Loose of limb with good shoulders, he is alluring in the eyes of the ladies who sit in the Sheridan stand at Sydney. In the Test match *v.* England at Sydney in January 1951, Hutton and Simpson were well-rooted and the score 128 for 1. England had lost at Brisbane and Melbourne; the rubber was now at stake. Before this third Test, England had prayed to win the toss. 'Let us only bat first on a good wicket', they had said. Well, England was, on this hot scorching afternoon at Sydney, batting first. And Hutton and Simpson seemed impregnable. The Australians were waiting without much hope for the new ball. Ten minutes from tea, Miller had strayed from the slips to the outfield. He stood in front of the Sheridan stand. He was communing between one ball and the next with the ladies. Then Hassett, Australia's captain, called on him to send down a few overs, merely to mark-time, till the interval and to give the other perspiring bowlers a rest. Miller reluctantly took the old ball, and at a deceptive medium pace relaxed like a fast bowler formally swinging his arm in the nets, he got rid of Hutton and Compton in an over, suddenly, from a short run, delivering streaked lightning. Immediately after tea he had Simpson caught at short leg. In twenty-eight balls he took 3 for 5, and by sheer improvisation he won the rubber for Australia.

He was, in fact, a great artist in improvisation. When he bowled, he often ran to the crease from different places and always did he attack along a shortish distance.

He couldn't bear to waste time. If a ball was played defensively from him he would clap his hands at the fielder retrieving the stroke, eager to 'get on with it'. At an inning's beginning his pace and bounce from the pitch were terrific and as though combustible. Certain England batsmen feared him even more palpitatingly than they feared Lindwall. He was 'at them' so abruptly, swinging round after his few impatient paces, his shoulders generating a last-second propulsive energy. 'If Keith had never gone in for batting', Cyril Washbrook one day told me, 'he would have been the most dangerous fast bowler ever.' He was quite dangerous enough. At Melbourne, he came close to equalling S. F. Barnes's wonder-bowling there, in December, 1911, when the Master took four wickets before lunch for one run, in five overs. Miller, at Melbourne in December, 1954, bowled throughout the ninety minutes before lunch, and took 3 wickets for 5 runs in 9 overs, despite a suspect knee. But when the mood to action visited Keith he was not conscious of physical impediments.

He was incalculable. Only mediocrity is always at its best. One day we would see Miller's bat trenchant and powerful, driving with a conquering swing, upright and free. Next day he might dismay us by pushing forward full stretch, groping at a good length ball, apprehensively groping. In 1945 he was the living embodiment of the game's and of London's resurrection from the ruin and the graveyard of the war. He came to Lord's, fresh from intrepid feats of battle in the air, and playing for the Dominions against England, enchanted the watching rationed English crowd by batsmanship glorious and visionary. He hit seven sixes and added 124 to a night before's score of 61 – in ninety minutes. An imperious drive off Eric Hollies landed on the roof of the broadcaster's box, but for which obstacle the ball would have cleared the pavilion, even as Albert Trott's gigantic hit had cleared it years previously.

Incalculable and unpredictable. One day he is in the slips interrupting conversation by a sudden leap or thrilling dive to take a sinful catch. Next day he is at cover, his mind wandering or pondering the 'odds' or the 'weights' and an easy chance, possibly from Washbrook in a Test, goes almost unnoticed by Keith, who hardly unfolds his arms. He is a law and lawless to himself. In fighting mood he could hurl a 'bumper' with the jubilant ferocity of a 'Digger' at Gallipoli throwing a hand grenade. In some other mood of his own fancy, he might go on to bowl like a middle-aged gentleman playing with young folk on the sands, rolling along donkey-drops square-arm. But the stronger the odds against him the greater his relish of the game – game of cricket or game of life.

His technique as bowler or batsman could not be described as classic. The energy in him galvanized him to action which could not take the form of Lindwall's smooth poise and balance. Miller was the romantic, sometimes even the eccentric. With the new ball he could rap the batsman's gloves, even threaten the breastbone, from a good length. He could swing away very late at a pace which seemed to accelerate cruelly after the ball had pitched. I fancy his fastest ball was one of the fastest in all cricket's history. As a batsman he delighted the most critical eye whenever he was on the attack. Defensively, he prodded most gingerly.

At Lord's, on the Saturday evening of 23 June, 1956, he had scored 30 and looked good for a century when he was caught at the wicket off a truly grand ball from Trueman. He at once raised his bat as a salute to Trueman. Another quite natural gesture of a cricketer who, with all his recurrent tantrums, was a chivalrous opponent.

When I was a resident in Sydney, Keith for a while lived in the same block of flats as myself.

He would come up to my room and ask if I would play the gramophone for him. 'What record, Keith?' Always he would ask for a piano concerto. Sometimes I would say, 'Why not a symphony this time?' No; it had to be a piano concerto. I imagine that he has scored hundreds of his runs and taken many, many wickets to the accompaniment, supplied mentally by himself, of the 'Emperor' concerto. The right music to go with his cricket at its greatest! Or perhaps something 'hotter' – say, 'Johnny and the Hurricanes'.

From *Cardus in the Covers* by Neville Cardus
(Souvenir Press, London, 1978).

Trevor Bailey

Jim Laker

My Test Match Special colleague Trevor Bailey was such a fighter he should have been born a Yorkshireman. An outstanding all-rounder for England, his stubborn batting saved England more than once, notably with Willie Watson in that celebrated drawn game at Lord's in 1953 against Australia, after which England went on to regain the Ashes. As third seamer for England he was better – and quicker – than many who now open for the country. Like all great cricketers he had an arrogance that could irritate as old England team-mate Jim Laker, writing in 1957 (when the old amateur/professional divide still existed), here describes.

F.S.T.

You have to tour with Trevor to understand him. First impressions are that he is a somewhat affected individual, prone to 'act' and even play his cricket selfishly. And, to be fair, there are times when Trevor, in his batting, tends to play for himself.

Yet he has a load of guts, a flair for the big occasion, and is very popular with his England and M.C.C. touring team-mates. Far from being a snob, he mixes well, and counts some of the professionals among his best friends.

It is said that he dislikes Australians. I think he probably *thought* he disliked them in his earlier days, and I believe he even said so at a party in Australia on the 1950–1 tour. He irritated the manager of that side, Brigadier M. A. Green, by his mannerisms, and later Green wrote that at one juncture early on Bailey was told that he would be ordered home if he did not make greater efforts on behalf of the team.

I was not in Australia at the time, so I would not know the strength of this report, but I do know that Trevor is less headstrong now than in his early days, and has mellowed with the years. With his great knack of rising to the occasion, he has served England well. In my opinion he has been hard done by in not receiving more responsibility in recent years.

Trevor went to the West Indies in 1953–4 as vice-captain, and did an excellent job as skipper when Hutton was resting. He is a keen student of the game, with a ready knack for summing up a situation and the weaknesses of opponents.

Of course, Trevor has been favoured in Test cricket through a lack of opposition from genuine all-rounders in post-war England. The tendency is more and more to specialize, but Trevor, though now well into his thirties, has maintained his bowling speed and seems still to enjoy bowling as much as batting.

Trevor Bailey plays cricket very seriously, with the studied approach of a professional. ... This trait was already evident when he was at school at Dulwich. As a fourteen-year-old he skippered one side in a house match, which he allowed to end tamely in a draw. He was called before his master, Mr S. C. Griffith, to explain why he had not gone for victory.

'I thought the risk of defeat was too great, sir,' young Bailey stated.

'Never mind that,' replied Griffith, 'you must play to win.' Griffith was then an experienced county cricketer, who had toured Australasia with an M.C.C. side. But Bailey was undeterred. 'That's not the way I play cricket,' he retorted.

You can see how this attitude was bound to be as a red rag to a bull as far as the volatile Miller was concerned. ... Trevor has traded on Keith's impatience.

In one Test match in which I was batting at the other end, Keith bowled a bouncer to Trevor. It hit him on the finger. Trevor immediately put on an absolute 'Hamlet'. He shook his glove, walked round the wicket half a dozen times, removed his glove, replaced it, prepared to take strike, then took off his glove for a second examination. The longer the delay, the greater Miller's anger.

The next ball was a 'beamer', straight for Trevor's skull. Bailey swayed out of harm's way and grinned impudently down the wicket. Keith said two emphatically uncomplimentary words, and hurried back to his bowling mark. He came in towards the wickets like a bat out of hell. He was about three paces away from releasing one of the fastest balls of all time, when Trevor stepped away from the stumps and began to look at his 'damaged' finger again. That was too much for Miller, and afterwards, his usually spot-on bowling was all awry.

In the Brisbane Test of 1954–5, Keith reached 49 by beautiful batting. Trevor, who was bowling, suddenly switched all but two of his fielders to the on side. Then he bowled leg theory in exactly the same way as he had done to save the Test at Leeds the previous year. Keith, who could not get near them, was hopping mad. The next ball was wide of the off stump, perfect for cutting. Keith slashed at it with all his might, got it on the side edge of his bat and dragged it on to his stumps ... bowled Bailey 49!

Matters did not always go Trevor's way, however. At Lord's in 1953, the forward defensive prod stalled Australia in the second innings, but not in the first. Keith bowled a slower one, Trevor pushed forward too soon and popped up a simple return catch. Keith made sure of holding it and then, as Trevor tore off his gloves in annoyance, drop-kicked the ball, Rugby-fashion, into the covers as a gesture of triumph.

But Miller missed the pleasure of seeing Trevor's one big Test match 'failure'. After being originally dropped for the Fifth Test against the South Africans in 1955, Bailey was reinstated at the eleventh hour through an injury to Tyson. There was quite a hue and cry in the Press about Trevor's original omission and, when he went in to bat, he received a terrific ovation. Incredibly, Bailey seemed to allow the wine of the moment to go to his head. He had a dip at Tayfield before he had scored, and was caught off a skier. Miller would not have believed his eyes, especially when Trevor was l.b.w. to Tayfield in the second innings with only one run to his name.

'I would have given fifty quid to have been there,' was Keith's comment when next I saw him.

Actually, the 'feud' is not carried beyond the cricket field. Trevor really admires Keith's gay abandon as much as Keith admires Trevor's tenacity. All the Aussies love a fighter; that is why Bailey is not so unpopular in Australia as we are sometimes led to believe.

Both Miller and Bailey are good friends. You could not wish to see a better catch anywhere than the one Bailey took 'round the corner' off Trueman to get rid of Neil Harvey in the second innings of the Lord's Test in 1953. Indeed, Trevor is often as much a source of irritation to Harvey — so often does he have a hand in his dismissal — as he is to Miller.

Keith, of course, has also picked up some blinding catches in his time. He still catches well in the slips in spite of his disarming manner of standing bolt upright, often with arms folded, as the bowler delivers the ball. Here again is an instance where Miller should not be copied!

He is a fine mover, and thrower away from the wicket, too, and all round he is better in the field than Bailey.

Yes, no matter which way you look at it, the vote for that all-rounder berth in our All-Star team must go to Miller.

Yet there can be no finer tribute to Bailey than that he could seriously be considered in the same light as a cricketer of Miller's almost unrivalled skill.

From *Spinning Around the World* by Jim Laker

(Muller, London, 1957).

Richie Benaud

Brian Johnston

Richie Benaud must rank as Australia's greatest all-rounder of recent times. Added to that he was a brilliant close-in fielder, a fine captain with a good tactical sense, and a very fair opponent. He was often a first-change bowler when the ball was still hard. Though he did not spin the ball a lot, he was quick for a leg spinner and that, combined with his high action and bounce, made him difficult to play, especially on overseas wickets which are much harder. And as a batsman few could hit the ball harder.

F.S.T.

Who is the nattiest-dressed cricket commentator? Who has the neatest coiffure? Who captained Australia in six series, winning five, and drawing one? Who took more Test wickets than any other Australian spinner? Who was the first Test cricketer to make 2,000 runs and take 200 Test wickets? I am sure your buzzers went after the first question, without need of further clues. Yes of course, it's Richie Benaud, who organizes every minute of his life more efficiently than anyone I know, helped, I hasten to add, by his wife Daphne, or Daphers as we call her.

I first met Richie during the 1953 Australian tour of England, when, to be honest, he was not a great success. He played in three Tests, took 2 wickets for 174, and made 15 runs in five innings, but he finished the tour with a flourish and a warning of things to come. Against T. N. Pearce's eleven at Scarborough he made 135 in 110 minutes, hitting eleven sixes and nine fours, his first hundred in England. He was always a fine driver of the ball, and as his career developed he became a complete stroke-player, which made him into a genuine Test all-rounder.

It was as a leg-spin bowler that he really made his mark, however. He had a fine high action which, especially on overseas pitches in Australia, South Africa and the West Indies, enabled him to get bounce into his deliveries. He was a great one for practising and spent hours in the nets perfecting his mixture of leg-breaks, googlies, top-spinners and flippers. He was not afraid to bowl the latter, which he picked up from Bruce Dooland, and took quite a number of his 248 Test wickets with it. He described it to me as a ball held in the tips of the first and third fingers of the right hand. It is squeezed or flipped out of the hand from underneath the wrist – rather like flipping a cherry stone. The object is to bowl it just on or outside the off-stump.

It hurries from the pitch, usually straight but sometimes from off to leg. It is a surprise ball which often traps a batsman who has played back.

Richie was not a big spinner of the ball, but he was always accurate and with his flight, line and bounce was difficult to score off. English pitches did not suit him, but in spite of a bad shoulder he did win the fourth Test for Australia at Old Trafford in 1961 by bowling his leg-breaks round the wicket into the rough outside the leg-stump. His analysis is worth noting – superb figures for a slow bowler, 32–11–70–6.

The fact that he was a brilliant close-fielder, especially in the gully, made him the complete all-rounder, but it was as a captain that he probably did most for Australia. He was certainly the best post-war captain whom I saw. He had everything a captain needs. He was a natural leader who inspired his teams to play above themselves. He was a motivator and he animated and encouraged them both on and off the field, where he placed great importance on a happy dressing-room. On the field I'm afraid he was really the starter of the hugging and kissing which goes on so much today. I asked him about it once and he said he was prepared to do anything if it helped to take wickets. Tony Lock carried on the habit when he came to captain Leicestershire – so much so that Maurice Hallam, normally an excellent fielder, once dropped two catches running down at long leg. When asked why he hadn't caught them, he is said to have replied: 'What, and be kissed by Tony Lock. Not bloody likely!'

Richie was an amazingly good reader of a game, and was quick to spot and memorize an opponent's weakness. He tried to be a positive captain and would attack whenever he could, but he was not prepared to 'play ball' unless the other side responded. A perfect example of this was the fifth Test at Sydney in 1963 against Ted Dexter's side. The series was level, and a thoroughly dull game followed England's desperately slow first innings of 321.

Off the field Richie was the best PRO of any captain I have seen. At the end of each day, however hot and tired, he would meet the press, TV and radio, and answer questions about the day's play. He was not afraid to be candid but was perfectly fair in his assessment of the day's events. It was still *his* opinion as Australian captain, however, and as a result the English newspapers, unintentionally no doubt, would often put over Australia's view of the match.

He took as much trouble to learn to commentate as he did to learn to bowl. When on tour here in 1956 and 1961 he took a great interest in our TV coverage, and managed to engineer a crash course for himself at the end of the 1961 tour. When still captain of Australia he joined TMS for radio commentary on the South African Tests in England in 1960. He soon picked up the tricks of the trade and joined BBC TV when he retired from Test cricket in February 1964. People often ask me why we have to have an Australian on BBC. The answer is simply that he is the best. He has tremendous knowledge of the tactics and techniques of the game, is quick-witted and knows when to talk or not to talk. He is also a very good summariser at the end of the day's play. He is fluent, knowledgeable, unflappable and remembers all the details of the play. What more can a producer ask for?

He also has a dry sense of humour and was great fun to work with in the box. Peter West, he and I always used to call the value of a run as soon as the ball left the bat. Richie was a pretty good judge and normally got it right. I wasn't so good, but if I said 'that's 4 all the way' and only 3 runs were scored I would either blame the slowness of the outfield or praise the speed and skill of the fielder.

I cannot end without explaining why Richie was indirectly responsible for my giving up wicket-keeping. One Sunday he and I were playing in a charity match at the Dragons School at Oxford. I was keeping wicket and he was bowling his googlies, top-spinners, flippers and leg-breaks. I read them all perfectly well, but most of them went for 4 byes. When the last man came in Richie bowled him a terrific leg-break. The man went down the pitch, and missed the ball by miles. It came into my gloves, and with all my own speed – so I thought – I whipped off the bails and appealed. The umpire raised his finger and there was I, an ordinary club cricketer, stumping someone off the Australian captain. No wonder I was looking pleased as I walked off. The bursar of the school confirmed my high opinion of my skill by coming up and saying: 'Jolly well stumped.' He then unfortunately went on to say: 'And I'd like to congratulate you on the sporting way you tried to give him time to get back.' I then realized that it was time for me to retire and hang up my gloves. I never kept wicket again.

In his spare time – which is very scarce – Richie is a dedicated golfer and thinks nothing, during a Test match, of getting up at five o'clock to play a game of golf before going off for a day's commentary.

From *It's Been a Piece of Cake* by Brian Johnston
(Methuen, London, 1989).

Richard Hadlee

Brian Johnston

I would put Richard Hadlee in the Lillee class with the new ball although he hasn't bowled really fast for almost ten years now. He is living proof there is life after fast bowling and off a slower run he has deadly swing and movement off the seam, so much so that he is now the first person to have taken more than 400 Test wickets. Even though now a controlled medium-fast, he can also slip in a very fast ball indeed – a surprise change of pace. With Botham's back restricting his bowling speed Hadlee is now the best all-rounder playing today. Here is Brian Johnston's assessment.

F.S.T.

There are many arguments for and against overseas players playing in the County Championship. Those *for* say that it enables spectators in England to see great players from all over the world regularly in action every summer, instead of every four years or so when their countries tour England. The county secretaries say that the acquisition of a top overseas player gives every county (except Yorkshire) a better chance of winning one of the four competitions. They also claim that it gives our young players the chance of playing with and learning from the overseas stars.

Those *against* say that our young players are denied opportunities in their county team. The overseas player so often gets preference in the batting order, or is given the new ball which would otherwise be taken by a home-bred player. They also point out that many who come here are not already stars. They come here to *learn* their cricket under English conditions and then use their improved skills and experience to beat England in Test matches. Personally I am in favour of the present restriction on overseas players, which will eventually mean that each county will only be allowed to register one player not qualified for England.

All this brings us to Richard Hadlee, who by playing over here from 1978 to 1987 has benefited both his county and himself. In this period, under the captaincy of South African Clive Rice, Nottinghamshire became one of the top counties: they won two Championships and a Nat West Trophy, were finalists in the Benson and Hedges, and came second twice in the Sunday League.

As for Hadlee himself, he came here as a fairly ordinary tearaway fast bowler who had taken 89 wickets at 31.58 apiece. In November 1988 in New Zealand he passed Ian Botham's total of 373 Test wickets, but what happens thereafter depends on Ian

Botham's recovery from his bad back and when Malcolm Marshall decides to retire from Test cricket.

The daily hard grind of county cricket forced Richard to adjust his methods. He cut down his run and learned to concentrate on swing and movement off the seam. He was nearly as fast as before and could still unleash a really fast ball which he used sparingly. Like Lindwall, Trueman, Lillee and Marshall, he simply relied on skill rather than speed.

He is a dedicated cricketer, and is number four out of five sons of Walter Hadlee, the old New Zealand captain. So he was brought up in a cricket atmosphere and was soon taught the finer points of the game. He has always set himself targets, and with his sense of purpose and determination has usually achieved them. He is said to have a number of slogans, which he keeps repeating to himself as occasion demands – a sort of self-hypnosis. And how well they worked for him, Nottinghamshire and New Zealand. He did the double in 1984 (the first since 1967) and topped the bowling averages in 1980, 1981, 1982, 1984 and 1987, but his slogans let him down slightly in 1987. I am sure he had planned to do the double in his last season for Notts. He just achieved his 1,000 runs, but only took 97 wickets. Even so, only two other bowlers did take 100, Neil Radford with 109 and Jonathan Agnew with 101. But they bowled 150 and 186 *more* overs respectively than Richard.

So what makes him such a great bowler? He is tall (six feet one inch), lean and wiry with long arms and a whippish action – not unlike Brian Statham in build. He has perfect sideways-on action and bowls from near the stumps. He swings the ball away from the batsman, and can then bring it back off the seam. His shortened run is about twelve yards, and he has a long raking stride. Because his arm comes over so high he produces a lot of bounce, and he keeps a good line and length with only the occasional short ball. Richard is a bowler whom any young player should copy to the last detail.

As a batsman he is a left-hander who used to go in at number eight or nine and then try to knock the cover off the ball, but he has gradually improved his defence without sacrificing his ability to strike the ball a long way, often high in the air. He has so much improved that he can now be called a genuine Test all-rounder. He has already made over 2,600 Test runs and in 1987 topped the Notts batting averages with 1,025 runs. (Needless to say, he also topped the bowling averages.)

His batting reached a peak in the NatWest Final at Lord's in 1987 against Northants. He made 70 not out in 61 balls, hitting 2 giant sixes and 4 fours. At one time Notts needed 51 off only 5 overs, but thanks to Richard and Bruce French this was reduced to 8 runs needed off the last over, to be bowled by David Capel. French was run out for a splendid 35 off the first ball. The next Hadlee hit for a towering six into the 'free' seats at the Nursery End. The third ball he pulled to the Tavern Stand for four, and Notts had won a thrilling game, coming from behind when all had seemed lost.

To complete his skills as an all-rounder Richard is a fine fielder anywhere, moving fast and with a good arm. What a chap to have on your side. He is always trying, is eager to win and as a bowler is feared by even the greatest Test batsmen. Like all cricketers, Richard has suffered his ups and downs, but he went out in a blaze of glory at the end of his time with Notts. Thanks to his fine all-round performance and the inspirational captaincy of South African Clive Rice, they won both the County Championship and the NatWest Trophy. They nearly did the hat-trick, finishing second in the Refuge Assurance League, only two points behind Worcestershire.

Both New Zealand and Nottinghamshire owe a debt of thanks to Wally Hadlee for producing such a magnificent all-round cricketer, and such a thoroughly nice person as well.

From *It's Been a Piece of Cake* by Brian Johnston
(Methuen, London, 1989).

After Botham's heroics against Australia in 1981, his return in 1989 was a bit of an anti-climax.

'*Call in the TCCB wicket inspectors! The ball failed to hit my bat!*'

Ian Botham – One Man's Ashes

Ray Illingworth and Kenneth Gregory

Ian Botham is the best all-rounder on figures that we've produced, and a fine catcher of the ball. At his peak as a young man he had a beautiful action close to the stumps and sideways on. He hit the ball as hard as anyone I've ever seen and played all the shots in the book. If he had tried to bat with the ability he had instead of trying to slog the ball out of the ground he would have got more runs. It didn't help playing opposite Vivian Richards at Somerset: if Viv got 80 in 40 overs then 'Both' wanted 90 in 39 overs. His batting in 1989 was pathetic, but he could still do a useful job for England at number four. He needed a strong captain and under Brearley in 1981 his prodigious talents all came together to win for England, almost single-handed, the Ashes. Three times, thanks to him, near-certain defeat was turned into victory at Headingley, Edgbaston and Old Trafford. It was a never-to-be-forgotten summer, described here by Ray Illingworth and Kenneth Gregory.

F.S.T.

For England joy came out of misery in 1981 – for Australia an unbearable collapse on the verge of victory. On 22 June England lost the first Test; at the close of the second on 7 July, her Selectors sacked the captain at a time when he told them he did not wish to continue his command on a match by match basis. The gamble had failed. Little more than a year previously, Ian Botham, aged twenty-four, had been pushed to the summit – perhaps because, more than anyone else, he was an integral member of the team; perhaps because he clearly had years of cricket ahead of him and would learn from experience; probably in the hope he could transmit the magnetism of his achievement into terms of leadership. But England's opposition in successive series was West Indies. Botham failed – as most likely anyone else would have failed – to inspire England above a normal potential. Worse, his own form suffered; he became something like a contemporary cricketer. Australia's strength lay in bowling – in Lawson who could be decidedly fast, in Hogg, the medium-pace of Alderman, *and* Lillee. Soon after reaching England, the last named had succumbed to pneumonia. But a Demon, though weakened is not put out by minor ailments; at fast-medium pace he does what he likes with the ball – and therefore with English batsmen. And so it proved. At Trent Bridge, under heavy skies and on a pitch that might have been ordered by Lillee and Alderman, England's two innings totalled 310 – Australia winning by 4 wickets. Much of Australia's close catching was brilliant, much of England's was not.

At Lord's the pitch was good, so the match was drawn. No individual made a hundred though Gatting, Willey, Boycott and Gower for England, Border and Wood for Australia, all passed 50. Botham fell leg-before-wicket to Lawson for 0, and was bowled by Bright (first ball sweeping) for 0. As a captain of England is not meant to get a pair at Lord's – especially against Australia – the Selectors reacted: 'let's send for Dr Brearley!' And so to Headingley.

Sunshine and showers, the weather experts were right. The sun shone on the Australian batsmen who, though not approving of the pitch, discovered they could play on it. England's bowlers rivalled the showers in being intermittently effective. The fielding – brilliant in Brearley's earlier reign – was undistinguished. Around five o'clock on the second day, with only 4 Australian wickets down and over 300 on the board, Brearley brought back Botham: 'You used to be able to move mountains, remove this lot.' Botham pranced in, took 5 wickets for 35 runs, prompting a declaration at 401 for 9.

Had the series just started for England? Not yet. On the third day Lillee, Alderman and Lawson bowled them out for 174, with Gooch gone in the second innings. The ball swung and cut, batting an impossibility; Botham made 50, Extras 34, ten other England batsmen 90. Botham's innings was interesting. It was as though George Gunn, a product of the Golden Age, had whispered, 'Never take any notice of the wicket.' That, surely, was one message of the Golden Age. How else can one explain Trumper and J. T. Tyldesley on unlikely surfaces? It is one thing to bat scientifically, another to be overawed by science.

England began the fourth day needing 222 to avoid an innings defeat. At lunch they were 78 for 4 – Brearley, Gower and Gatting out. Still 124 in arrears. Half an hour after lunch Willey left, 103 for 5. The new batsman (and at moments of crisis we should note vital statistics) stood, or rather marched, an inch over six foot, weighed sixteen stone, and carried an implement shaped like a bat but clearly – in the hands of a Botham – about as subtle a weapon as a Stone Age club. To emphasize further his non-contemporary character, Botham did not wear a helmet.

Boycott departed at 133, Taylor 2 runs later, England 135 for 7, the 92 runs still required to make Australia bat again were out of the question. Or so the jubilation of the fielders suggested. Dilley, Old and Willis had their pads on. Three straight balls? How the Australians rejoiced!

Their three bowlers were, of course, tiring a little. In a day and a half, Lillee, Alderman and Lawson had sent down 99 overs; a fourth bowler, Bright, had not been used – being a slow left-arm over the wicket bowler, he probably did not expect to be used in the circumstances. True Dilley batted left-handed – and Bright's normal delivery would have pitched in the rough outside his off-stump. But one of the three faster men would soon account for Dilley. Meanwhile Botham was getting a sight of the ball. As he hit the 57th ball of his innings to the boundary, the crowd applauded his half-century – eight 4s, two 3s, three 2s, and seven singles. Botham's rate of progress was not rapid – a mere 28 runs an hour. The Australians were bowling only 14 overs to the hour, containing Botham while they snipped off England's tail.

However, Dilley was thumping anything pitched up past cover. He looked most unsnip-off-able.

Botham's method was simple. He became more selective yet more violent. From the next thirty balls bowled him, he did not score off sixteen. Those he felt safe to plunder realized one 6, eleven 4s, and two singles. Botham's hundred came in just over two and a half hours — in far distant days a commendable though hardly remarkable time. But 103 from 87 balls and 31 scoring strokes: incredible at any time. Had Australia bowled their overs in 1921 fashion, Botham's century would have been made at about a run a minute. At the close on the fourth day England were 351 for 9 — Dilley 56, Old 29, and the Man Without A Helmet 145 not out.

Australia had not won with an innings to spare, but a target of 130 suggested a need for concentration rather than a reason for consternation. Willis and Old had opened the bowling when they began batting five days ago, now Brearley tried his two heroes, Botham and Dilley. Dilley wasn't very straight and Botham, in spite of an early wicket, appeared relatively amiable. So Brearley hastily erased Dilley and substituted Willis. Willis labouring is a bowler conscious of his knees — or lack of knees; the Willis knees have undergone such surgery that the wonder is he can stagger, not alone run, to the crease. But Willis rampant . . . When Willis is rampant, the batsman sees a 6 foot 5 inch giant with hair uncut since Bob Dylan was mobbed at Heathrow — a species of stump-ding ostrich in huffy mood. Half an hour before lunch, with Australia 48 for 1, Brearley brought on Willis at the Kirkstall Lane End, the breeze behind him.

At once Willis began to make the ball lift. At 56 Trevor Chappell got a brute, the wicketkeeper Taylor running forward to take the catch. Then, with only a few minutes to go before the interval, the bottom fell out of Australia's world: Hughes touched Willis to second slip where Botham dived and came up beaming. Yallop fended off a shortish delivery only to see Gatting hurl himself forward at short-leg. If, with Australia 56 for 1, Brearley thought England would win, he was an optimist; at 58 for 4 it was time to discard pessimistic ideas. After lunch Old bowled Border, Dyson was caught by the wicketkeeper hooking at Willis, Marsh hooked and connected with Dilley waiting at long-leg, Lawson snicked and was swallowed up. Australia 75 for 8, Bright and Lillee added 35 in 4 overs before Willis had Lillee caught, then removed Bright's middle stump. In 61 balls Willis had taken 8 wickets, his innings analysis 15.1-3-43-8. England had beaten Australia by 18 runs after being made to follow on. It had happened before, at Sydney in 1894. No one could remember that.

Botham saved England from an inevitable and humiliating defeat. In the context of 1981 he had only just begun. The fourth Test at Edgbaston — when Australia in perfect conditions required 151 to win, reached 105 for 4, 114 for 5, then collapsed to 121 — that was Botham. In twenty-six balls he took the last five wickets for 1 run. However by then Australia deserved to lose, a side which totters to 114 from 352 balls should not be surprised if some Botham says, 'Enough of this nonsense!' and sweeps it into the dustbin. After Edgbaston England were two-one up in the series with two matches left. Without Botham they would probably have been three-nil down — and the Ashes in Australian hands. One man had saved England.

In the second innings of the Fifth Test at Old Trafford Botham scored 100 in 86 balls, and in all 118 out of 149 in only 102 balls which included 6 sixes and thirteen 4's.

After 7 Alderman–Lillee overs with the new ball had brought Botham 66 runs, the Australian captain opted for a bowling change. Bright applied cunning. Botham swept him for 6 to reach a century. Bright applied more cunning. Botham hit him over the sight screen. On 118 Botham was caught at the wicket off Whitney, his last 90 runs made from 49 balls in 57 minutes. For the first time in England–Australia Tests a man had struck six 6s in an innings. Knott and Emburey cashed in on Botham's act of mayhem with half-centuries, and Australia were set 506 to win. Yallop batted brilliantly for 114. Border 5 minutes under 7 hours for 123 not out. A score of 402 spelled defeat for Australia but recaptured pride. The final drawn Test at the Oval was a match for individuals: Border with 106 not out and 84, Wellham with a second innings of 103 in his first Test against England, Boycott with 137, Botham's 10 wickets in the match and Lillee's 11. The Master Demon was quite at his supreme best.

'We are both good for each other,' said Brearley of Botham. 'He needs a father figure as I need a younger brother to help me out.'

From *The Ashes: A Centenary* by Ray Illingworth and Kenneth Gregory (Collins, London, 1982).

Beefy Has a Beef

There is very little common ground between me and the average player. Frankly I think most famous cricketers are too big to play county cricket.

Ian Botham to his former captain at Somerset, Peter Roebuck.

I'm told that Peter Roebuck is flying out to have a man-to-man talk with me. I suggest he stays in London. He'll be a whole lot safer there.

Ian Botham in Australia after hearing confirmation that Somerset were sacking Richards and Garner.

6

GAMBLING AT THE CREASE
Side bet

Godfrey Evans

Taken overall, Godfrey Evans was our finest post-war wicket-keeper, though on a bad turning wicket I reckon Don Brennan of Yorkshire was his equal. Don never got the recognition he deserved, and most emphatically nor did Jim Binks. It was a constant source of mystery to the Australians why Jim never played for England – except for the once in India when he was sent out as a replacement and seemed to cross officialdom. He was never chosen again. Godfrey could play a few pranks on tour – and place a few bets. Here's how he did Compton out of £200.

F.S.T.

In 1953, playing against our old adversaries Australia, we won the Ashes for the first time since the infamous Bodyline tour of 1932–3. Our captain, Len Hutton, led us to victory in the fifth Test at the Oval.

I remember it well: Denis Compton sweeping the ball to the leg boundary off the bowling of Arthur Morris, to score the winning runs. A keen cricket enthusiast rushed up to Denis and gave him £100. 'I'll double it if you do the same in Australia,' the man said.

In the winter of 1954–5 we went to Australia to defend the Ashes. We lost the first Test at Brisbane, won the second at Sydney, and the third at Melbourne. A victory at Adelaide would give us the series and ensure that we kept the Ashes. England were in the box seat and wanted just 94 in the last innings to win. Keith Miller had us struggling, capturing the first three wickets for 18 runs. Trevor Bailey and Denis Compton were taking the score nearer and nearer the winning total, then Trevor was out with six runs to go.

I was next in. My first ball we scampered a leg bye. This gave me the bowling, with Keith Miller still trying like mad. We took two to third man; the next was an horrific bouncer I just managed to avoid. The third ball, well up on the leg stump, I whacked for four. We had won the series and retained the Ashes, to cheers from the dressing-room.

As we came off the field, Denis said: 'You bloody fool, Godders! What did you want to do that for?'

'To win the series!' I said excitedly.

'If you had let me hit that winning run, I would have won £200,' said Denis.

'Why didn't you tell me, we could have shared it.'

'I didn't want to put you off,' came his reply, smiling all over his face.

Denis was really thinking of the party he could have had with £200. As it was, he said, 'Well done, Godders'. We had a hell of a party anyway.

From *Tales From Around The Wicket* by the Lord's Taverners
(A Graham Tarrant Book, David & Charles, Newton Abbot 1989).

BACKING ENGLAND TO WIN AT 500–1

Dennis Lillee

I still can't believe we lost that Leeds Test in 1981. When England were 7 for 135 in their Second innings on the fourth day, still needing 93 to make us bat again, we all thought we were home and hosed. But Botham was at his irrepressible best.

There was quite some controversy surrounding this game as far as Rod Marsh and I were concerned. It hinged on the fact that we had a bet on the outcome. Not that having a bet on a cricket match is anything out of the ordinary. The trouble was, Rod and I backed England to win. That sounds unbelievable, but so were the odds that flashed on the new scoreboard at Headingley on the fourth day. England were set at 500 to 1! We were in the dressing-room during lunch at the time and I said to the guys. 'Have a look at that. Five hundred to one! In a two-horse race there's just no way those odds can be right. I'm going to put fifty quid on that, because I can't believe anybody would offer odds of that nature. I'm prepared to risk fifty on the off-chance that I might get twenty-five thousand.'

The others said not to be stupid, there just wasn't a bet at that stage because England were so far gone. I said, 'You're right, there's no bet, but it's a chance of a lifetime with such stupid odds.' At no stage did any of us think there was anything wrong with taking the odds and betting against Australia, just that it would be stupid to throw the money away. The boys talked me out of wasting fifty pounds, but I decided I'd still throw ten pounds at the bookies.

I asked our bus driver, Peter, to go and put the ten on for me. As we were walking down the stairs to go out on the field Marshy saw Peter going round to the betting tent and yelled out 'Pete!' When Peter turned round Marshy showed him five fingers, indicating a five-pound bet. When we got out to the middle we forgot all about the bet and got on with the game. Peter later told us when he got half-way round to the tent he'd decided it was ridiculous to waste the money. He had stopped and turned back to the dressing-room, saying to himself that he'd give us our money back at afternoon tea time. But he had stopped again, thinking, 'I've heard of these things happening and I'd better not take the risk.' So he put the money on for the two of us.

That meant that when Australia were losers in the Test, Marshy and I were winners. Even though we weren't all that happy about being winners in those circumstances, we reasoned that there have been many instances when teams have bet against themselves or against a number of runs being scored or the like. Nobody could claim that because of the bet either Rod or I weren't trying as hard as we possibly could. At that time we realized we'd won the money we felt a bit bad about it, but what could you do ... the odds were ridiculous and it was just one of those stupid bets. But after we'd collected our 'ill-gotten gains' Marshy and I did spend a little of it buying the lads a few drinks.

From *Lillee: My Life in Cricket* by Dennis Lillee
(Methuen, London, 1982).

Australia introduce Dennis Lillee, a sort of Fred Trueman with a built-in kangaroo hop.

7

SOME GIANTS OF THE ENGLISH POST-WAR ERA

Alec Bedser

Neville Cardus

Alec Bedser was the greatest medium-fast bowler I have ever seen, with a complete command of length, line and swing and a magnificent leg-cutter. It was a great pleasure and privilege to me to be playing at the opposite end to him in my first Test at Headingley against the Indians in 1952. His haul of Test wickets was 236 (100 of them Australian) and he would probably have been the first to take 300 Test wickets if it hadn't been for six lost seasons in the war. He commanded the respect of all the great players, notably Hutton and Bradman.

F.S.T.

Alec Bedser is a big man, squarely shouldered, with the gentlest face, frank and kind eyes, and the smile of a friend – that is when he is talking to you off the field of play. I have seen him waiting in the 'middle' for a new batsman to come in, and then his brow has seemed shadowed with thunder, and his mouth grimly closed.

When a game is about to begin, he measures his run as deliberately as once upon a time boys measured paces in the street when playing a game called 'Piggy'. He strides the last two lengths, then rolls up the sleeve of the right arm, and with the other signals his wishes to his captain as the field is placed.

He moves into action as though going slightly uphill; it is not a flowing rhythmical action like Lindwall's. Bedser runs to bowl in small galloping strides until the ball is released by energy at the shoulders, which swing round from a classical left side pointing to the batsman's position. The right hand follows through full, or nearly full, circle. The hint of stiffness before the ball goes its stinging, swinging way is the proof of compressed, concentrated power.

He is a natural bowler. He learned his cricket less from instruction than from the example of others while playing entirely for fun. As a boy his first love was 'soccer', as it was mine. He then played at Woking, and after they had looked at him (and at his brother) at Kennington Oval, he was encouraged by advice and pats on the shoulder from Alan Peach the Surrey all-rounder, who not many years ago would arrive at the wicket at five o'clock on a warm afternoon and thump runs all over the field, pavilion or Vauxhall end, gasholder, Tenison's Grammar School, or Westminster and the Houses of Parliament. For years Bedser remained a bowler by instinct and steady application of muscle. But nothing distinguished can be done in this world without some amount of hard thinking thrown in.

Bedser was a splendid bowler when first he visited Australia with Hammond's team in 1946–7; but though he put all his skill and determination into his every arduous over during that tour, he was coping with Bradman, with Barnes, with Morris at his best, with Hassett also at his best. Since those gruelling days he has often found success coming to him after efforts less strenuous or challenging than those given so wholeheartedly to the ill-starred cause of Hammond. A cricketer's career, like that of any public performer, may easily change direction by hazard; a single wind turns fortune's weather-cock.

He bowled Bradman for 0 at Adelaide in 1947. And here, in England in 1948, he harried the great man sorely, getting him out in four consecutive Test innings, an achievement of itself enough to guarantee any bowler's posterity.

Bedser came into his own once and for all during the Australian rubber of 1950–51, under the captaincy of F. R. Brown. In the summer of 1950, against the West Indies in England, he was not outstandingly a great bowler. Critics in fact, were saying: 'Look at his arm. Getting low.' In Australia in 1950–51 he began indifferently. Illness handicapped him. On the eve of the first Test match at Brisbane, his bowling was hit about right and left by Miller and Morris in the match M.C.C. against New South Wales at Sydney. If Bedser had failed in this first Test match of F. R. Brown's campaign is it certain we should today agree that he is the greatest 'new ball' bowler since Maurice Tate – and perhaps the equal of Maurice Tate?

In praising this famous bowler we do not often enough remember (though Alan Ross has reminded us) that Bedser for long had to work for England on a lonely trail. He had no Statham, no Trueman, no Lock or Laker, to help him at the other end. And it was in a vulnerable England XI, a losing England XI, that he staked his claim to greatness, and to the attention of the game's historians for ever. I imagine that his 'finest hour' came to him at Nottingham in June 1953. Australia won the toss, and in showery weather which made the ball hard to grip even in a hand as capacious as Bedser's, Australia were sitting pretty with 243 for 4 at lunch on the second day. Bedser then crashed through the Australian innings like a 'bulldozer'. Hutton cleverly nursed Bedser so that with a new ball, he took, in three spells, one for 7, two for 5 and four – all bowled – for 2. Australia were all out for 249. Bedser in this rubber took 39 wickets at 17.48 runs each, which was the largest 'bag' in international games until Laker helped himself to 46 v Australia in 1956.

Bedser resents constant allusions to himself as essentially an inswinger. He exploits the inswinger cleverly enough, goodness and Sir Donald Bradman knows.

But a few years ago he began some private experiments with the ball's seam held horizontally; after much diligent practice he was able to pitch between leg and middle and cause the ball to turn to the off and remain dangerously near the stumps. The effect was that of a genuinely spun leg-break; it was not a case of cutting under the ball. Bedser at his best brought this superb ball – the best of any bowler's tricks – under almost sure command. At Melbourne in 1950 I saw him pitch it between Harvey's off and middle and just miss the leg – Harvey, of course, is a left-hander.

With this ball, known of old as the 'Barnes ball', Bedser has taken his place among the truly great of his craft. No bowler can live on inswingers alone. Every batsman will agree that the really dangerous spin is that which 'leaves the bat'.

Bedser believes in the direct attack on the wickets; he does not use his slips and short-legs as so many hopeful accessories; he likes to see catches sent to them from strokes played mainly in defence of the stumps. Naturally, being human, he likes to take a wicket as soon as a match begins. And being frank and open of disposition he shares the Englishman's love of a 'grouse' and also his love of a hint of encouragement.

From *Close of Play* by Neville Cardus
(Sportsman's Book Club, London, 1957).

Denis Compton

Trevor Bailey

In 1947 Middlesex were probably the strongest batting side ever seen in county cricket and the supreme players of that golden summer were, of course, the Middlesex Twins – Denis Compton with 3,816 runs and an average of 90.85, Bill Edrich with 3,539 runs, average 80.43. Compton, as I learnt more than once, had shots no one else had ever thought of, including the famous sweep which he seemed to paddle past leg slip almost straight behind the stumps, though he could place it almost anywhere. I remember once, when he had been retired for four or five years, we turned out together for the international cavaliers at Sabina Park, Jamaica. Wes Hall and Garry Sobers were both bowling at him and agreed: 'We'll let the old boy have a few to start with.' By the time he reached 20 they were doing their best to get him out – but he went on to make over 100. In these pieces Trevor Bailey assesses his brilliance and the great man himself describes his farewell.

F.S.T.

Of all the great English batsmen I have bowled against Denis Compton was the most unorthodox and the most brilliant. When he was in his prime, and in the mood, he was not only very difficult to dismiss, but his wide and often unconventional range of strokes, combined with his ability to extemporize, made him hard to contain. An outstanding example of his capacity to *ad lib* when at the crease occurred when he was playing for Middlesex against the Rest. Denis, as was so often his wont, had advanced down the wicket to that fine off spinner, Tom Goddard. He slipped and fell. Quite unperturbed by this mishap, he was not merely content to make contact, but proceeded to hit the ball to the boundary from his prone position much to the indignation of the understandably incensed bowler.

Against the faster bowling the initial movement of Denis was the same as that of the majority of overseas players, back and across. No doubt that this was to some extent due to the fact that he was brought up on the fast, true pitches which prevailed at Lord's before the War. He also had the good fortune that in his formulating years the net wickets at Headquarters were outstandingly good, and almost lived up to the ideal of being better than the middle. When he became established, nets had little appeal for him, except as looseners, after all he did spend a not inconsiderable portion of his life at the crease, but they helped originally.

His initial movement back and across, combined with his wonderful eye, quick reactions, backlift towards third man, and physical courage meant that he was an exceptionally good hooker and a fine player of really fast bowling. It is interesting to note that today even when there is not all that amount of genuine pace about most batsmen wear one and often two thigh pads, but Denis never bothered with one even when facing Lindwall and Miller at their peak.

Like all great players Denis used his feet and he was never happier than when gaily trotting down the track to some unfortunate spinner. Conversely when he played back he gave himself the maximum time by going right back to the stumps, and indeed this did on occasions lead to him treading on his own wicket.

Denis used rather more right hand in his batting than a classical stylist, but this did not prevent him from being able to cover drive with ferocity as I know to my cost. Young and naïve, I allowed myself to be stationed at silly mid-off with Denis batting and the eight stitches I had to have inserted in the webbing between my fingers are a permanent reminder of the power of his drive.

Although he had all the shots, both defensive and offensive, the stroke that will for ever be associated with his name is the sweep. This can be a dangerous shot if a fieldsman is stationed at deepish backward short leg for the top edge and the South Africans did, rather optimistically, plan to trap him in this way. However, Denis overcame the problem as a result of his own interpretation of the sweep. He played the shot later and hit the ball down with the blade of his bat slanting and not parallel to the ground. In addition he had an almost uncanny ability to place this very difficult stroke. On one occasion at Lord's I watched him sweep three successive boundaries off Peter Smith. I was stationed at deep square leg and the first one went to fine. I was moved there, only for the next to go to the exact spot I had vacated. This was the signal for another fieldsman to join me, but it made no difference as he smote the final delivery to very fine leg.

Denis had a long career which would have been even longer, but for the famous 'knee' which was to restrict his mobility in his later years. Despite a handicap that would have caused a less determined individual to retire, he did still make runs, because he could afford to forget about quick singles and rely on boundaries, but it could make batting with him for ordinary, limited players like myself rather difficult. However, there is no doubt that the golden year for the golden boy was 1947 when he scored more runs and made more centuries than anyone in the history of the game, records likely to stand for eternity. At the close of that summer when it was 'roses, roses all the way' I found myself batting with Denis against the South Africans in the Hastings Festival. Thousands turned up mainly in the hope of seeing him break the record. My one fear was that I should run him out which seemed to be the only thing likely to prevent him achieving this feat. I was also aware that an event of this nature was by no means improbable as the 'golden boy's' calling was unpredictable in the extreme, and it had been remarked, with every justification, that his first call merely meant that he was prepared to open negotiations. Fortunately we managed to avoid this calamity largely through some unexpected co-operation from the South African fieldsmen. It was a less satisfactory story some years later in a Test match at Old Trafford, when Denis had me half-way down the wicket after his first affirmative, halted me there with a frantic 'wait', and had me slightly puzzled as he passed me at full speed saying 'no'. On my way back to the pavilion I realized that I had merely become yet another victim of the Compton three-call trick!

Denis was infinitely more than just a great batsman. He was an entertainer and one of the biggest box office draws ever to have played the game. Some of the more dour of the Northerners may have regarded with suspicion the light-hearted way he tackled the serious business of amassing runs, but in general he was a source of delight to crowds all over the world. The feature of his play I most admired was its essential gaiety. He not only made batting look easy, he also made it look fun. It contained a mixture of genius, mirth, and more than a suggestion of schoolboy impishness.

Like all entertainers he thrived on situation and a large audience. These brought the very best out of him, so that he tended to sparkle more brightly in a tense Test match at Melbourne than in a comparatively unimportant, badly attended county match in the Midlands.

Although it is sometimes forgotten, Denis was a useful 'chinaman' and googly bowler. He spun the ball considerably, but lacked the discipline and singleness of purpose necessary to reach the heights of this department. He might produce the unplayable delivery, but his length and direction tended to be wayward. Until increasing age and the handicap of the 'knee' took their inevitable toll, Denis was also a brilliant and decidedly unpredictable fieldsman. Away from the bat and when the game was proving somewhat dull he had a tendency to wander both mentally and physically which somewhat increased the problems of captaincy. Close to the wicket he liked to stand nearer to the batsman than most fieldsmen.

Quite apart from his ability as a cricketer Denis would always be one of my first selections for an overseas tour, because so much of the charm of his batting is reflected in an essentially sunny disposition. In consequence he is a pleasant and easy companion. It is easy to disagree with him on occasions, but I find it difficult to believe that anyone, who knows him well, could dislike him as an individual. Few people have possessed so much charm, a charm moreover that appealed to young and old, male and female, friend and foe.

Of course Denis has never been famed for his punctuality, reliability, and sense of responsibility and these have from time to time led to minor disagreements with the authorities, but as one perplexed official once remarked to me, 'You can't be cross with Denis for long.'

From *Playfair Cricket Monthly* 1967

End of An Innings – Denis Compton

On that last journey out to the wicket, and as I faced the Worcestershire bowlers, I thought more than once about Patsy Hendren. He had loved his career in cricket and so had I. I had played in the same side with him in his last season for Middlesex; I, very young and relatively inexperienced, going in No. 5 or No. 6, and Patsy, senior and genial and distinguished, going in at No. 4. I could remember how he used to walk down the wicket to me when we were out in the middle together, and give me

Denis Compton makes the winning hit to regain the Ashes for England in 1953. (*Syndication International*).

Denis Compton was one of the first cricketers to make a handsome sum from advertising. (*Syndication International*).

Left: Colin Cowdrey, classic stroke-maker with a sound defence – in the B & H final, Kent v. Worcestershire at Lords in 1973. (*Patrick Eagar*). *Below*: Peter May, greatest amateur bat of the post-war era, faces Australia in the friendly against the Duke of Norfolk's side at Arundel in 1968. (*Patrick Eagar*).

Above: Wes Hall still capable of
ferocious pace in 1966. (*Patrick Eagar*).
Right: Jim Laker has Maddocks l.b.w.
on his way to taking 19 wickets against
Australia in the 1956 Test at Old
Trafford. (*Sport and General*).

Above: Clyde Walcott hits out on the West Indies 1957 tour of England. (*Sport and General*). *Below*: The late Sir Frank Worrell off-driving in the dramatic Lord's Test against the West Indies in 1963, when any one of four results was possible till the last ball. (*Sport and General*).

Left: Everton Weekes, one of the three W's, who with Walcott and Worrell dominated the West Indies batting for many years. (*Sport and General*). *Below*: 'Thou shalt not pass'. Allan Border, as resolute in defence as he was prolific in attack, carried Australia's batting for years. (*Patrick Eagar*).

The great W. G. Grace, the most commanding figure in Victorian cricket, strides out to bat. Supposedly an amateur, his earnings from the game dwarfed all others till modern times. (*Sport and General*).

No finer sight in cricket than David Gower in flow, here making 215 against Australia at Edgbaston in 1985! His victory as captain in that series was almost as one-sided as England's defeat under his command in 1989. (*Patrick Eagar*).

information – he never gave me advice on how to play the ball, wisely of course – but just gave me useful information: this bowler was bowling or might bowl out-swingers, and that one could spin it quite a lot from the leg, if he wanted to, so I had better look out, and so on. He was a great help, and it was a great experience to be at the wicket with him. Then he retired and I had taken his place in the Middlesex team at No. 4. In his last game Patsy got a century in his first innings.

I too had made a century in the first innings of my last game.

Now I was in my second innings, and Bill Edrich and I were at the wicket together. Horton was bowling to me, and I had nearly reached my half-century. Then Horton sent down one which I thought should be hit, and I opened my shoulders and hit the ball, and watched it climb towards the boundary. It looked like being a six. Then I saw Outschoorn going back for it. The ball began to drop from the top of its arc, and it seemed to be coming down unbearably slowly ... and just across the boundary ... but no, Outschoorn was there, leaning across the boundary, and first juggling, then taking and holding the catch. I was out, for the last time. It was as nice a way as any to be dismissed.

I started the walk back from the wicket, over the familiar turf, in the friendly surroundings: I had scored 48 runs and I was caught Outschoorn bowled Horton. Out of the corner of my eye I noticed that someone near the Tavern was holding up a glass of beer towards me as I walked in.

The Worcestershire players were all looking at me and clapping, and so was Bill. Applause from the crowd was ringing the ground with noise; many people were standing, some, I think, were cheering, and there was what I thought was a sympathetic buzz of talk and comment. As I approached the pavilion, I could see that the members too were standing and clapping and smiling. Once or twice I raised my bat in acknowledgment, though I wanted to keep my head well down.

Then I opened the white gate, ascended the steps between the standing members as some of them patted me on the shoulders, and went back into the pavilion.

From *End of an Innings* by Denis Compton
(Oldbourne, London, 1958).

P. B. H. May

A. A. Thomson

Peter May retired young because of business pressures and illness, otherwise he would certainly have made 100 centuries. To my mind he was the best batsman we have produced since the war and the best amateur captain. He hit the ball very hard, especially against the West Indies quick bowlers, one of whom I remember was cracked for six clean over his head to hoist May's century in Jamaica. He had played with a winning side at Surrey in the fifties and had been brought up under an astute skipper with Stuart Surridge. So he liked to win and he was used to winning.

It was one of the great reversals of fortune after his triumph against the Australians in 1956, when our immensely strong side of 1958–9 was badly beaten in Australia. but I would not blame May. We never played to our potential and suffered appallingly from the umpiring and the throwing, which had not then been purged from the game, of the Australians Meckiff and Rorke.

F.S.T.

Peter May took over the England captaincy in 1955. He brought to the post certain fundamental advantages: for one thing, now that Hutton had retired, he was incomparably England's best batsman and, even then, very nearly the greatest batsman in the world. He was modest and courteous in demeanour and, though somewhat retiring, he was not difficult to like. Perhaps his greatest advantage of all was that he had received, so to speak, his basic training in stern schools: in county cricket under the ebullient Surridge, who was at the time in full spate, hurrying Surrey to the top of the championship and keeping them there; and his Test experience had taken place under Hutton, and this in itself was a rich education for a young man. Even though May retired through ill-health and for business reasons at an early age, he captained England forty-one times, which is more than anyone else had ever done....

His first rubber as captain was played against the South African tourists in 1955, and was won by three games to two in a succession of hard struggles in which no quarter was given or taken. May himself batted superbly – in his prime there was nobody like him – and he still had the benefit of Compton's and Graveney's experience, but conquest was really clinched by the bowlers, by Statham and Tyson in the first two Tests and by Laker in the last.

The seasons of 1956 and 1957 were May's high summers of success, with England established on the heights, and May unchallenged leader of England. In neither year was the fight won without a struggle. The Australian team of 1956 was in no sense a feeble one and after a drawn first Test at Trent Bridge and a second, at Lord's, which was deservedly won by the Australians, the battle for the third was the vital point of the struggle. The Test itself was memorable in many ways, but especially for the return of Washbrook, who had not played for England since the 1950–51 tour of Australia, in which he had been only moderately successful. With three England wickets down for 17, May saw Washbrook striding purposefully to the crease. 'I have never felt so glad in my life', he said afterwards, 'as when I saw who was coming.' Their stand was historic and before they were separated they had put on 187. England's batting position was assured and the bowlers Lock and Laker did the rest.

The position of the teams was now all square with two to play. In the fourth Test, at Old Trafford, the most fantastic of all Test bowling performances took place, breaking records right, left and centre. England's leading batsmen did all that was wanted of them and Evans hit out with his usual exuberance. But the true triumph belonged to Laker, and his incredible toll of nine for 37 and ten for 53. There has never been anything like it and never will be. England once more had easily the best of a draw at the Oval and if heavy rain had not intervened, the Australians, who had already lost five wickets for 27 in attempting to get 228, would have hardly succeeded in saving the game. . . .

The magic of victory remained for one more season and England's win over a strong and widely talented West Indies side was directly due to the gifts and influence of May. The complete reversal of the result in the first Test at Edgbaston was symbolic of England's power of recovery and May was its most efficient instrument. Winning the toss on an amiable wicket, England fell flat for the miserable total of 186 before the cunning spin of Ramadhin, who took seven for 49. By tea-time on the third day West Indies piled up a huge score, mainly through the punitive efforts of Walcott, Worrell and the lamented O. G. (Collie) Smith, and England, 268 to the bad, lost two wickets before the end of the day. One of the most welcome sights in all the cricket of the period was that of watching May come in at this point of peril and without ceremony attack Ramadhin with two searing cover-drives.

England, still in jeopardy, resumed on the Monday morning and Close, who had helped May to put on 48 useful runs, was out at 113. Before the West Indies captured the next wicket over 400 runs had been added. At first with resolution and then with zest, May and Cowdrey, the most gifted young English batsmen of their generation, proceeded to subdue and then to destroy the West Indies attack. They remained together the whole of Monday and when Cowdrey was caught in the deep he had made 154 and the stand lasted eight hours and twenty minutes. May went on to score 59 with Evans in another half-hour and, when he declared, England were 583 for four. His own magnificent total was 285 not out, worthy to be reckoned for a place among the finest of all Test innings. . . . At this point West Indies might have slipped quietly away to a draw, but so strong now was England's grip on the game that they were able to give the batsmen the fright of their lives, first through some thunder and lightning from Trueman and then some spin-bowling of diabolical cunning by Lock and Laker. Five wickets went crashing down for 43 and when time came West Indies had lost seven wickets for 72, while the fieldsmen were crowding menacingly round the bats of the two defenders who survived.

England won the next game at Lord's, which contained another handsome 159 by Cowdrey, who was now in magnificent form, not to mention some astonishing bowling by Bailey....

The fourth and fifth Tests England won by an innings, with Loader as the destroyer at Headingley and Lock (eleven for 58) making hay at the Oval. Success in this splendid series marked the highest point of May's Test career.

England's decline and fall did not, of course, come immediately. The visitors of 1958 came from New Zealand and suffered both from the English weather and from injuries to some of their most talented players....

The tour to Australia of 1958–9 was anticipated with confidence and its unsuccessful result was the cause of massive disappointment. The chosen team included many players who had formed the backbone of England's previously victorious side, but several of them, unfortunately, showed themselves to be either out of form or past their best....

It was one of those rubbers which the victors thoroughly deserved to win, but the losers hardly deserved to lose by quite so much.

After the storm and stresses of the Australian tour the season of 1959 at home was a placid affair, with no echo of the alarums and excursions of the previous winter. Earlier in the year May married and did not turn out for his county till the end of the season's first month. He played for Surrey, in fact, in only seven matches. England won all five Tests with ease against the sadly weak opposition of an Indian touring side. May appeared in only three of them.... The fourth Test, at Old Trafford, provided an easy victory but sounded a warning note. May had to call off owing to illness and Cowdrey assumed the captaincy of the England side for the first time. May watched the first two days of the match. On the third day he underwent an internal operation.

With the start of the 1959–60 tour of the West Indies we are back in sombre vein. May, believing himself to have recovered more completely from the operation than was in fact so, went out to the Caribbean as captain, leading a team which included a number of players bent on winning their spurs.... What clouded the series from its earliest days was the serious recurrence of May's illness. He believed himself fit to play in the earlier matches and this courageous if misguided resolve was not shaken even when the operation wound opened up before the second Test. He played in horrid discomfort, known to no one but himself.

In the third Test he made his highest Test score, a meagre 45, even though it was the next best to Cowdrey's 114 and 97. After this the facts of his illness became known and he was flown home for treatment....

The season of 1961 saw another Australian visit, led by Richie Benaud, who had captained his side with such consummate skill against May's men in 1958–9.... May came back into the team at last for the second Test at Lords....

A win in the fifth Test would at least have halved the rubber, even if it had left the resting place of the Ashes unaffected, but England seemed incapable of reasserting any kind of grip. In cricketing terms the real delight of the second innings was May's

33, which included seven fours; all of them superbly driven, as though in scorn of the whole proceedings. As matters turned out, this was his last Test innings.

He enjoyed a period of complete domination from the time he took over the captaincy until the unhappy tour in Australia of 1958–9 and the serious illness that brought him home from the West Indies in 1959–60 and kept him out of cricket for the whole of the following summer. While he remained fit and willing to play, nobody could seriously challenge his status as the best-equipped batsman in the world. He has undoubtedly been the most accomplished stroke-maker between Compton and Dexter. He was likable and well liked. His Test career was full of innings of which you could say: 'No captain ever served his side better....'

From *The Great Captains* by A. A. Thomson
(Stanley Paul, London, 1965).

Bowled H.R.H.

Tom Graveney

We used to call him Elegant – a magnificent player on all wickets. They say he had a weakness with leg spin but I never noticed it. He was unusually strong on the front foot – and you never caught him LBW like so many of our England players in 1989, because of failure to get well forward with the left pad. How he was overlooked for England as often as he was by the selectors was a mystery to me and to most players in the first-class game, including the Australians. His character had all the charm of his batting as this little anecdote about himself shows.

F.S.T.

I was taking part in a match for the Playing Fields at Arundel in the mid-sixties: the Duke of Edinburgh's XI v the Duke of Norfolk's XI.

Having got a dozen or so runs, I was suddenly faced with Prince Philip bowling his off-spinners round the wicket; he wasn't a bad bowler, incidentally. He bowled one down the leg side and I swept at it, getting a top edge. The fielder at mid-wicket ran round and caught it. I was out – caught Wing Commander Chinnery, bowled His Royal Highness, the Duke of Edinburgh. You can't get out better than that!

I don't know whether it had any bearing on future events, but I was awarded the OBE in the next Honours List!

From *Tales From Around The Wicket* by the Lords' Taverners
(A Graham Tarrant Book, David and Charles, Newton Abbot, 1989).

Colin Cowdrey

Brian Johnston

Colin Cowdrey should have made 150 first-class centuries rather than the 107 he did make. He played a great innings when he felt like it but he was never quite the killer that less-talented players made themselves into. Peter May could hit the ball with great ferocity whereas the Kipper, as we always called him (because he could cat-nap at the drop of a hat or a wicket), scarcely seemed to strike the ball. Yet, if you were fielding at cover or mid-off, it went past you just as fast as May's drive did. His technique and defence were perfect and though he was an old man in 1974–5, when he was called up as a replacement to face Thomson and Lillee, he looked better than all the other England players, with the possible exception of Freddie Titmus who, hailing from the previous decade, had a sideways-on stance which gave the Aussie thunderers less to aim at.

F.S.T.

On 30 July 1946, I went to Lord's to sit in the sun and watch some schoolboy cricket. The previous day in the Clifton *v.* Tonbridge match a thirteen-year-old playing for Tonbridge had made 75 out of 156 and then had taken 3 wickets with teasing leg-breaks. Michael Cowdrey, the papers called him and he was said to be the youngest player ever to play at Lord's. I thought I would have a look at this infant prodigy. I was rewarded by seeing him make 44 in his second innings and then win the match for Tonbridge by taking 5 for 59 with his highly tossed leg-breaks; three times he enticed the batsmen down the pitch and was rewarded by three stumpings. He was small but already had a slightly rotund figure. I enquired about him and was told that his father – a great cricket enthusiast – lived and worked in India and had deliberately given his son the initials MCC. It didn't need an expert to predict a promising future for the young boy, and for once the promise was fulfilled – though not so far as the leg-spin went. Like so many small boys who bowl leg-breaks, as he grew taller they seemed to lose their teasing flight, but his batting got better and better. Three years playing for Oxford University were followed by his selection for Len Hutton's MCC tour of Australia in 1954 at the age of twenty-one. Sadly, his father died before Colin played his first Test, but he did know that Colin had been chosen for the tour and that the MCC gimmick had borne fruit.

From then on Colin was an essential and seemingly inevitable member of the

England team: 114 Tests with 7,624 runs, 22 hundreds and 120 catches, captain 27 times, 6 tours of Australia, vice-captain 4 times. An incredible record, and yet somehow it might have been even better.

As a batsman, though heavily built, he was remarkably light of foot with an exceptional eye – two assets which made him such a fine racquets player. He always played straight and had every stroke in the game – and stroke is the right word. He never seemed to hit the ball, but by superb timing seemed to 'waft' it away to the boundary. The late-cut, the off-, straight- and on-drive, and his own particular sweep were strokes I remember best. His sweep was more of a paddle, with the bat vertical rather than horizontal, and played very fine. His defence was as solid as a rock, and he developed – perhaps over-developed – a skilful use of his pads as a second line of defence. The best example of this was his 154 in a record partnership of 411 with Peter May in the first Test against the West Indies in 1957. It is still the highest fourth-wicket partnership in all Test cricket, and successfully put paid to the mystery spin of Ramadhin. By sound judgment of where his off-stump was, Colin used his pads not just as a second line of defence but also a first line. It proved effective, but wasn't pleasant to watch.

He not only played spin well but was even better against fast bowling. He showed his class by always seeming to have plenty of time to play the ball, and never had to hurry. He often opened for England and played some of his biggest innings when going in first. But he was equally happy and effective batting lower in the order.

I am not the only one to think that, great player as he undoubtedly was, he could perhaps have been the greatest. So what was the flaw which stopped him reaching even greater heights? Strange to say, it was a lack of confidence in his own ability. He would often start off an innings brilliantly and then suddenly for no apparent reason shut up shop and get into all sorts of difficulties. In spite of his tremendous successes he would every now and again begin experimenting with a new grip on his bat or a new stance for his feet. Perhaps too he lacked the final killer instinct. But no matter – he was a great batsman in every sense of the word.

He was in the highest class as a slip fielder, that class including Hammond, Miller, Simpson, Sharpe, G. Chappell and Botham. Of course the quickness of his eye helped, but he believed in practice and you could always see him taking part in the catching sessions round a slip machine. It was the same with his batting. He had a net and a bowling machine in his garden. This not only gave him practice but helped him to coach his sons, two of whom – Christopher and Graham – have followed him into the Kent side, with Chris having also played in six Tests.

This lack of confidence and a killer instinct perhaps prevented Colin from being a great captain, though he was a sound enough tactician and a natural leader of men. On a tour he ran a happy ship and always included the media in this. He was a good communicator and his public relations were superb. Nothing was too much trouble, and he paid innumerable visits to schools and hospitals, as well as striking the right note at all the social functions. If a problem cropped up on or off the field he was strangely indecisive, however. A perfect example of this was the fourth Test in Trinidad in 1968. Sobers had sportingly declared to set England to score 215 in 165 minutes. At tea England had lost Edrich and were behind the clock, but Boycott and

Cowdrey were batting well and, with so many wickets in hand, it seemed definitely worth while for England to take risks and go for victory. Colin had to be persuaded that it was possible, his inclination being to play safe. As it was, he and Boycott attacked the bowling and England won with three minutes to spare. But it has taken quite a lot of persuasion by Ken Barrington, in particular, to persuade Colin that he was capable of playing in the way he finally did.

Out of his six tours he was vice-captain four times – 'always the bridesmaid ...' – but he had his compensation with his successful captaincy of Kent for fourteen years. He was a great cricketer, a very nice person and achieved perhaps his final ambition when he was elected president of MCC in their bicentenary year. Again he was struck down by bad luck. There were a few 'local difficulties' at Lord's, resulting in a special general meeting, but by this time Colin had suffered from heart trouble. After an operation and a slow recuperation, he is now happily fit again.

As usual, he showed great courage throughout his troublesome presidency and it is something which he always showed on the cricket field. I remember him well coming down the steps at Lord's in that marvellous Test against the West Indies in 1963. He had had his left forearm broken by Wes Hall, but with two balls left and six runs needed for victory he came out to join David Allen, his wrist in plaster, and the prospect of facing a ball from Wes Hall. If he had had to do so he had decided to bat as a left-hander, with his right hand holding the bat.

Another occasion was at Kingston, Jamaica, during the famous tear-gas riot. I can see him now walking towards the stand from where the crowd was hurling bottles. With his hands held up he advanced into the shower of bottles to try to pacify the angry crowd. He didn't succeed, but he proved what a worthy captain of England he was.

From *It's Been A Piece of Cake* by Brian Johnston
(Methuen, London, 1989).

Jim Laker *v.* Australia, Old Trafford, 1956

Patrick Murphy

No one had more to do with Surrey's record seven championships in a row in the fifties than Laker and Lock. Jim Laker, Yorkshire born, was the greatest off-spin bowler on a wet or dry wicket that I have ever seen. You could hear his finger click when he delivered the ball. He had a beautiful loop to his bowling and was never afraid to give the ball a lot more air than they do today. I can't see his record nineteen wickets in a Test match at Old Trafford in 1956 ever being beaten. The great question is why his bowling twin, Tony Lock, a left-arm spinner, only took one wicket in that match. The answer is that he bowled too short.

Laker was a magnificent bowler when he wanted to be, but Lockie never gave up and never knew when he was beaten – not even when his action was found to be suspect. He then remodelled it entirely in mid-career, for which he earns my 100 per cent respect. He became an inspired captain for Western Australia before coming home to give valuable service to Leicester.

F.S.T.

Laker's Match. Enough said. Australia lost the Old Trafford Test by an innings and 170 runs to J. C. Laker, Esq. If ever a record could claim to be imperishable, it is Laker's feat of taking 19 for 90 in a first-class match. No one else has taken more than seventeen wickets in a first-class match, and it would take either a highly developed imagination or a fantastic sequence of events to create another nineteen-wicket scenario for one man. Just for a change, the use of hyperbole is justified: it was a fabulous achievement.

One of the more remarkable sub-plots of Old Trafford 1956 is that Laker had already taken all ten wickets that summer against the Australians, this time for Surrey. He had been up all night with two sick children and hoped that Surrey would bat first thing. Yet Laker had to bowl forty-six overs on a very good batting wicket and Stuart Surridge, his captain, cajoled him to take 10 for 88. There was little turn for him at the Oval compared to Old Trafford and most of his wickets were catches at slip or behind the wicket. When sceptics point out that Laker was indebted to the wicket's vagaries at Old Trafford, they might remember a classic piece of spin bowling on a good wicket earlier in the season.

They might also consider the case of Tony Lock. Laker's Surrey team-mate could only take one wicket at Old Trafford, despite his customary commitment. Lock was one of the game's great triers and would be expected to pick up a shoal of wickets in such conditions. Yet he tried too hard and ended up with 1 for 106 in the match. Godfrey Evans, the England wicket-keeper that day, says: 'Locky kept pulling the ball down and I was taking it chest-high. When it turned for him, it just went too far. Jim had the right idea – pitch the ball up and let it turn a little off the pitch.' Peter May, England's captain, feels the crucial difference lay in the fact that Lock's stock delivery was going away from the right-hander and so they could leave a few that were spinning viciously. 'Jim just dripped away at their nerves, realizing that they had got a little obsessional about him and the wickets that year. To be honest, the wicket was not that difficult.' Whatever the reasons, only one England player was less than chuffed in the after-match celebrations, as everyone else toasted Jim Laker.

Before the game, Cyril Washbrook, England selector and alleged expert on Old Trafford, prophesied that it would be the greatest batting wicket of all time. The chairman of selectors, G. O. Allen, disagreed and voted against playing an extra seamer. For the first day and a half, Washbrook looked to have got it right, as England piled up a score that at least put them beyond defeat. The off-spinner Ian Johnson and the leg-spinner Richie Benaud did not look very penetrative, and it seemed to augur a lot of work for Laker and Lock. At tea on the second day, Australia were 62 for 2. Thirty-five minutes later, they were all out for 84. Why? The light was fine and the pitch dry with a small degree of turn. The only ball that did anything untoward was the one that pitched on Neil Harvey's leg-stump and hit the off. Laker took seven wickets in the space of twenty-two deliveries and the batsmen were simply mesmerized by his reputation and control. Peter May was right: they had got themselves into a state about the turning wickets in a damp summer and the likes of Mackay, Miller and Archer looked as if they had never held a bat in their lives.

Laker's 9 for 37 had only been bettered in Test history by George Lohmann's 9 for 28 for England against South Africa in 1895/6, but little did we know that a new record would be established within a few days. Laker finished off the second day with another wicket when Australia followed on, but it was not one to brag about – Neil Harvey hit a full toss straight to mid-wicket to complete a 'pair'. Yet Australia ended the day in a comfortable manner which suggested that they would, as usual, battle to save the game. Now the weather came to their aid. Just forty-five minutes' play on Saturday saw Jim Burke caught in the leg-trap for 33 and, in another fifty minutes on Monday, Ian Craig and Colin McDonald added another 27 runs and Australia ended on 84 for 2. The wicket was very damp indeed and all Laker could seemingly offer was accuracy. England began to resign themselves to a moral victory.

On Tuesday it rained hard until dawn. The captains disagreed about the condition of the pitch and play started ten minutes late. Until lunch the batsmen were not troubled; the pitch was sluggish and it was taking too long to dry out for England's peace of mind. Craig and McDonald looked immovable. Over lunchtime the clouds dispersed and a strong wind joined forces with a bright sun and began to work its influence on the pitch. At 2.25 Craig was beaten through the air and off the pitch and trapped lbw, after four hours and twenty minutes of watchful, mature batting. The roof started to cave in around the Australians as Laker bowled with six fielders around the bat. Archer turned an off-break into the leg-trap with the air of a man giving catching practice, Miller used his pads instead of his bat and was yorked, while Mackay's torment ended when he offered a supine catch to slip. They had gone from 114 for 3 to 130 for 6 with the time now 2.55. At last McDonald found a doughty partner in Richie Benaud. They stayed together for eighty minutes – McDonald picking up runs on the leg-side off a frustrated Lock, and Benaud wasting time by asking for a guard each over and gardening the pitch after every ball. This served only to increase the frustration of the volative Lock, whereas Laker viewed the proceedings with his usual calm, detached manner at the other end. It was a time for cool heads and there was no better man in such a situation than Jim Laker.

The pair were still together at tea, and May had even rested his two spinners in favour of Oakman and Bailey. That had not worked, so the Surrey spinners were reunited with four wickets needed in two hours. The second ball after tea turned sharply and McDonald turned it into the hands of Oakman at short-leg. He had batted magnificently for 337 minutes, and given the bulk of his team-mates an embarrassing lesson in skilled defensive play. At five o'clock, Benaud played back to Laker and the ball hurried through to bowl him. Laker had now equalled the first-class record of seventeen wickets in a match and everyone on England's side (apart from Lock) was willing him to take the last two wickets. At 5.15 Lock secured the record by catching Lindwall. Lock bowled the next over with all his usual demonic fervour, but he could not break through. At 5.20 Laker bowled the second ball of his fifty-second over to Len Maddocks, the Australian wicket-keeper; Maddocks went back instead of forward, the ball hit his pads and he was out lbw. Maddocks went forward to shake Laker's hand, and a few England players walked up and patted the bowler on the back. Laker strolled off the pitch with that detached air, softly whistling to himself while his colleagues followed a respectful pace or two behind, contenting themselves with measured applause. Judging by Laker's demeanour, you would have thought he had taken nought for plenty.

A quarter of a century later, Jim Laker and I talked about that astonishing day. He was simply philosophical about the chain of events that made history: 'If that game was played again a million times over, you'd never get the same situation. I wasn't particularly excited inside – nobody kissed me, that's for sure. I was doing my job and I tried to detach myself from everything. I gave a thought to every ball I bowled.' Colin Cowdrey stood at slip for most of the game and he cannot forget Laker's calmness: 'The batsmen played and missed so often, yet you couldn't tell from his expression. He was in perfect rhythm. Jim made the batsmen play at every ball, with a little drift in the air and just enough turn.'

How much was it a case of great bowling or mesmerized batting? Certainly Laker had the 'hex' on the Australians throughout that year. In the previous Test at Leeds, he and Lock had taken eighteen of the twenty wickets and, whenever he went into their dressing-room at Old Trafford, the Australians stopped playing cards, looked at him, then at his fingers as if he were a magician. Yet McDonald, Burke and Craig showed the wicket was not hopeless for batting; perhaps it was yet another case of a great bowler exerting psychological pressure on vulnerable players who were out of form.

So many amusing vignettes came out of this historic match. There was the sight of Tony Lock cursing and throwing the ball away whenever he took a catch off Laker. The hero of the day toasted the crowd in Lucozade and, when he stepped back into the dressing-room, Lock had changed and gone to his car. Alan Oakman has dined out on his five catches ever since, so much so that the youngsters in Warwickshire's second eleven groan whenever their coach is asked his memories of the game. 'Twenty years later, I sat next to Jim at a dinner and when I was billed as the man who took all those catches in Laker's Match, Jim leaned over and whispered, 'Christ, you're not still living on that are you?' but you've got to make the most of it, haven't you?'

That is the one thing Jim Laker did not do. He was too great a bowler to rely on one performance for a place in the Pantheon and he was too self-mocking and whimsical a man to talk about it unless pressed. On the way home from Old Trafford he stopped for a pie and a pint in a pub at Lichfield. He stood in a corner of the bar, munching away contemplatively, listening to the chatter of the regulars about this chap Laker. He watched about eight of his wickets on the television in the bar, drained his pint and walked out. Nobody recognized him. Jim thought that was very funny.

From *Fifty Incredible Cricket Matches* by Patrick Murphy
(Hutchinson, London, 1990).

*   *   *

Jim Laker once asked Everton Weekes how he got his first name: 'My Dad was a soccer nut and when I was born Everton won the championship.'

'Really,' said Jim, dry as ever. 'Bloody good job it wasn't West Bromwich Albion.'

ENGLAND *v* AUSTRALIA
(Fourth Test)

At Old Trafford, Manchester, 26–31 July 1956

ENGLAND

P. E. Richardson c Maddocks b Benaud	104
M. C. Cowdrey c Maddocks b Lindwall	80
Rev. D. S. Sheppard b Archer	113
*P. B. H. May c Archer b Benaud	43
T. E. Bailey b Johnson	20
C. Washbrook lbw b Johnson	6
A. S. M. Oakman c Archer b Johnson	10
†T. G. Evans st Maddocks b Johnson	47
J. C. Laker run out	3
G. A. R. Lock not out	25

J. B. Statham c Maddocks b Lind-
wall   0
B 2, 1-b 5, w 1...........................   <u>8</u>
                                               459

1/174 2/195 3/288 4/321 5/327 6/339 7/401 8/417 9/458 10/459

Bowling: Lindwall 21.3–6–63–2; Miller 21–6–41–0; Archer 22–6–73–1; Johnson 47–10–151–4; Benaud 47–17–123–2.

AUSTRALIA

C. C. McDonald c Lock b Laker..	32	– c Oakman b Laker	89
J. W. Burke c Cowdrey b Lock.....	22	– c Lock b Laker	33
R. N. Harvey b Laker	0	– c Cowdrey b Laker	0
I. D. Craig lbw b Laker.................	8	– lbw b Laker	38
K. R. Miller c Oakman b Laker....	6	– (6) b Laker	0
K. D. Mackay c Oakman b Laker	0	– (5) c Oakman b Laker	0
R. G. Archer st Evans b Laker.....	6	– c Oakman b Laker	0
R. Benaud c Statham b Laker.......	0	– b Laker	18
R. R. Lindwall not out.................	6	– c Lock b Laker	8
†L. V. Maddocks b Laker	4	– (11) lbw b Laker	2
*I. W. Johnson b Laker	0	– (10) not out	1
Extras	0	– B 12, 1-b 4	16
	84	–	205

1/48 2/48 3/62 4/62 5/62 6/73 7/73 8/78 9/84 10/84   1/28 2/55 3/114 4/124 5/130 6/130 7/181 8/198 9/203 10/205

Bowling: *First Innings* – Statham 6–3–6–0; Bailey 4–3–4–0; Laker 16.4–4–37–9; Lock 14–3–37–1. *Second Innings* – Statham 16–10–15–0; Bailey 20–8–31–0; Laker 51.2–23–53–10; Lock 55–30–69–0; Oakman 8–3–21–0.

Umpires: D. E. Davies and F. S. Lee.

England won by an innings and 170 runs.

8

BLACK MAGIC

Cricket has always been more than a sport to the West Indies. All the people of the Caribbean identify with their cricket team even though they belong to many different islands and several different countries. When the proposed West Indian Federation broke up in 1961, cricket remained the great unifying influence. The West Indians won millions of friends with their crowd-noisy carefree Calypso cricket, especially 'Those two little pals of mine Ramadhin and Valentine' who humiliated us in 1950 (though actually Valentine was six feet tall).

They were never really mastered until May and Cowdrey got hold of them at Edgbaston in 1957 (May 285 not out, Cowdrey 154). That broke the West Indies' spin and after that England went on to win three times in the series by an innings. But before that it wasn't just the Englishmen who suffered. Australia's top batsmen were spellbound too.

Valentine had a slow looping left-arm delivery and spun the ball with a terrific rip – indeed I would say he spun the ball more than any other finger spin bowler who has ever played the game. It is said that he needed a skin graft on his spinning finger after the 1950 tour.

Little Sonny Ramadhin had the off spinner as his stock ball, but mixed it up with the leg cutter and you couldn't tell one from t'other. Leonard Hutton told me he had never known an off-spinner who turned the ball so much. Even so Yorkshire almost beat them at Bradford in 1950.

The West Indian crowds have always been volatile and I remember running for my life after the bottle-throwing riot at Trinidad in 1959–60, though I felt easier when they shouted, 'Don't worry Fred. We're not going to touch you. We want the umpires.'

But in the last two decades a lot of the Calypso spirit has vanished. At Old Trafford in 1976 Clive Lloyd allowed his quick men Roberts and Holding backed up by Daniel to unleash for fully 80 minutes as ugly a spell of intimidatory bowling on Brian Close and John Edrich as I've ever seen go unchecked by the umpires. It was bouncer after bouncer with not a chance for the batsmen to score.

Then in the third Test at Port of Spain in 1990 we had what former Aussie skipper

Ian Chappell called West Indies 'criminal over rate', not to mention a very unpleasant war of words waged by acting captain Desmond Haynes when fielding against the English batsmen. Then more intimidatory bowling against Lamb and Smith under skipper Viv Richards at Antigua – not to mention Viv's extraordinary outburst against *Daily Express* journalist James Lawton when he should have been leading his team onto the field.

In this piece Jamaican Prime Minister Michael Manley, a life-long cricket fan since his father took him as a ten-year-old to watch George Headley make 270 not out against England at Sabina Park, explains how the Calypso image has been transformed and how Lloyd got his idea for a relentless four-man pace battery – or should it be battering? – from the success of the Australian's four-prong pace attack against them in 1975–6. Manley, twice elected Jamaican Prime Minister, found time to write his 575 page history of West Indies cricket during his years of opposition – a tribute to the hold the game has on all walks of life in the Caribbean and to the brilliance of a side which he believes to have been consistently greater than any other in history.

F.S.T.

The All-Conquering Kings of Speed

Michael Manley

> Cricket, lovely cricket
> At Lord's where I saw it
> Yardley tried his best
> But West Indies won the Test
> With those little pals of mine
> Ramadhin and Valentine.

As is the tradition, great events in the West Indies are heralded in song. In 1950 first Lord Kitchener led a jubilant band of West Indian supporters on a march around the famous Lord's ground in London; second, a few days later, Lord Beginner composed the famous calypso. They were celebrating the West Indies' first Test match victory in England. This triumph had been twenty-two years in the making and remains till today, thirty-six years later, perhaps the single greatest moment in West Indies cricket history.

The 1950 West Indian team were quickly dubbed the 'calypso cricketers'. It was as much a tribute to the sparkle and style they brought to the game as a commentary on their latent unpredictability.

It was a brilliant side. The batting began with the elegant Jeffrey Stollmeyer and the patiently assured Allan Rae. They laid the foundations exploited with devastating effect by three great players, 'The Three Ws': Frank Worrell, all grace; Everton Weekes, whose ferocity all but concealed a superb technique; and Clyde Walcott with his awesome power. In 1950, these three between them broke the hearts of England's bowlers and captured English imaginations in the process. Two young spin bowlers completed the rout: Ramadhin, stoical of manner, with his twinkle-toed approach and magical twirl of the arm, seemed to mesmerize all and sundry. Opposite him was Valentine, left-arm, as awkward as Ramadhin was neat, but imparting a ferocious tweak to the ball which, they said, hissed through the air before breaking sharply off the pitch.

From the islands of the West Indies had come a group of cricketers who could delight with their play. The fact that they seemed to give the home side a chance of winning may have added a touch of affection to the admiration which they commanded by their skill. And so, the 'calypso cricketers' image, part reality, part myth, was born. Hence, West Indian fans lived from 1950 to 1975 with a constant faith that their teams were unbeatable. Yet seemingly strong sides, lavish with stars, proved no different to the other cricketing élite, the Test-match-playing countries of England, Australia, New Zealand, India and Pakistan. They won some and they lost some. They had their good periods and their bad, and the latter invariably evoked for them the critical connotations of calypso cricketers. Yet, this had now changed; unpredictability and suspense giving way to unqualified and consistent success.

Today, they still excite by their style of play and are probably the biggest drawing card in cricket. But, the calypso image has been transformed to that of a tough, uncompromising group of professionals, who for the last decade have systematically ground all opposition into the dust.

In November 1975 in Australia, a young, talented and vastly promising West Indies team under the leadership of a new captain, Clive Lloyd, played the first Test of a series against a great Australian side. The match was at Brisbane, traditionally the scene of the opening Test exchanges 'down under'. The West Indies group had a devastating new fast bowler from Antigua, Andy Roberts. They also boasted two young batting stars in Lawrence Rowe and Alvin Kallicharran. Rowe, a Jamaican, had made an incredible debut in 1972 against New Zealand with a double century, 214, in his very first innings, followed by 100 not out in the second. Shortly after he performed with credit against an Australian side. Rowe then set the West Indies itself on fire when, playing as an opening bat with the left-hander Roy Fredericks, who was nearing the end of his career, he made an exquisite 120 at Sabina Park against England. Next, at the Kensington Oval in Barbados, he made a triple century, 302, which Barbadians remember with a mixture of delight and reverence. It was utterly chanceless, utterly majestic, utterly beautiful by the accounts of everyone who watched. It captured the hearts of that most knowledgeable of cricket crowds.

As if this were not enough, Rowe had gone on to a turning wicket at the Queen's Park Oval in Trinidad and performed with the sort of circumspection and control in difficult circumstances which are among the more notable claims to fame of his immortal predecessor, George Headley, and that other giant, still arguably the greatest English batsman of them all, Jack Hobbs.

At this point Guyana's Alvin Kallicharran had also shown poise and class in the course of his own only slightly less memorable six Test centuries; while the new West Indian captain, Clive Lloyd, was a giant of a man whose stature belied his speed as an outfielder and his marvellous footwork as an attacking middle-order batsman. It could be argued with equal purpose that his amiable personality gave no hint of the relentless leader whose side was, first, to defeat, then overawe and finally annihilate all opposition in the future. This team had just beaten India and, more to the point, had won the first one-day International Cricket Festival, the World Cup. It seemed highly relevant that they had defeated this same Australian side in a memorable encounter in the final.

But the 1975–6 series proved a disaster. Despite centuries by Rowe and Kallicharran, Australia won the first Test comfortably. The West Indies redeemed this with a magnificent victory on the super-fast surface at Perth in the second Test. There Roy Fredericks and Clive Lloyd, with 169 and 149 respectively, launched a bold counterattack against the Australian fast bowling quartet of Dennis Lillee, Jeff Thomson, Max Walker and Gary Gilmour.

Chancing their arms and going for their shots, Fredericks and Lloyd laid the foundation for a resounding West Indies victory by an innings and 87 runs. This was cemented by some great fast bowling particularly from Andy Roberts, who took 9 wickets for 119 in the match.

The respite was short-lived, however. The Australian fast attack could be confronted in a single game, but the daring of the West Indies counterattack at Perth could not be sustained. Australia proceeded to grind down the West Indies in the next four tests, winning them by margins of 8 wickets, 7 wickets, 190 runs and 165 runs, and the series by 5 matches to 1. Rowe, after his century in the first Test, never achieved another innings of significance till the fourth Test when he managed a slightly shaky 67.

In terms of the batting, coming events were to cast what then seemed to be no more than a faint shadow in the steady improvement of another Antiguan star, the batsman Vivian Richards. He had scores of 30, 101, 50 and 98 in the last two Tests. Together with the manner of his scoring them, these runs gave more than a hint of the talent that was shortly to blossom.

On the credit side also was the promise of the untried, loose-limbed 6ft 4½in of slender grace that was the fast bowler, Michael Holding. Holding only took 10 wickets for 614 runs in that series, but he was possessed of that unmistakeable quality, class; and, as it was to turn out, that vital capacity, speed.

It was not lost upon the highly intelligent Clive Lloyd that, in the course of a long series, the sheer weight and intimidatory reality of four pace bowlers had proved more than his talented array of young batting stars could handle. They were capable of a magnificent counterattack but, in retrospect, the Perth victory was more like some premature Götterdämmerung than evidence of a side equal to its opposition and taking its turn at victory.

The present success of the West Indies began, therefore, with an analytical response to the disaster of the 1975–6 series in Australia. Obviously, the West Indies needed a four-pronged pace attack of its own.

As it turned out there began to emerge, from the sometimes inscrutable workings of the region's culture, a stream of fast bowlers who, as the years passed, looked more like a river than a stream and have since taken on the characteristics of a flood.

In the very next Test series, in 1976, the West Indies defeated India 2–1 with one match drawn. Not an overwhelming result on the face of it. But this series, played in the West Indies, was notable for the fact that Lloyd took the field in every match with four fast bowlers, although he employed considerably more throughout the series because of the need to experiment. This was to culminate in a turn of events in the last Test which pointed clearly to the future. Some would say that the portents were ominous for, quite frankly, the Indian team was suspended somewhere between anxiety and indignation, a circumstance which they sought to conceal behind claims of 'injury'. Perhaps this was just as well since it served the purposes of diplomacy no less than those of honour.

The experiment against India may have been vital in confirming the lessons of the Australian tour in Clive Lloyd's mind. Up to 1975, the use of four quick bowlers in a side was considered a gamble at best, and in all likelihood a recipe for disaster.

Apart from a brilliant West Indies' victory behind four speed merchants at Sabina Park in 1935, experiments in the past had proved generally unsuccessful. The 'body-line' bowling employed by England when they routed Australia in 1932–3 can be regarded as a precedent. It involved a special type of attack which was eventually condemned as too dangerous to allow.

England's first professional captain, Len Hutton, a believer himself in the advantage of good quick bowling, had played four fast men, conventionally deployed, in the first Test of the 1953–4 series against the West Indies. Statham, Trueman, Moss and Bailey had laboured diligently, bowling 155 overs and taking 11 wickets for 475 runs. England lost the match and their selectors reverted to a more conventional balance for the rest of the tour.

One year later against Australia, Hutton experimented again. At Brisbane, he employed Bedser, Statham, Tyson, Bailey and Edrich in the first Test. In this instance, they bowled 129 eight-ball overs and for their efforts were rewarded with 7 wickets for 582 runs. Again, Hutton lost heart. Yet it is instructive to note that over the last four Tests of that series Statham and Tyson bowled England to a spectacular series triumph, taking between them 43 wickets. With Bailey bagging 7 wickets, 50 of the 76 Australian wickets lost fell to pace.

Hutton's experiment failed because, first, the quality of the attack was not consistent, and second, because he abandoned it too quickly. One wonders, had a young Trueman rather than a not fully fit Bedser gone to Australia in 1954, would Hutton's plan have succeeded?

Lloyd, however, was convinced that if three good fast bowlers were effective, then four could be devastating. He had witnessed and personally experienced the fire of sustained pace and quality. It had been indelibly imprinted in his mind that it is virtually impossible for any batting side to stand up to hour after hour of this type of attack. Sporadic counterattack is possible. Sustained response is not. The combined mental and physical effort required cannot be maintained indefinitely.

Following the triumphant experiment against India, a new strategy was to take root. The team next took on England in England.

The composition of the touring party made an interesting comparison with that of their predecessors some twenty-six years before. Whereas in 1950 the West Indies travelled to England with only three recognized quick bowlers – Hines Johnson, P. E. Jones and Lance Pierre – plus four recognized spinners, the 1976 contingent had five fast bowlers and only two spinners.

In this series Roberts, Holding, the Barbadian Wayne Daniel who spearheaded the Middlesex attack for many years, Vanburn Holder, another Barbadian, and the all-rounder, Collis King, ensured that the West Indian effort unfolded behind a four-pronged pace attack throughout the series. In fact, of the 908 overs bowled by the West Indies this group completed 772 of them and took 88 of the 92 England wickets to fall in the five Test matches.

One does not pretend that the only thing memorable about that series in 1976, which the West Indies won by 3–0 with two matches drawn, was the effect of the sustained pace attack. That summer was literally set ablaze by Viv Richards's batting at all stages; as it was, too, by Michael Holding's feats in the final Test at The Oval when his bowling was the stuff of which legend is made. The summer of 1976 was a time of glory for the West Indies.

For the next ten years, nine of them under Lloyd's own leadership and then under Vivian Richards, the West Indies were to sweep everything before them.

And what of the other components following the lesson of 1975–6 and the use of the flow of fast bowlers? The other factors peculiarly at work in building this side were the captaincy itself of Clive Lloyd; the evolution of a new approach by the West Indies Cricket Board of Control and particularly under the leadership of Allan Rae; and the effect of that fascinating aberrant episode in cricket history known as the Packer intervention. This was to cement the process by which the West Indies cricket team became truly professional. Finally there is an added level of physical fitness which sets them apart from other sides in cricket history.

In the ten years 1976–86, and if you exclude the matches organized under Kerry Packer in Australia, the West Indies played 17 Test series, winning 15, drawing 1 and losing 1. They won 37 matches while they drew 29 and lost 5. Further analysis shows that they were in a winning position in the majority of the matches that were drawn. The one series that was lost was highly controversial, involving a tired and overconfident side in New Zealand after a tough tour of Australia and it involved bitterness about the quality of the pitches and the umpiring. One offers this not by way of excuse, but to indicate that the only lost series occurred in controversial circumstances, to say the least.

Throughout this period the most powerful side, apart from the West Indies, was probably England. The comparison is instructive. England played 28 series and 102 matches. They won 14 of their series, losing 11 and drawing 3. They won 31 of their matches, drawing 39 and losing 32. Put another way, while they were losing 16 games without a single victory against the West Indies, England were winning two Tests for every one they lost against their other opponents.

Only two sides in cricket history can seriously compare with the West Indians of this period. Both are Australian, under Warwick Armstrong in 1920–21 and under Don Bradman in 1948. The first beat England 5–0 in Australia and went on to win the first three Tests in England in 1921. The second defeated the same opponents 4–0, with one match drawn.

Armstrong's side needed to bowl 57 balls for every wicket they captured. Bradman's side averaged 74. In beating England 5–0 in 1984, the West Indies dismissed a batsman with every 49 balls. In the 1986 series, in which they went on to create history by extending their victory streak against England to 10 straight matches they were to require only 39 balls per wicket taken. The difference lay mainly in those four fast bowlers. They do not bowl deliberately at the batsmen. But there is a cumulative effect to all those thunderbolts lifting off the wicket. The batsmen now face the fire under helmets, gloves and many pads. All of these can protect the body but cannot relieve the apprehension nor fully still the fear.

It is difficult to find a comparable ten years in which a single team has so utterly dominated a sport. In baseball the great sides of the New York Yankees, first in the days of Babe Ruth and Lou Gehrig and later with Mickey Mantle, Roger Maris and the pitcher Whitey Ford, come to mind. So, too, with what is perhaps an even more dominant phenomenon in American sport, the Boston Celtics in basketball. Their record under the astute leadership of George 'Red' Auerbach included a phenomenal period spanning the 1950s and 1960s in which they captured ten championships in thirteen years. But with the expansion of the National Basketball Association and more teams competing, the Celtics, while still a dominant force, have had to settle since then for a more modest record.

Perhaps, with the same explanation, the outcome remains similar in the case of the Green Bay Packers under their coach Vince Lombardi in the late 1950s and the 1960s in American football.

If we turn to soccer we find Brazil as the glamour side of history, but only once able to put together back-to-back World Cup victories; and today's Argentinian side had to step aside for Italy, West Germany and Brazil in 1982 before they could follow their 1978 triumph with a comparable success in Mexico in 1986.

From *A History of West Indies Cricket* by Michael Manley
(Andre Deutsch, London, 1988).

Michael Manley's reference to baseball, basketball and American football is a timely reminder that cricket is no longer quite so dominant in the West Indies as it used to be. West Indies' best-known commentator Tony Cozier says, 'The kids are growing up with new idols because of the amount of American sport that is being beamed in from the US. Every satellite dish you see is aimed at the strength of West Indian cricket. Baseball, basketball, they are flooding our screens and cricket is losing out.' Sir Garfield Sobers says, 'Yes, we may be coming to the end of an era. We have to hope young players will come along to make new heroes.' But will the kids want to become pitchers and batters for the New York Yankees? The answer could be on the golden sandy beaches of the Caribbean where the baseball diamond is now almost as common a sight as the wickets.

F.S.T.

Quick Quotes

Clive Lloyd's West Indians of 1980 would have given
Bradman's 1948 'unbeatables' a real run for their
money. We'd have won, but only just.

> Neil Harvey, former Australian Test cricketer.

*   *   *

The West Indies pacemen have switched the attack
to me to the body. It's not very pleasant.

> Allan Border explaining his chest protector
> and other armour in the second Test
> v West Indies in Perth in 1988.

We don't breed brutal cricketers.

> Clive Lloyd, West Indies manager, rejecting
> charges that his side played violent cricket.

*   *   *

We bowl short at them, they bowl short at us –
it's as simple as that.

> Geoff Lawson, Australian paceman, as fast
> bowlers got caught up in the bumper war, in the Second
> Test in Perth. Lawson's jaw was broken by Curtly
> Ambrose.

*   *   *

Within a decade every top team will field four
fast bowlers pitching short with no one in front
of the bat. Adventurous batting will be reserved
for one day games. Ruthlessness and violence will
be indistinguishable.

> Peter Roebuck, Somerset batsman and
> journalist writing in 1989.

'*Fantastic! I never thought that they'd do that in my lifetime!*'

The Four W's

Brian Johnston

To me a great cricketer is just that, regardless of the colour of his skin. I first met the legendary three Ws of West Indies cricket – Worrell, Walcott and Weekes – when they were in league cricket in England and we got on well. Then when Len Hutton took the MCC team on the 1953–4 tour to the West Indies he made it clear he didn't want us to fraternize with the West Indian players. But there was no way I was going to follow that advice with my pals the three Ws. In this piece Brian Johnston cheats a bit and writes about the four Ws, the fourth being Wesley Hall, whom everyone called Wes. Like me and Ray Lindwall, Wes could bowl the outswinger – the one that gets the great players out. Wes was one of the best fast bowlers of all time.

F.S.T.

Sir Frank Worrell during his short life had more influence on West Indies cricket than possibly any other West Indian. He was the first black man to captain them, and welded together the various islands with all their differences into a team. He was dignified, calm, friendly and had that indefinable attribute of charisma. He was captain in 15 Tests, winning 9, losing 3, drawing 2 and tying 1, and his behaviour both on and off the field was always impeccable. He could have played in more Tests had he not decided to study economics first at Manchester University, and later in Jamaica, where he went to live and became a senator in their Parliament. He was, like the other three, both in Barbados but for some reason was unhappy there. The highlights of his captaincy were undoubtedly the famous Brisbane tie in 1960, and the dramatic last-over finish at Lord's in 1963 which ended in a draw. On both occasions it was his calm leadership which controlled the natural exuberance of the West Indian players. The 1960–61 Australian tour ended with an unprecedented tribute to him and his team. They paraded through the streets of Melbourne in a motorcade cheered by an estimated 500,000 people lining the route. His own personal accolade came in 1964 when he was knighted by the Queen for his services to the game. He retired after the 1963 tour of England and sadly died of leukaemia at the early age of forty-two. Again, uniquely for a cricketer, a memorial service was held for him in Westminster Abbey. It was a tribute and recognition, not just of his captaincy and prowess as a cricketer, but of his outstanding qualities as a man.

The emphasis on his captaincy and character tends to overshadow his skills as a player. He was a graceful batsman with plenty of strokes, good footwork and immense powers of concentration. He played in 51 Tests, scoring 3,860 runs with the remarkably high average of 49.48 and scored 9 hundreds. He enjoyed playing a long innings, as scores of 261 and 197 not out against England will indicate. He was also a useful left-arm bowler, sometimes slow but more often fast-medium, and took 69 Test workers, though they were fairly expensive at 38.72 apiece. I shall always treasure the memory of keeping wicket to him in a charity match in Kent. I remember standing up to him, so he must have been bowling his slows. Sadly I cannot remember whether I caught or stumped anyone off him, but the odds are that I didn't!

Clyde Walcott was a complete contrast to the feline grace of Worrell. He was six feet two inches tall, burly, immensely strong and one of the hardest hitters the game has ever known. There was never much competition to field at mid-off or mid-on when he was batting. He drove with great power off both the front and back foot and, as if this was not enough, was a fierce square cutter and hooker. In 74 Tests he scored 3,798 runs at the high average of 56.68, eleventh best of all Test cricketers. Like Worrell he enjoyed going on after reaching a hundred. He scored fifteen hundreds in Tests, including 220 and 168 not out against England. Perhaps his best ever achievement was in the West Indies against Australia in 1955. He was at the pinnacle of his career and in 5 Tests scored 827 runs at 82.70, including 5 hundreds, and twice scored two hundreds in one match – a Test record. This was a tremendous feat against bowlers like Lindwall, Miller, W. A. Johnston and Benaud. He must also hold another unusual record. In a Test against India at Bridgetown in 1953 he had scored 98 when he was given out (lbw) by his uncle (J. H. Walcott)!

He was a versatile cricketer. In spite of his height and bulk he was a more than competent wicket-keeper, especially to the slows, but I cannot quite remember seeing him flinging himself about as Dujon has to do today. He eventually gave it up after slipping a disc and having his nose broken. At a pinch he could also bowl, medium-paced in-duckers or off-cutters – whatever they were, he did take 11 Test wickets. He has continued his versatility since he retired from Test cricket in 1960 and went to live in Guyana. He has been cricket organizer and coach, commentator, manager of the West Indies side to England in 1976, and is now president of the West Indies board – a just reward for a big friendly man.

Everton DeCourcey Weekes has the broadest grin in cricket, and was the most prolific scorer of the three W's. He played in 48 Tests and scored 4,455 runs with an average of 58.61, putting him seventh in the list of Test averages, 0.06 behind Ken Barrington but above Hammond, Sobers and Hobbs. He was smaller than Walcott but seemingly equally powerful, with every known stroke in the game. Words like 'plunder', 'murderous', 'savage' and 'thrash' are constantly used by writers describing some of his innings, and he could be quite merciless in the way he tore into even the strongest attacks. He had two special assets: nimble footwork and guts.

People who played against him in the Test at Lord's in 1957 say that his 90 in the second innings was one of the best and bravest innings they have ever seen. Trueman, Bailey and Statham were exploiting the famous ridge at the Nursery End, and the ball rose sharply every time they hit it. Weekes suffered a cracked bone in a finger of his right hand. In spite of this – and he was obviously in great pain – he attacked the bowling for two and three-quarter hours and hit as many as sixteen fours in a superb innings – a tremendous display of guts. I am sure that Godfrey Evans was sorry to have to appeal when he finally caught him off Trevor Bailey.

Everton's most prolific spell of batting came in 1948–9. He scored 141 against England at Kingston in the fourth and final Test of Gubby Allen's tour in March. The following November the West Indies toured India and in the first three Tests he scored, 128, 194, 162 and 101. In the fourth Test at Madras he was run out for 90! I suspect that just for once there was no grin on his face! He might have gone on to score many more Test runs but he was forced to retire early because of a bad thigh injury. Since then his chief claim to fame has been as a world-class bridge player – appropriately enough, since he was born in Bridgetown. But he is always there to welcome visitors to Barbados, and is an equally welcome visitor whenever he comes over here.

Lastly, the intruder, W. Wes Hall. One of the fastest ever Test bowlers, with probably the longest run-up to the wicket. I remember being in the commentary box at Sabina Park and Wes starting his run from just below us. If we had had longer arms we could very nearly have patted him on the head. He was tall (six feet two inches) and gangling with long arms and legs. In spite of his long run he had tremendous stamina and could bowl for long spells. In 1963 at Lord's in England's second innings on the last day he bowled for nearly three and a half hours unchanged. This of course meant a very slow over-rate, which made England's task much harder. If you were a spectator it was a joy to watch him as he ran up, gaining pace and lengthening his stride as he approached the stumps. The batsmen, I am sure, held a different view, as they waited for the ball to be hurled at them at something like 90 m.p.h. He could move the ball in the air but it was primarily his pace which won him most of his 192 Test wickets at 26.38 apiece. He had a lovely action as he delivered the ball, left arm high in the air, right arm stretched right back, rather as if he was about to throw a javelin. He followed through a long way down the pitch, often ending up a few yards from the batsman. He could – and did – bowl a fearsome bouncer, but though batsmen feared and hated him *on* the field, he was one of the most popular cricketers *off* it.

He became a smiling gentle giant, witty, friendly and a superb mimic. He seldom stopped talking and he is reported to have told a reporter when he first became a senator in Barbados: 'if you think my run-up was long, wait till you hear my speeches!' He has now progressed from senator to minister in charge of tourism and sport, and has selected a most suitable assistant – Garry Sobers. Wes works tremendously hard to supply tourists with more facilities than just the sun and the beaches.

It was a coincidence that on the occasions of both the Brisbane tie and the 1963 draw at Lord's he was the bowler to bowl the last over. In Brisbane Australia needed 6 runs off an 8-ball over to win with 3 wickets still to fall. At Lord's England needed 8 runs to win with 2 wickets to fall. Wes, under the calming influence of Frank Worrell, kept his head on both occasions, and made certain that he did not bowl a no-ball.

Like most bowlers, he fancied himself as a batsman and there was fierce competition between himself and Charlie Griffith as to who went in above the other. In fact, at the Brisbane tie Wes made his top Test score of 50, and on Colin Cowdrey's tour in 1968 he saved West Indies from defeat in the first Test at Port-of-Spain. He put on 68 for the ninth wicket with Garry Sobers, and batted throughout the final session. As a batsman he had, and played, all the strokes – many of them brilliantly spectacular. The only trouble was that on most occasions he failed to make contact with the ball!

He will always remain one of the greatest characters of cricket, and I treasure the memory of him running up to bowl with the gold crucifix hanging from his neck, glistening in the sun. Like so many West Indians he was always passionately fond of horse-racing, and has had shares in racehorses in Barbados. What I didn't know until the other day was that it had been his ambition as a boy to become a jockey. With his six-foot-two-inch frame and well-built body I bet the horses are glad that he didn't.

From *It's Been A Piece of Cake* by Brian Johnston
(Methuen, London, 1989).

You think my run-up was long. You should hear my speeches.
Wes Hall, West Indies fast bowler, now a Barbados Senator.

Viv Richards – Black Bradman?

Trevor McDonald

Vivian Richards is the only batsman today that I would still go a long way to see. He is unorthodox, often playing across the line on the on-side, and his brilliance depends on the quickness of his eye. I suspect that eye is not as quick as it once was now that he has turned thirty-eight, but he will remain a crowd-puller and a man who always promises something electric for as long as he chooses to play. He has been called the Black Bradman but such comparisons are all but impossible to make. The Don was fairly orthodox and would think more than twice before hitting a ball outside the off stump over mid-wicket's head for four as Viv so often does. For his 6,996 Test runs at an average of 99.94 the Don played in only fifty-two tests between 1928 and 48 – there were fewer tours then as well as six war years, whereas Viv has played in over 100 Tests for almost 8,000 runs at an average in the fifties. But both had the power to dominate a series as Viv undoubtedly did in the summer of 1976, here described by Trinidad-born TV newscaster Trevor McDonald.

F.S.T.

> *We will make (the West Indies) grovel*
>
> Tony Greig
>
> *Nobody talks to Viv Richards like that*
>
> Viv Richards

Richards is serious about his talent; and he is fiercely proud of it. He comes very close to believing that it's God-given and that he was charged with the responsibility of using it to its best advantage. That makes him humble. But he is not in the least apologetic about the fact that he can see the cricket ball and pick up its line earlier than any other living batsman.

That gives him time to play his shots. It's the key to the confident, uninhibited manner in which he plays, and the glorious freedom with which he strokes the ball.

His approach – a combination of humility, seriousness and burning pride – was shaped by the class structure which has always dominated the West Indian game and nurtured by the politics of contemporary cricket. That's why, on the eve of that first test between England and the West Indies in 1976, the England captain, Tony Greig, touched a raw nerve with his 'grovel' remark. And not only with Viv Richards.

It had perhaps never occurred to Tony Greig that for the South African captain of an English team to publicly threaten to make the West Indies 'grovel' in 1976 was probably the closest any cricketer ever came to making a formal declaration of war.

In any event, that's how the West Indians read it; and that's certainly how Greig's words were perceived by the twenty-four-year-old player from Antigua, Vivian Richards.

He says:

> It came as a bit of a shock really to hear what Tony Greig had said. I suppose on one level you could say that Greigy was just trying to reassure an England side that was not too good a team. But still I was taken aback. We all were. Wayne Daniel, Andy Roberts and I had gone into the room where the team meeting was about to be held. We were early and the television was on. We weren't watching, but when news about the cricket came on we all paid attention. And then we heard the 'grovel' remark. We all knew the kinda guy Tony was, you know, he always played the game hard, but always with a lot of chat also. But even so we thought he went a bit too far. Wayne didn't say much, but Andy was quite mad. I felt it was not too brilliant a thing for a South African to say about West Indian players and it made me more determined to do well.
>
> The senior players tried to make us put the remark behind us, to forget it. But I can tell you, what Tony had said hung over that particular team meeting and I think it made us all feel that we could not afford to let the folks down.

So when the Test match started, Vivian Richards went into battle wielding his bat like a broadsword.

And on the first day of that first Test match at Nottingham, in the words of one correspondent: 'The graduation of Vivian Richards from student of the highest potential to master of the batting art, stuffed Tony Greig's battle cry down his throat.'

Continuing the magnificent run of form which saw him take one century against the Australians and three against the Indians in the seven months preceding the Nottingham Test, Richards tore the England attack to shreds. He was undefeated at stumps on the first day with 143 to his name. When his wicket fell, at about half past two on the second day, he had accumulated 232 brilliant runs. In his seven-and-a-half-hour occupation of the wicket he'd struck four sixes and thirty-one fours. He had shared in a third wicket stand of 303 and had set his team on an irrevocable path to victory.

'Cultural violence' was how one cricket writer described it. And so it had been. A blend of seemingly outrageous flair and prudence when required. Perfectly balanced, with wrists of steel and a marvellous quickness of eye and reflex, Richards had never been hurried into making a stroke. Even when he played and missed outside the off stump, his supreme confidence gave the bowler not the slightest bit of encouragement.

Tony Greig's England team was given a brief reprieve in the second test, but only from Richards. He'd been kept in bed for a week with 'flu.

At Headingley Richards scored 66 and 38 in his two knocks, but with his first run in that Test he had taken his aggregate for 1976 to 1,381, overhauling the record set in 1964 by Australia's Bobby Simpson.

Richards ended the series against England on the same high note on which he'd begun. The Oval Test was dominated by the silken grace and menacing speed of fast bowler Michael Holding. On a singularly unhelpful pitch, he took 14 England wickets for 149 runs. But if Holding delivered the *coup de grâce*, the slaughter had been started by Richards. He went out to bat after Greenidge had been trapped leg before by Bob Willis for a duck, and launched into an innings which was to be of epic greatness.

Throughout the day, without mercy, he cut and drove the ball over the hard brown Oval outfield, to the most distant boundaries. Ruthless with any deliveries short of a good length, he was capable of defending stoutly when the need arose. But the unending feature of that memorable late summer's day was the sight of England fieldsmen despairingly chasing and then retrieving the ball from behind the boundary ropes, as Richards piled on the agony. To many, there were distinct echoes in Richards' batting that day of the almost mechanical brilliance of Bradman and Ponsford in the 1930s.

By stumps on the first day of that fifth Test match, Richards had scored 200. He had driven the honest medium pace of Mike Selvey as though Selvey were a slow bowler. He had been always devastating on the onside. He flicked Willis to the long-leg boundary with a kind of graceful contempt. In a moment of delightful malice he struck Underwood over the long extra cover boundary for six.

His 200 on the first day were not to be the end of the story. He went on to make 291, before he was bowled playing a tired drive at a delivery from Tony Greig. His score of 291 on the second day included 38 fours and was the highest-ever by a West Indian batsman at the Oval. It was also the highest-ever by a West Indian in a Test in England, and Richards' own highest score in Test cricket. Another 'Calypso Run Carnival' as one writer described it.

From the moment he passed 250, all West Indian thoughts became fixed on Garry Sobers' score of 365. To this day, Richards maintains that nothing was further from his mind:

> You can't play an innings in that way, going after a record. Every ball has to be played on its merit and concentration is important throughout. And thinking about how many runs you want to make, or about some batting record set by someone else could disturb your concentration. I was out there to bat and to stay as long as I could. I never let myself think of making 365.

With Richards gone, the West Indies declared at a massive 687 for 8, the highest score ever made by the West Indies against England.

Tony Greig himself could never get his bat down quickly enough to keep out Holding's faster ball. Holding got him for 12 in the first innings and uprooted his middle stump in the second, when Greig had scored only one run. In the end England lost the Oval Test by 231 runs.

England had managed a draw at Trent Bridge and at Lord's. At Old Trafford they had gone down by the humiliatingly wide margin of 425 runs, and they had been convincingly beaten at Headingley and at the Oval.

Viv Richards was undoubtedly the man of the series. He'd topped the batting averages and his aggregate for the tour of 829 runs set a new record for the West Indies against any country.

To his countrymen in the Caribbean, Viv Richards' exploits on the cricket field meant far more than beating the old enemy at cricket. His greatest admirer, the then Deputy Prime Minister of Antigua, Lester Bird, put it this way:

> The country needed a focal point, a touchstone, which could form the basis of communal unity in common cause. He (Richards) represented that touchstone: he was the embodiment of an opportunity for a whole nation to be galvanized for a single purpose ... Viv Richards' success on the international cricket stage. ... He personified what we perceived ourselves to be: young, dynamic and talented but yet unrecognized in the world.

Mr Bird went even further. He said: 'Richards was a stabilizing force at a time when politics threatened to disrupt the very fabric and fibre of the society.' Not for the first time, a West Indian politician had found West Indian success on the cricket field a suitable metaphor for political progress in the islands themselves.

In Viv's first-ever Test series in England, senior players regularly lectured the team about the need to make sure that their showing in Test matches did not disappoint the hundreds of thousands of West Indians living in Britain. It's a responsibility that Richards bears willingly and ably.

The best-selling author and former Member of Parliament, Jeffrey Archer, writing a tribute to Viv Richards on the occasion of his benefit year, tells a story which goes some way to explaining why the contemporary West Indian cricketer must see his role in a far wider context than that circumscribed by the game alone:

'My son William, aged nine, was reading an article in *The Times* about the Brixton riots, and when he finished I tentatively asked him how he felt about the National Front's view that black people were somehow inferior.

'"Pathetic," he replied, "none of them can have seen Viv Richards at the crease."'

It's a story which comes close to explaining how Viv Richards sees himself and his cricket, and it's a story that Richards himself delights in telling. 'Yeah, man,' he says, 'it was very good of Jeffrey Archer to recount that story in my testimonial brochure.'

From *Viv Richards – The Authorised Biography* by Trevor McDonald
(Pelham, London 1984).

When you have two work horses and shoot them in the back I think it's evil. You don't treat animals in this way. I was blind-folded, led up an alley and assassinated.

Viv Richards, when told in 1986 that Somerset were not renewing his or Joel Garner's contracts

Sacking Viv Richards is like sending Shergar to Argentina for dog meat.

Ian Botham, who quit Somerset when the two black stars were sacked.

9

GENIUS IS LEFT-HANDED
David Gower – Golden Boy

Trevor Bailey

He is such a beautiful timer of the ball that at times he looks lazy – but that is only an impression. He is a touch player and when he is on form there is no more elegant sight. 'David Gower is sheer class. He is without doubt one of the best timers of the ball I've seen,' says Viv Richards. 'He is the difference between players of average ability and those of exceptional pedigree. He has time to play his shots, he is really sensational to watch on his day … he can light up the park.' I agree with every word of that and over 7,000 Test runs testify to it. But I also think David's batting technique has let him down too often because his feet are often in the wrong place and he has never had a consistent defence.

F.S.T.

In the 1970s and 1980s there have been better, more spectacular, and correcter batsmen than David Gower, yet I preferred to watch an innings by David more than anybody else, because he had so much to offer in terms of style as well as runs. In addition to being a cricketer, he looked the part, with the tall lean build, rather languid manner, handsome features, blue eyes and blond hair of a matinée idol of the 1920s, while his cavalier approach was reminiscent of the Golden Age. Whenever he strolls nonchalantly out to the crease, one knows that, if he remains, the runs must flow quickly and elegantly. He reminded me of another wonderful left-hander, Frank Woolley, the same relaxed stance, high backlift and follow-through with the full swing of the bat which will despatch fast and slow bowling to all parts of the ground. Although both men hit the ball very hard, they gave the impression that they were *caressing* boundaries. It was this ability to stroke fours and sixes, and to make batting look easy when clearly it was not, which so appealed to me.

David Gower was able to make scoring runs appear simple because he always appeared to have so much time; and he was also a beautifully balanced mover. These characteristics applied as well to another England left-hander, Willie Watson, about whom Sir Len Hutton once complained that it all came too easily to him, both his cricket and his football. Willie would glide over the ground very quickly without seeming to be in a hurry, and David has the same deceptive pace which makes him dangerous in the field and such a delight to bat with, as his judgment of what constitutes a run and his own pace between the wickets is excellent.

One of the many charms of David's batting is that it is largely instinctive. This can hardly be better illustrated than by the first ball he received in Test cricket. He was selected for the first Test in 1978 against Pakistan who, denuded of their five most accomplished players, casualties of World Series Cricket, were the weakest team that country had sent to England for twenty years. David arrived at the crease with England comfortably placed, 101 for 2 facing a total of 164 and Sarfraz Nawaz, the only class bowler in the Pakistan attack, injured. Liaquat Ali responded with what might be described as a friendly bouncer, which David contemptuously pulled to the mid-wicket boundary. He went on to provide the only batting of true international quality until the arrival of Ian Botham at no. 7. Although England did reach 452 for 8 declared, a batting line-up of Brearley 1, Wood 2, Radley 3, Roope 5, Miller 6, explains why this twenty-one-year-old left-hander lifted the tone, so immediately and dramatically.

When David Gower remains at the crease for any length of time, whatever the situation, he automatically accrues runs both sweetly and swiftly, because he is not only an instinctive stroke-maker; but his footwork is frequently at fault, and this enables him to hit the balls into areas which a more orthodox player would not. His square-drive off his front foot played with his bat a long way from his body and his two feet in a half-cock position provides a perfect example, indeed he scores many runs from over-the-crease positions, neither forward, nor back. His methods depend upon the keenness of his eye and one would not fancy his chances of still being able to churn out the runs like Geoff Boycott did in his forties. David's technique means that he is often giving opposing bowlers a chance, especially outside the off stump, because it is only a matter of time before he will attempt to drive a widish ball through the covers without moving his front foot outside his off stump, or to cut without his left foot moving towards the off side, with the bat brought down on the ball and the wrists rolled. As a result he is obviously more effective on true firm pitches where the bounce is true and he can hit through the line with confidence, so that David is usually more successful overseas than in England.

At the commencement of the 1988 summer, I saw him batting for Leicestershire on a heavily grassed, guaranteed-result pitch, where the bowlers were able to make the ball deviate and rise sharply off the seam. Although these conditions were well exploited by Leicester's four-man pace attack, they did not suit David's highly individual style. Wickets like these are better for batsmen like Peter Willey – who is prepared to wait, drop the rising ball dead by giving with the bat at moment of contact, and dab, nudge and push – or, the sound and solid Nigel Briers, than for a daring stroke-maker with the mercurial touch. The inevitable outcome was that David neither spent the time at the crease, nor acquired runs in the quantities one would expect from him on the standard Grace Road wickets of yesteryear; it also meant that he went into the Tests against the West Indies without the confidence which stems from making runs in the middle. The outcome was sad and predictable. The 'golden boy' of English cricket, who with 7000 runs in 100 Tests had proved his ability at the highest level, found himself struggling against a good West Indian attack on wickets which, in the main, were far less helpful to pace than they had been on England's last tour to the Caribbean. There he had headed the English averages by a not inconsiderable margin when the bowling was considerably more hostile. The outcome this time was that the selectors dispenses with his services for the final Test when, ironically, the Oval wicket would have suited him far more than any of the other four.

David's most unenviable task, was to lead England against the West Indies in 1984 and again in 1985–6, when all ten Tests were lost and England was 'blackwashed' by the World Champions. Whoever had captained in England, when Peter May and his fellow selectors appeared to have no idea of what constituted our strongest side and used twenty-four players in the series, was destined to lose heavily. However, I believe David should have done better in the Caribbean, because there the England team played below its potential. David himself batted bravely and was the only player to average over 30, but his relaxed style of leadership, which had worked so well in India in 1984–5, was unsuited to this situation. He sorely missed his vice-captain, Mike Gatting, who had his nose broken by a ball from Malcolm Marshall before the Tests began and was out of action until the final Test, by which time the England party had become a bitter, beaten and bemused outfit. On the tour to India and Sri Lanka the Gower–Gatting combination had provided a nice balance, not unlike one often encountered in a platoon during the war, with Gower in the role of the rather aesthetic, intelligent lieutenant with a public school background and Gatting as the vital sergeant, who could be relied upon to supply a touch of down-to-earth realism in a crisis. When a team is winning, such matters as indifferently organized practice and voluntary nets go unnoticed and unmentioned, but not when the side is being thrashed and the media are looking for reasons other than the superiority of the opposition.

Those two horrendous 'blackwashes' which his team experienced against the West Indies tend to make people forget just how well David captained England in India in 1984–5 when he won the series 2–1 against formidable opposition with a quite ordinary side. My one criticism on that tour was that his Press conferences were inclined to be a shade too condescending, though it must have been difficult to treat some of the questions seriously. I am sure that I would have enjoyed playing under David. All I ever wanted or expected from a skipper was a tactical awareness, ability as a player and occasional suggestions, allowing me to do my job to the best of my ability without interference. David's laid-back style would have suited my temperament admirably.

In some respects David Gower is a throw-back to the amateur of the past. His approach to life reminds me of that of Colin Ingleby-Mackenzie, who led Hampshire from 1958 to 65 with gaiety, humour and considerable charm. His much-quoted recipe for the success of his team, his insistence that his players be back in the hotel in time for breakfast, would have appealed to David. Although Colin, again like David, gave the appearance of being a carefree cavalier, underneath there was a hard, realist centre. Both were of course, flamboyant and somewhat unconventional left-handers, but whereas Colin was no more than a lively middle-order county player, as a career average of nearly 25 shows, David is a high-class international batsman. Both are very good company with great joie-de-vivre, who consider good parties an essential and who opens a magnum of champagne with the easy nonchalance that stems from dexterity and practice.

Neither believed in giving anything to the opposition, their tactics were never over-generous, and their field settings often tight and distinctly frugal. Both did lose their wickets from time to time with an over-ambitious stroke, but it is unlikely in the long term that they would have made more runs with more cautious methods which were foreign to their nature.

From *The Greatest Since My Time* by Trevor Bailey
(Hodder & Stoughton, London 1989).

Allan Border – Little Man, Big Heart

Trevor Bailey

For about five years when Australia took to the field it was Border versus The Rest. Time and again he played the big innings or rescued them when they were up against it. If he has a weakness it is to the ball swinging into him (the away swinger to the right-hander) and Richard Ellison did him twice through the gate in this fashion during the Aussie's unhappy tour (for them) of 1985. But he led his side to an ample 4–0 revenge when Australia returned in 1989. A tough, fine competitor. Here my Test Match Special friend Trevor Bailey, as fine a cricket writer as he was an all-rounder for England, assesses the enormous technical strengths of Allan Border's batting. (The piece was written before England's annihilation in the 1989 Ashes series.)

F.S.T.

Just before the end of Allan Border's first season with Essex (1986), I asked Keith Fletcher for his opinion of his ability as a batsman. He thought for a moment and said that Allan was the best player he had ever batted with. That is an enormous tribute when one takes into account the number of outstanding batsmen Keith has partnered at the crease in over twenty years of first-class cricket. In addition, Keith Fletcher, like most top-class cricketers, is chary in making assessments; but his view of Allan Border certainly substantiated my own belief that the Australian is a truly great batsman, who has not always received sufficient recognition because his style is practical rather than spectacular, and rugged rather than beautiful.

At Colchester, while Allan was hitting a chanceless, almost faultless, undefeated 130 against Nottinghamshire in 1988, Graham Gooch voiced similar admiration for one master craftsman by another. He believed that Allan's success stemmed from his careful selection – he literally treats every ball on its merits. He would inspect each delivery before taking the appropriate action, whether to drive, to block, to sway, to hook or to cut, which reduced his chance of making a mistake. Another major virtue for which both Essex captains were especially appreciative and, as outstanding batsmen themselves, could appreciate better than most, was Allan's ability to make runs and come up with the big innings when it was most wanted. This is exactly what he did at Castle Park against Notts. Apart from Gooch, who had contributed an effortless 36, all the front-line Essex batsmen struggled, eventually settled, played an inappropriate shot and then departed, but Border not only prospered, he made batting look – which it certainly was not – an easy, uncomplicated business. In so doing, he underlined why he has scored, and will continue to score, so heavily and regularly. Everything about his batting is well organized and technically correct, starting with a stance with his weight equally balanced on both feet. This helps him to move either forward or back easily, which he does, like most of the finest players, very late and also ensures that his head is in alignment, and still, at the moment when bat hits ball.

One of the charms of watching Allan Border at the crease, which was especially noticeable in this particular innings, was the way he, having first assessed each delivery, obtained his runs all round the wicket, in that wide obtuse angle stretching from fine leg to third man, with sound text-book strokes. He would be quite content to play a maiden over and await the arrival of a ball, not necessarily a bad one, from which he could score without risk. Like many small men, though not so many left-handers, Allan is a marvellous square-cutter. It is not merely the power of the stroke, but the correct footwork and the way he places the shot, so that one was able to predict with confidence a boundary whenever Eddie Hemmings dropped one fractionally short outside his off stump. It was to be expected that he should be strong off his legs whether pushing, clipping the ball to mid-wicket, hooking, pulling, glancing or sweeping, as these come easily to a small, high-class left-hander. What is surprising, however, is the quality and the straightness of his driving, not of a full toss, or half-volley, but a ball which is only fractionally over-pitched. It is his driving along the ground using a full swing of the bat which makes him so difficult to contain. Another asset is the speed of his footwork which enables him to reach the slow bowlers on the full pitch or the half-volley, and explains why he is so effective against the spinners and, indeed, is not unreminiscent of Neil Harvey in his prime.

Although Australians possess probably the two finest coaches in the world, climate and space, they have an inbuilt competitive streak, and this last characteristic is why, per head of the population and including all sports, they are probably the finest sporting nation in the world. It is this attitude which fires Allan Border, makes each innings a personal challenge and helps to explain his desire for large scores. He still has an insatiable appetite for runs, which is seen in the way he scampers between the wickets in an effort to turn ones into twos, and twos into threes, irrespective of whether the shot has been played by himself or by his partner.

The respect and affection with which Allan Border is held in Essex was increased by his performance at Edgbaston on one of those notorious 'there will be no need for any declarations, and it should end early' types of pitch, which were among the least satisfactory features of 1988. He was hit on the head by a bouncer from Merrick and required fourteen stitches in his ear. I can think of a number of cricketers who would have then called it a day, but very few who would not only have come back, let alone a guest player, to win his personal battle with the bowler by scoring a remarkable century. That took more than ability, that took strength and depth of character.

Border is relatively more effective in first-class cricket than in the limited-overs game, for in the former he can afford to treat each ball on its merits and does not need to improvise. This does not mean that he has failed to score heavily in one-day matches, for his ability to hit all round the wicket makes containment difficult. His off-side repertoire includes the run-down through the gulley area, the genuine cut off both front and back foot, the square-drive off the back foot, the cover slash, the cover drive and the straight drive, while his on-side range is similarly extensive. Even so, his basic technique and his temperament are even better suited to Test cricket, where he has an average of over 50, despite the handicap of playing a high percentage of his matches for a weak and struggling Australia.

Australia has never had the same belief in born and raised-to-be captains which was derived from the Victorian Public School system, as England. Their selectors pick what they consider to be the strongest combination, and then decide the most appropriate skipper, working on the assumption that one of the group should be able to do a reasonable job. Sometimes they have been unfortunate, though rarely; while they have always avoided the danger of including a captain who could not justify his place as a player. Allan is not a natural leader in the Richie Benaud or Ian Chappell moulds, but he takes his cricket very seriously, is liked and respected by his compatriots and has had the considerable advantage of being easily the best batsman in a team which, at the highest level, was short of class players.

Although I would prefer to watch David Gower batting I would want to have Allan in my side because, from the moment he walks out to bat after early wickets have tumbled and the bowling looks full of menace, one feels that here is the man to rescue the situation with a big innings, a fighter who revels in the challenge and who possesses the technique and the temperament to claw back the ground lost. How often opposing Test captains must have said, 'We had Australia on the floor, and then in came Border'!

From *The Greatest Since My Time* by Trevor Bailey
(Hodder & Stoughton, London 1989).

10

SHAMATEURS – THE TWO FACES OF W. G. GRACE

I always thought the business of Gentlemen and Players was ludicrous and was thankful when the distinction was abolished. The Gentlemen were the amateurs and the Players were the professionals and both Yorkshire and England tried for years to appoint an amateur captain, even one of inferior ability. It was ridiculous because, apart from the many privileges they enjoyed, many of those amateurs were drawing £1,000 a year in expenses when we were getting paid around £750. I described them as 'Shamateurs' and made myself somewhat unpopular. The snobbishness in my early days was unbelievable. As we shall see the business of shamateurism was nothing new. Indeed the great Dr Grace himself, who had scored no less than 6,008 runs for the Gentlemen against the Players, in fact grossed over £120,000 from cricket – and that was in the days when the pound was worth perhaps 50 times what it is today! But first a highly analytical tribute, worthy of Holmes himself, to the greatest of cricketers.

F.S.T.

The Greatest of Cricketers – W. G. Grace

Sir Arthur Conan Doyle

Sir Arthur Conan Doyle did more than create Sherlock Holmes. A doctor by training he also played occasional first-class cricket. 'Although never a famous cricketer he could hit the ball hard and bowl slows with a puzzling flight,' said Wisden. He once took 7 for 63 playing for MCC against Cambridgeshire and carried his bat for 32 against Leicestershire. It is said that Shacklock of Notts inspired the Christian name of Holmes and that Holmes's brother Mycroft was named after the Derbyshire cricketing brothers. Conan Doyle also played against Dr Grace, as he describes in this obituary piece.

In all first-class cricket in a career from 1865 to 1908 Grace scored 54,896 runs at an average of 39.55 and took 2,864 wickets at 17.99. He scored 126 centuries, many on much worse wickets than today's.

F.S.T.

27 October 1915 The world will be the poorer to many of us for the passing of the greatest of cricketers. To those who knew him he was more than a great cricketer. He had many of the characteristics of a great man. There was a masterful personality and a large direct simplicity and frankness which, combined with his huge frame, swarthy features, bushy beard, and somewhat lumbering carriage, made an impression which could never be forgotten.

In spite of his giant West-of-England build, there was, as it seemed to me, something of the gipsy in his colouring, his vitality, and his quick, dark eyes with their wary expression. The bright yellow and red cap which he loved to wear added to this Zingari effect. His elder brother, the Coroner, small, wizened, dark, and wiry, had even more of this gipsy appearance. I speak, of course, only of the effect produced, for I have no reason to think that such blood was in his veins, though, following Borrow, I am ready to believe that there is no better in Europe. There was a fine, open-air breeziness of manner about the man which made his company a delight and added a zest to the game. He was, of course, a highly educated surgeon, but he had rather the fashion of talk which one would associate with a jovial farmer. His voice was high-pitched, considering the huge chest from which it came, and it preserved something of the Western burr.

His style and methods were peculiar to himself. In his youth, when he was tall, slim, and agile, he must have been as ideal in his form as in his results. But as this generation knew him he had run to great size and a certain awkwardness of build.

As he came towards the wicket, walking heavily with shoulders rounded, his great girth outlined by his coloured sash, one would have imagined that his day was past. He seemed slow, stiff, and heavy at first. When he had made 50 in his quiet methodical fashion he was somewhat younger and fresher. At the end of a century he had not turned a hair, and was watching the ball with as clear an eye as in the first over. It was his advice to play every ball as if it were the first – and he lived up to it. Everything that he did was firm, definite, and well within his strength.

I have had the privilege of fielding at point more than once while he made his hundred, and have in my mind a clear impression of his methods. He stood very clear of his wicket, bending his huge shoulders and presenting a very broad face of the bat towards the bowler. Then, as he saw the latter advance, he would slowly raise himself to his height, and draw back the blade of his bat, while his left toe would go upwards until only the heel of that foot remained upon the ground. He gauged the pitch of the ball in an instant, and if it were doubtful played back rather than forward. Often he smothered a really dangerous length ball by a curious half-cock stroke to which he was partial. He took no risks, and in playing forward trailed the bottom of his bat along the grass as it advanced so as to guard against the shooter – a relic, no doubt, of his early days in the sixties, when shooters were seen more often than on modern grounds.

The great strength of his batting was upon the off side. I should not suppose that there was ever a batsman who was so good at controlling that most uncontrollable of all balls, the good-length ball outside the off stump. He would not disregard it, as is the modern habit. Stepping across the wicket while bending his great shoulders, he watched it closely as it rose, and patted it with an easy tap through the slips. In vain, with a fast bumpy bowler pounding them down, did three quivering fieldsmen crouch in the slips, their hands outstretched and eager for the coming catch. Never with the edge of the bat but always with the true centre would he turn the ball groundwards, so that it flashed down and then fizzed off between the grasping hands, flying with its own momentum to the boundary. With incredible accuracy he would place it according to the fields, curving it off squarely if third man were not in his place or tapping it almost straight down upon the ground if short slip were standing wide of the wicket.

In no shot was he so supremely excellent, and like all great things it seemed simplicity itself as he did it. Only when one saw other great batsmen fail did one realize how accurate was the timing and the wrist-work of the old man. When he was well on towards his 60th year I have seen him standing up to Lockwood when man after man was helpless at the other wicket, tapping those terrific expresses away through the slips with the easy sureness with which one would bounce a tennis ball with a racket. The fastest bowler in England [*usually said to be Ernest Jones, the Australian*] sent one like a cannon-shot through his beard with only a comic shake of the head and a good-humoured growl in reply.

Of his bowling I have very clear recollections. He was an innovator among bowlers, for he really invented the leg-theory a generation before it was rediscovered and practised by Vine, Armstrong and others. Grace's traps at leg were proverbial in the seventies. His manner was peculiar. He would lumber up to the wicket, and toss up the ball in a take-it-or-leave-it style, as if he cared little whether it pitched between the wickets or in the next parish. As a matter of fact this careless attitude covered a very remarkable accuracy. His command of length was absolute, and he had just enough leg spin to beat the bat if you played forward to the pitch of the ball. He was full of guile, and the bad ball which was worth four to you was sent, as likely as not, to unsettle you and lead you on.

Those who knew him will never look at the classic sward of Lord's without an occasional vision of the great cricketer. He was, and will remain, the very impersonation of cricket, redolent of fresh air, of good humour, of conflict without malice, of chivalrous strife, of keenness for victory by fair means, and utter detestation of all that was foul. Few men have done more for the generation in which he lived, and his influence was none the less because it was a spontaneous and utterly unconscious one.

The Disguised Professional

Ric Sissons

'Nice customs curtsey to great kings' was how *Wisden* in 1897 explained away the substantial and widely-known payments to W. G. Grace. They were considered 'anomalous'.

Ten years later Sir Home Gordon, writing in the *National Review*, took up 'the amateur question' in more forceful terms:

> The case of Dr W. G. Grace became an accepted anachronism and that of the late Mr W. W. Read was also treated as a thing apart. For those two then there are probably a score today, and the matter is euphemistically cloaked under the guise of 'expenses', the item for washing alone being on occasion preposterous.

These were not new revelations. In the 1878 edition of *John Lillywhite's Cricket Companion* Frederick Gale had criticized the 'gentlemen professionals' who posed as amateurs. During the 1890s the Rev. Holmes, through the pages of *Cricket*, had occasionally drawn attention to the matter. In 1893 he criticized the 'idiotic class barriers' which ensure there are 'amateur-professionals' or 'highly paid pros who pose as amateurs'. Two years later he attacked 'the snobbishness of the disguised professional'.

Joe Darling captained Australia on 18 occasions, toured England four times between 1896 and 1905 and was subsequently elected as an Independent in the Tasmanian Legislative Council. In 1926 he stated that 'very few of the amateurs in England in my time – or today – were amateurs. They were highly paid professionals.' Darling cites Grace, Stoddart, MacLaren, Jones and Jessop as the prime offenders.

It is clear in retrospect that for many years the MCC and the county Committees either turned a blind eye to the amateurs' remunerations or were directly party to contravening the ethics of the game as they claimed it should be played.

W. G. Grace

Examples of Grace's earnings from cricket are well-documented. In Eric Midwinter's biography of the 'Old Man' it is estimated that he grossed £120,000 from cricket.

For the 1873–4 tour to Australia Grace was paid £1500 or 10 times the amount each professional received, yet the party included such talented professionals as Harry

Jupp, Richard Humphrey and William Oscroft. Eighteen years later Lord Sheffield obliged with a fee of £3000, generous expenses and a locum for Grace's medical practice for the tour of Australia. Lord Sheffield lost £2000 on the 1891–2 tour, in part, according to Alfred Shaw, because of the captain's 'princely fee'. Arthur Shrewsbury, through the intermediary of his business partner Shaw, had given pre-tour financial advice to Lord Sheffield, but on being told he had substantially under-estimated the tour costs he wrote:

> I didn't know that Lord Sheffield had to pay for Grace's wife and family expenses in Australia. I thought he had repudiated that before leaving England. If he hadn't taken Grace out, Lord Sheffield would have been £3000 better off at the end of the tour, and also had a better team.

As secretary-captain of London county from 1900–04, Grace received an annual payment of £600 which was virtually double the earnings of the best paid professionals, despite his being well past his best by this time. The most blatant examples of payments to Grace were his two testimonials. The first, in 1879, raised £1458. The MCC hoped that the money would be used by Grace to buy a medical practice. The second, in 1895, was much more substantial. It totalled almost £6000. The *Daily Telegraph's* 'National Shilling Fund' accounted for more than £4000, the *Sportsman* and the MCC contributed £3000 and Gloucestershire a further £1500. In *Background to Cricket* Sir Home Gordon claims that 'a substantial portion went to pay his betting debts'. Before the turn of the century the highest sum ever achieved in a player's benefit was £2000 for Bobby Peel in 1894.

W. W. Read

Although always regarded as an amateur, Walter Read was the best paid pre-War Surrey cricketer. Until 1897 he held the nominal position of assistant secretary at the Oval with a salary package as follows:
 * £150 per annum,
 * a railway season ticket to and from the Oval,
 * four guineas per match,
 * an annual bonus of £100, albeit proportional to the number of matches he played.

It is obvious from the Surrey minutes and correspondence that there was never any question of Read working as assistant secretary. The payments to Read clearly contravened the MCC definition of an amateur, that 'no gentleman ought to make a profit from his services on the cricket field'. In 1895 Read was given the Surrey versus England match as a testimonial. It netted him £829, including £200 from the Club. The same year Bobby Abel's benefit raised £621, including 50 guineas from the county.

Walter Read retired in 1897 having scored 22,349 runs for Surrey. He may have batted like an amateur and been considered one socially, but he was paid as a professional.

A. C. Maclaren

A. C. Maclaren, the most notable Lancashire amateur, was the only cricketer at Old Trafford honoured with a 'star' contract and it was worth twice the annual earnings of the club's leading professionals.

S. M. J. Woods

Australian-born Sammy Woods was captain and secretary of Somerset from 1894 to 1906 on a salary of £200 per annum. After his retirement from first-class cricket he remained secretary until 1923. Sir Home Gordon, a good friend of Woods, commented that 'grey matter was not predominant in his powerful physique'. He recalled Woods telling him that 'there is one thing I have steadily tried to do: to drink more beer for the years I have lived than any other man who has ever come down from Cambridge'.

As in the case of the appointment of Mr V. F. S. Crawford as Leicestershire secretary in 1903, Somerset were keen that Woods would be in a position to play for the county on a permanent basis. In May 1907 Sammy Woods was rewarded with a testimonial which exceeded £1600.

The players in the 1880s and 1890s may have been some of the first popular sports' stars but within the cricket world they remained second-class citizens. Their subordinate position was perpetuated by a combination of paternalism, dependence, defence and strict discipline. Again in this respect they were no different from any other Victorian workers.

The 'irritating restrictions' and 'petty distinctions' which segregated the professionals from the amateurs included:
* separate dressing rooms;
* separate entrances on to the field of play – the amateurs used the pavilion's centre gate;
* separate travel arrangements to away matches – first-class for the amateur and third-class for the professional;
* different hotels or lodging houses for away games and
* if the professionals were invited into the luncheon room, separate tables and menu.

From *The Players – A Social History of the Professional Cricketer* by Ric Sissons (The Kingswood Press, London, 1988).

In 1952 Len Hutton became the first professional to captain England. In twenty-three Tests under him England won eleven times and lost four. He also regained the Ashes in 1953 and successfully defended them in 1954–5. Prior to that under three post-war amateur captains, Hammond, Yardley and Brown, England beat Australia just once in fifteen games, with eleven defeats. In county cricket Doug Wright (Kent), Dennis Brooks (Northants) and Cyril Washbrook (Lancashire) captained their sides from 1954. In 1959 only thirty-nine amateurs played in county cricket compared with over two hundred pre-war. Several of the regular amateurs were employed as county secretaries like Donald Carr (Derby), Trevor Bailey (Essex) and Wilf Wooller (Glamorgan), thus gaining their livelihood from cricket. In November 1962 MCC bowed to the inevitable and abolished the distinction between amateur and professional. Now all were simply cricketers. The same meeting voted to inaugurate a knockout competition and so limited-overs cricket was born, starting in 1963 with the Gillette (now NatWest) Cup.

F.S.T.

11

WARS OF THE ROSES

When I first played in the Roses matches spectators had to get there at least three-quarters of an hour before the start of play or they might be locked out – and those were the days, before police restrictions, when Old Trafford and Headingley could take crowds of 30,000! Mind you, they were some spectacle in terms of talent with the Yorkshire side fielding as many as ten internationals – Hutton, Lowson, Close, Yardley, Watson, Appleyard, Wardle, Brennan, Coxon and myself. Lancashire were almost as rich, with Washbrook, Ikin, Place, Hilton, Tattersall, Berry, Pollard, Greenhough and Statham. In these pieces Neville Cardus and Mike Parkinson both give us the feel and the atmosphere of the great Roses games of time gone by. Today some of the atmosphere is undoubtedly lacking in the crowd and you'd be lucky to get more than a few thousand. But the players still look to the Roses game with relish. It is the big one, with the rest of the country completely forgotten about. After all, it's none of their business anyway.

F.S.T.

Honest Cheatin' in Conformity wi' the Law

Neville Cardus

The Lancashire and Yorkshire match was every year like a play and pageant exhibiting the genius of the two counties. To watch it rightly you needed the clue; for years I myself had missed the point. There is slow play and slow play at cricket. There are batsmen who cannot score quickly because they can't, and there are batsmen who can score quickly but won't. In a representative Lancashire and Yorkshire match of 1924–34, runs were severely discountenanced. No fours before lunch, on principle, was the unannounced policy; and as few as possible after. But fours or no fours, runs or no runs, the games touched greatness because of the North of England character that was exposed in every action, every movement, all day. Imagine the scene: Bramall Lane. Factory chimneys everywhere; a pall of smoke between earth and sun. A crowd mainly silent; hard hats or caps and scarves on all sides. Makepeace is batting to Rhodes; old soldier against old soldier. Makepeace has only one purpose in life at the moment, and that is not to get out. And Rhodes pitches a cautious ball wide of the off-stump – pitches it there so that Makepeace cannot safely score off it; Makepeace, mind you, who is not going to put his bat anywhere near a ball if he can help it.

Maiden overs occurred in profusion. Appeals for leg-before-wicket were the only signs of waking life for hours. Often I thought that one day during overs, while the field was changing positions, somebody would return the ball from the outfield and accidentally hit a batsman on the pads, and then eleven terrific 'H'zats!' would be emitted by sheer force of habit. 'Aye,' said Roy Kilner, 'it's a rum 'un is t'Yarksheer and Lankysheer match. T'two teams meets in t'dressin'-room on t'Bank Holiday; and then we never speaks agean for three days – except to appeal.' The ordeal of umpiring in a Lancashire and Yorkshire match during 1924–30 was severe. One day at Leeds, Yorkshire fell upon the Lancashire first innings and three wickets – the best – were annihilated for next to nothing. Two young novices nervously discovered themselves together, holding the fourth Lancashire wicket, while thirty thousand Yorkshire folk roared for their blood; and the Yorkshire team crouched under their very noses, a few yards from the block-hole. By some miracle worked on high, the two young novices stayed in. Not only that; they began to hit fours. One drive soared over the ropes. George Macaulay, the Yorkshire medium-paced bowler (a grand fellow off the field, and on it a tiger with the temper of the jungle) glared down the wicket until his eyes were pin-points of incredulity and frustration. And Emmott Robinson, grey-haired in the service of Yorkshire and whose trousers were always coming down, an old campaigner who would any day have died rather than give 'owt away', kept muttering 'Hey, dear, dear, dear; what's t'matter, what's t'matter?' The two novices declined to get out; the score mounted – forty for three, fifty for three, eighty for three, one hundred for three. At that time the Yorkshire captain was not a good cricketer though a very nice man – an 'amateur' of course; for even Yorkshire continued to observe the custom that no first-class county team should be captained by a professional; even Yorkshire carried a 'passenger' for the sake of traditional social distinctions. But he was only a figurehead; the leadership was a joint dictatorship; Rhodes and Robinson. This day the situation got out of hand; the novices each made a century. One of the umpires told me, after the scalding afternoon's play was over: 'Never again; no more "standin'" in Yorkshire and Lancashire matches for me. Why, this afternoon, when them two lads were knockin' t'stuffin' out of t'Yorkshire bowlers, the row and racket on t'field were awful. George Macaulay were cussin' 'is 'ead off, and Emmott were mutterin' to 'isself, and poor owd captain 'ad been sent out into t'outfield so's 'e couldn't 'ear. At last I 'ad to call order; I said "Now look 'ere, you chaps, how the 'ell do you expect me and me pal 'Arry to umpire in a bloody parrot 'ouse?"'

Roy Kilner, Yorkshire to the end of his days and for ever after, once said that umpires were only 'luxurious superfluities' in a Lancashire and Yorkshire match. 'They gets in t'way. What we want in Yarksheer and Lankysheer matches is "fair do's" – no umpires, and honest cheatin' all round, in conformity wi' the law.'

The joke about Yorkshire cricket is that for Yorkshiremen it is no laughing matter. It is a possession of the clan and must on no account be put down, or interfered with by anybody not born in the county. When Hammond was an unknown young player, I went to look at him at Huddersfield one day when Gloucestershire were playing Yorkshire. I had been told he was more than promising. He came to the wicket and began well. I watched from behind the bowler's arm, through Zeiss glasses. Suddenly a ball from Emmott Robinson struck him on the pad, high up. Every Yorkshireman on the field of play, and many not on it, roared 'Howzat!' Involuntarily I spoke aloud and said, 'No, not out, not out'; through my glasses I had seen that the ball would have missed the wicket. Then I was conscious I was being watched; you know how you can somehow feel that somebody behind you is looking at you. I turned round and saw a typical Yorkshireman eyeing me from my boots upward to the crown of my head, his hand deep and aggressively thrust in his pocket. 'And what's the matter with thee?' he asked.

No writer of novels could make a picture of Yorkshire life half as full of meaning as the one drawn every year in matches between Lancashire and Yorkshire. Cricket on the dole; nature herself on the dole. The very grass on the field of play told of the struggle for existence; it eventually achieved a triumphant greenness. 'Tha can't be too careful.' If it happened to be a fine day, well – 'maybe it'll last and maybe it won't.' And, if things are at a pretty pass all round, well – 'they'll get worse before they get better.' 'Ah'm tekking nowt on trust.' At Sheffield there is a refreshment-room situated deep in the earth under a concrete stand. I descended one afternoon for a cup of tea. A plump Yorkshire lass served me and I asked for a spoon. 'It's there, Maister,' she said.

'Where?' I asked.

She pointed with her bread-knife. 'There,' she said, 'tied to t'counter, la-ad.' So it was; a lead spoon tied to the premises with a piece of string.

*   *   *

Emmott Robinson was a grizzled, squat, bandy-legged Yorkshireman, all sagging and loose at the braces in private life, but on duty for Yorkshire he was liable at any minute to gather and concentrate his energy into sudden and vehement leaps and charges and scuffles. He had shrewd eyes, a hatchet face and grey hairs, most of them representing appeals that had gone against him for leg-before-wicket. I imagine that he was created one day by God scooping up the nearest acre of Yorkshire soil at hand, then breathing into it saying, 'Now, lad, tha's called Emmott Robinson and tha can go on with new ball at t'pavilion end.' Emmott cherished the new ball dearly; he would carry it between overs in person to the next bowler needing it after himself; and he would contain it in the two palms of his hands shaped like a sacred chalice. If some ignorant novice unnecessarily threw the new ball along the earth, Emmott gave him a look of wrath and pain. He was not a great cricketer in technique; but by passion and by taking thought he became so. But for me he will be remembered for the Yorkshire stuff in him. He had no use for the flashing bat school, 'brighter cricket' and all such nonsense. He dismissed it with one good word: 'Swashbuckle,' he called it. Life had taught him to take no risks. It was sad to see him passively looking on if Yorkshire happened to get into trouble. The Yorkshire team without him was never the same again. After he had been absent from the side for a year or two, some mishap unexpectedly deprived Yorkshire of two men at the beginning of the second day of a Lancashire and Yorkshire match; and Emmott was requisitioned as one of the substitutes; there, once again, we saw him taking the field against the ancient enemy on an August Bank Holiday. He had not been in the field five minutes before he yapped out a violent appeal for leg-before-wicket. He was standing at backward-point and nobody appealed with him, not even the bowler, who was George Macaulay. The umpire who dismissed the appeal was the old Derbyshire cricketer, Arthur Morton; 'Not out,' he said derisively, and added, 'An' look 'ere, Emmott; that's not pla-aying' in this match – so keep thi mouth shut.'

From *Autobiography* by Neville Cardus
(Hamish Hamilton, London, 1984).

Not What It Was

Michael Parkinson

There is no more certain indication of the decline of cricket as a popular spectator sport than the pathetic attendance at the present day Roses game. Once there were glorious encounters as important as test matches played to full houses and the noise of battle on and off the field.

The fact of the matter is that today, except for a few nostalgics like myself, the prospect of a Roses game quickens as many pulses in Leeds and Manchester as the news that the Turkish Bank Rate has been increased to $6\frac{1}{2}$%. Today the Wars of the Roses is a tired headline to sell a story that people stopped reading a long time ago.

It still means something in 1947 when I went to my first Roses game. We queued for three hours outside Bramall Lane, Sheffield, and in that blessed moment when I was jostled through the turnstile, I felt as if I had arrived in Paradise. We sat on the hard concrete terracing of the football ground, knees drawn up under our chins, arms pinioned by one's neighbours, and there we remained for the next eight hours in a state of acute physical discomfort sustained only by the knowledge that this was no ordinary cricket match.

To stand up to relieve cramped muscles was to invite an apple core or a pork pie crust to the back of the head along with the usual polite advice to 'Sit thissen down Gladys.'

The Bramall Lane crowd has never been in sympathy with the physical discomfort of others. A few seasons later I was sitting on the same piece of concrete watching Yorkshire play Middlesex. It was during Compton's golden days when his face shone from every [hoarding] advertising hair dressing. In Yorkshire, among the rank and file cricket supporters, at least, there was always a guarded attitude toward Compton. He was too flash for their tastes, too much of a fly boy. Brylcreem and cricket don't mix in Yorkshire.

On this particular occasion Compton was granted a privileged insight into the way that the cricket lovers of Sheffield feel about the suffering of their fellow men. Yorkshire were batting when play was held up by the apperance on the field of what is called a Sheffield mongrel, which is to say a dog of exceedingly dubious parentage. The dog careered around the field defying the energetic attempts of the Middlesex side to catch it. It should be explained at this point that the sympathies of the Yorkshire crowd were entirely with the Middlesex men, it being a commonly held view in Yorkshire that dogs are for racing and not for petting.

Eventually it was Compton who caught it. It had to be, it was his year. He swooped low as the dog raced past him and scooped it triumphantly aloft. The crowd was relieved that the game could go on but remained unimpressed by Compton's panache. Still brandishing the dog Compton trotted towards the pavilion and as he did so the creature, being born in Sheffield and therefore no respecter of personalities, bit him smartly on the arm. Compton dropped the animal and stood rubbing the bite. The huge crowd watched the performance dispassionately and then someone from the football terraces shouted 'Put some bloody Brylcreem on it Compton.'

I digress only to acquaint you with my neighbours on that lovely Saturday in 1947 when I saw my first Roses game. There was a roar as Sellers, broad as a muck stack, won the toss and chose to bat. In the opening over I caught the sense of tradition and meaning that set these games apart and made them special. There was an atmosphere, a tenseness about the play which I have never tasted since, not even in a Test match. When Yorkshire lost their first wicket with only twelve scored the ground was in mourning. There came to the wicket an unknown called Smithson playing in his first Roses game.

In a situation calling for trench warfare Smithson decided on a cavalry charge. No one who sat in Bramall Lane that day could forget his innings. By any standards it was a good one, but in the context of the grim Roses games it was sensational. He defied tradition by hitting three fours and a three in one over, he made old men wince with his daring strokeplay and when he was out two short of his century every spectator creaked to his feet and applauded.

In his excellent book 'The Wars of the Roses' the late and very lamented A. A. Thomson recalls the innings and tells how, before Smithson went in to bat Emmott Robinson told him: 'Na, lad, what tha' has to do is shove thi' bat in t'blockhole and keep it there, chose 'ow.' When Smithson was out for 98 and with the cheers of the crowd still warming his ears, Emmott sought him out and reprimanded him for his 'outrageous levity'. At the end of the telling off Emmott was seen to shake his head despairingly and mutter, 'We'll never learn that lad.'

At the end of the day as we streamed out of grimy Bramall Lane, a scruffy, jostling, happy crowd, I felt privileged to have been initiated into cricket's most secret ritual. Warned by the presence of 30,000 others I felt part of a tradition that would last for ever no matter what became of the rest of the game. In fact I was in at the beginning of the end. The tradition of the Roses game has not been enough to protect it from cricket's present maladies. What was once a meaningful occasion is nowadays just another three-day match.

Two years ago I went to Old Trafford for the Roses game. The morning sun shone, Old Trafford was beautiful, Trueman had his tail up, the Yorkshire fielding was of the highest and all these treasures were witnessed by a crowd so small it might have arrived in one double-decker bus. My mind drifted back to Sheffield in 1947 and I would willingly in that moment have swapped my seat in the stand for that concrete step if it meant a taste of the old excitement. I pitied any young boy being blooded that day at Old Trafford. His head full of dreams and Cardus beforehand, he must have felt bitterly let down by what he saw.

In the bar I tried to start an argument but no one wanted to know. Completely disenchanted I found myself a lonely place in the sun and sat there sulking. Nothing altered my mood, not even the fact that at close of play Yorkshire were well on top.

I went home knowing that things would never be the same again, that to recapture what used to be I must now rely on memory, Sir Neville and my old man. The consolation is that tradition dies harder with the players than the spectators and this fact at least will ensure that what happens in the middle during a Roses match will continue to be very different from the sort of thing that happens in any other kind of cricket match. The players of both counties are sufficiently well versed in their heritage to regard the Roses games as something special no matter how large the public apathy. I cherish one story told me by that fine Yorkshire cricketer Ken Taylor, now coaching abroad, that accounts for the reason why the Roses game will always be held to be different by the players. Taylor's first game against Lancashire was at Old Trafford. Yorkshire were doing badly as he walked down the pavilion steps on his way to the wicket. The Lancashire crowd was baying for blood. As he approached the pavilion gate it was opened for him by a uniformed attendant who, as Ken passed, politely saluted and then said out of the corner of his mouth: 'Best of luck lad, but think on, don't be long.'

Taylor was still bemused by this quote as he took guard. Unfortunately he was bowled first ball. He made his way sadly and slowly back to the pavilion. At the gate the same man was waiting. He opened the gate, touched his forelock and said: 'Thank you lad.'

From *Cricket Mad* by Michael Parkinson
(Stanley & Paul, London, 1969).

12

CIDER AND SIXES – THE LIGHT AND THE DARK

When the Strain Tells

From the end of April to the middle of September the professional cricketer is a very busy man indeed. With the advent of Sunday cricket the modern county player is on call for 120 or so days out of 140 and of the remaining 'Free' days he will probably appear in a local game for his county's beneficiary. In the so-called Golden Age of cricket before World War I the schedule was much easier, each county arranging its own fixtures, which varied between eighteen to twenty-eight games or fifty-four to eighty-four playing days, with only the star players on call for extra festival games. Added to the hours on the field there is extensive travel, and even more now that the Sunday game comes in the middle of a county game and may not even be in the same location. I always wonder there are not more accidents with county cricketers pounding down the motorways at unsociable hours.

Peter Roebuck in his book *It Never Rains* described the Somerset dressing room on a Saturday in August in Derby: 'Seven of our party are lying around sound asleep, heads on pads or towels. I've never seen a team so white and drawn ... the barrage of travelling and concentration has taken its toll ... County cricket is rather like trench warfare at times; the qualities you most need to survive are graft and endurance.' Not surprisingly some players do crack under the strain. But of course there are many lighter moments too – not least from the big-hitting cidermen from Somerset. That's why I have called this section 'The Light and the Dark'.

F.S.T.

Harold Gimblett

David Foot

The first county match I ever saw was Somerset versus Sussex at Eastbourne – a long way from my native Yorkshire. Indeed, it was the first time I'd been away from home. I was seventeen in that year of 1948 and had just been picked for the Yorkshire Federation Tour, in which Yorkshire Colts played the Colts of other counties. So we found ourselves in Sussex and were taken to see a county championship game. It was a memorable one because Harold Gimblett, prince among Somerset batsmen, scored 310. He was one of the few opening batsmen who would dare to hit the first ball of an innings for six and his cover drive was in Hammond's class. He loved to hook fast bowlers 'as if he were tossing hay back at Bicknoller'. I was to play against him a few years later, little realizing the mental turmoil he was undergoing, which caused his premature retirement from first-class cricket in 1954. Indeed, I was bowling at him at Taunton in his very last game for Somerset.

F.S.T.

*   *   *

Harold Gimblett is the greatest batsmen Somerset has ever produced.

He wiped the mud off his farm boots and as part of a West Country romance, quoted more graphically and affectionately than Exmoor's own Lorna Doone, he hitched a lift to Frome before scoring a sensationally fast and fearless century on his county debut. No one has yet scored more runs, hit more hundreds or reached a higher score (310 at Eastbourne) for Somerset.*

Gimblett has no native rival and my lofty assessment cannot readily be challenged. Lionel Palairet came from Lancashire and Ian Botham from Cheshire, Sammy Woods from Australia and Vivian Richards from Antigua. Harold Gimblett was born in a creeper-clad Bicknoller farmhouse, on the other side of the Quantocks from the county ground in Taunton. This undulating, red-earthed corner of West Somerset also nurtured J. C. White. The home of Bill Greswell, one of the innovators of late inswing bowling and subsequently the county president, was only a few boundary lengths away. Those rolling hills had the tang of freshly cut grass and linseed oil.

* Since beaten by Vivian Richards 322 at Taunton v. Warwickshire in 1985 and Jimmy Cook's 313 not out at Cardiff v Glamorgan in 1990.

In a county renowned for the muscle and imprudence of its batsmen, Gimblett could be the most audacious of them all. Very few opening batsmen have hit more steepling sixes, have so readily dismissed caution in the first over of the day, delighted more schoolboys or threatened more diehards, short of imagination, with apoplexy. He played for Somerset from 1935 till 1954 and cattle market trade, across the road from the cosy county ground, fluctuated according to Gimblett's prowess at the wicket: the farmers left the pens and put their cheque books away when he was in full flow. On early closing day in Taunton, the cricket attendance depended on him.

Marguerita (Rita) Gimblett told me: 'I used to find out from the radio whether Harold was going well. If he was, I'd rush along to the ground. Sometimes, by the time I got there, the spectators would be streaming away, glum and silent. And I always knew what that meant – he was out!'

He played just three times for England and not only Somerset's cricket lovers, who doted on his deeds, were aggrieved. Some would argue that he contributed to that kind of wanton neglect by a defensive, tetchy manner that found less than favour with the game's hierarchy including Sir Pelham Warner. Gimblett was never servile or particularly tactful; his withering observations, not always out of earshot, could easily be misconstrued. Some of his verbal strokes had every bit as much venom as those that scorched past extra cover. It should also be remembered, to adjust the perspective, that in the post-war years, Hutton and Washbrook were two other valid reasons for his scant recognition as a Test player.

Harold Gimblett was a marvellous cricketer by so many standards. At times, his batting, instinctively classical when the mood was right – and more exhilarating than any of his contemporaries – came near to genius. The farmer's boy diligently improved his defence, learned how to hook, from one of his great idols, Herbert Sutcliffe and became a stylist who could fashion his innings as handsomely as Palairet once did. His cover drive was even envied by Hammond, though the pair had no natural rapport; the straight drive for six, a mischief maker off the first ball of the innings, was flawless in its ruthless execution.

I first saw him play during the Thirties in my home town of Yeovil. It was an annual fixture for Somerset, and Gimblett was the attraction, along with Wellard who was expected to put balls out of sight over the Westland hangers.

Hero worship is healthy; but such doting dreams are fragile. Harold in the flesh, as I discovered some years later, was not always an engaging person.

Two years before he died he phoned me one evening from his home, then at Minehead. Would I help him write a book? 'I don't want it to be like any of the other cricket books. I want the public to know what it is really like being a professional sportsman, when you're a worrier. The mental battles for me have been enormous and maybe it would be a good idea to put it on record.' I got the impression that he also saw the exercise as a form of therapy.

He told me he had bought a small cassette recorder and I encouraged him to start putting thoughts, as they occurred to him, down on tape. He could let me have the various cassettes and I could use them as the basis for a book.

The meeting never took place. I waited for the summons. Then, with a ghastly suddenness, I read of his death.

At home I listened to the cassettes. They were like very private documents that he wanted now to make public. They were subjective: astute, perceptive, belligerent, unhappy and at time on the point of being irrational.

> David, this is my attempt at a possible book. The only thing I'm absolutely certain of is the title. At the ripe old age of 62, I feel the title must be 'No More Bouncers' ... not that I was ever afraid of 'em.

He took more than his share of bouncers, on and off the field.

At the age of 38 Gimblett was inclined to look an old man. He was still far and away Somerset's best batsman. The straight drive was as potent as ever; the cover was in Hammond's class. But, for reasons which came from within him, his career was almost over. I leave the words to him. They came out in a whisper, adding to their poignancy.

> I couldn't take much more. I was taking sleeping pills to make me sleep and others to wake me up. By the end of 1953 the world was closing in on me. I couldn't offer any reason why and I don't think the medical profession knew, either. There were moments of the past season that I couldn't remember at all. The Christmas was a complete blank to me. My doctor studied me and said: 'I think you ought to see the doctor in charge of Tone Vale' [mental hospital]. He in turn saw me at Musgrove Hospital in Taunton but I had a complete blackout from the moment I sat down in the waiting room until an hour later when my wife came in. The doctor turned to Rita and said: 'I think Harold had better come out with us for a few days.'
>
> I was put on E.C.T. [electro-convulsant therapy] treatment. There were several of us having it twice a week. I felt like death but I remember joking to the others: 'Well, I open for Somerset so I may as well go first.' Rita came to see me and couldn't believe the difference. I had some colour back in my cheeks ...
>
> I stayed there for sixteen weeks and then it was spring again. Time for the nets once more. But I'd felt so safe at Tone Vale. No one could get at me. I just knew I wouldn't complete the next season. The first match was at Notts. I just folded up and had to stop the game while I was batting. I desperately tried to pull myself together. Reggie Simpson said: 'Go off, Harold.' I looked at Reggie and said: 'No, I mustn't. If I go off, I'll never come back again.' Of course, they didn't understand. I struggled to make 29. Back in the dressing room I was at the bottom of the pit ...

He slumped on the bench and went into a bitter little monologue. 'I wanted to get it all out of the system in one go.' As a result of that outburst, he claimed, he was reported to the secretary for setting a bad example. Versions vary about what precisely happened during that match at Trent Bridge in early May and the one, immediately afterwards, against Yorkshire at Taunton.

There has been much vague talk about how Gimblett walked sullenly out of the ground after making a duck in the Yorkshire match.

> I went out to the wicket and tried – I really tried. But I got caught off my gloves when Trueman was bowling. I came in and said I couldn't take any more. I was finished. It was my last game for Somerset. I knew I shouldn't have played. I packed my bags and went home. I moped about the house. Soon I was to return to hospital as a voluntary patient.

In fact, he never played for the county again. For weeks he distanced himself from the county ground. He rarely checked the scores in the stop press. Now we come to a quite remarkable incident. I relate it again in Gimblett's own words.

> Towards the end of the season the Indians were playing at Taunton. I suddenly thought I'd like to go and see some cricket. I self-consciously walked along St James Street with Rita. 'Nip up to the scorebox and ask Tom Tout if I can sit with him.' Tom agreed and found a chair for me. I didn't want anyone to know I was there but it got around.
>
> Tom went down to tea and he got the kitchen staff to bring me up a cup of tea and a bun. Believe it or not, they charged me. Soon after, I got a message that the secretary wanted to see me. I went down to his office ... and he ordered me out of the ground. I was speechless. I just turned and went back to collect my wife. On the way I bumped into Ron Roberts, in those days a cricket writer covering Somerset. 'If you want a story, Ron, here's one for you. I've just been ordered out of the Somerset county ground.'
>
> That had to be the final severance with the county I had joined in 1935.

Harold Gimblett took his own life with an overdose in March 1978.

Dr K. C. P. Smith, a consultant psychiatrist with great experience in advising on the anxieties of professional sportsmen, said that a low-key man like Gimblett, needed high excitement. When he failed to reach it, he became phobic: hence talk of too much responsibility, ill health, money anxieties. 'He had strong 'anti' feelings of aggression. He enjoyed hitting a ball around the ground, having revenge on the world at the same time. He could become enjoyably paranoid – as in the case of the M.C.C. – and play a new type of game against the establishment. But he couldn't keep it up, so became depressed again.'

'His religious life,' says his brother Dennis, 'Was emotionally-based and somewhat unstable. It was subject to his being the centre of its activity, rather than its being centred on God. He lacked the inner strength to resist the temptation to commit suicide. He was inclined to put himself first and God second. There was also a pantheistic streak which revealed itself in his love of natural beauty and belief in the divine presence of nature. From this, he drew peace and harmony. He was at heart a true countryman – he believed in God as the creator and not so much in God the redeemer. I have always thought his life would have been much happier and more full of contentment if he'd found a country job, out of the public eye.'

Throughout his perplexed adult life he was periodically burdened by phobias and various forms of paranoia. He catalogued what he saw as broken promises and rejection. Some of the festering complexes were still on his lips in the closing days of his life. He was unforgiving: for instance, he claimed that no one from the county went to visit him in hospital at Tone Vale, when he first went there for a course of E.C.T. That, he repeated years later, was especially hurtful to him. He came to hate officials and some committee members of the Somerset club, and the game of cricket as a whole.

He worried incessantly about money when often there was no need. In his last cassette, recorded in a weak, faltering voice, he returns repeatedly to the theme of insecurity and fears about providing for his wife and himself in their old age.

This brings us to his overriding sense of rejection. Although in truth he chose to leave Somerset, he was upset when the committee vetoed the comeback that R. J. O. Meyer and others were advocating. Eric Hill, by then on the committee, told me: 'The decision was made partly on medical advice but mainly because of the effect we felt failure might have on Harold and the team.'

It is a melancholy and not irrelevant fact that other fine cricketers, for a variety of reasons, have killed themselves.

William Scotton played for his country fifteen times between 1881–6. But by 1893 he had lost his place in the Nottinghamshire side and this, according to the inquest that followed his suicide, preyed seriously on his mind. Certainly his loss of form depressed him.

The magnificent Arthur Shrewsbury, immortalized by Dr Grace's sweeping compliment, shot himself one May evening in 1903, the season after he gave up playing for Nottinghamshire. Latterly he worried unnecessarily about an illness and pined for summers' days back at the wicket. Arthur played 23 times for England and was the outstanding professional of his day. Those glories no longer sustained him; he could not bear to think that his cricket was over for good.

Albert Trott played for both his native Australia and England. From 1898 he played for Middlesex and, it could be wryly claimed, he had indelible links with Somerset. He was given the Somerset fixture for his benefit match in 1907 and with exquisite timing he spectacularly demolished the West Country side's second innings. Trott started by taking the wickets of Lewis, Poyntz, Woods and Robson in four balls; then he finished off the innings with another hat-trick. In spite of such dramatics and some magnificent hitting, Trott was already on the wane and was no longer seen, arguably, as the best all-rounder in the world. He had suffered various rejections, like being left out of the ninth Australian side to tour England. His private proclivities were apparently a matter of some concern and there were innuendos about his liaisons with a Taunton woman of, as they quaintly said in those priggish, hypocritical days, 'easy virtue'. He was a great cricketer but by 1914, with war looming, he had had enough of life. He shot himself in his lonely London digs.

That was a year before A. E. Stoddart, of Middlesex and England, who twice captained his country in Australia, shot himself through the head.

And then there was R. C. Robertson-Glasgow, who enjoyed his cricket like Gimblett for Somerset; and who, like him, died from an overdose of drugs. He was a lovable player who traded on gentle eccentricity and was apt to bamboozle various captains by disappearing into the beer tent at Bath and Weston between wickets. His felicitous prose also hummed with humour. His private pain he kept to himself.

Is it just a quirky coincidence that half a dozen especially talented cricketers – no doubt there are others – killed themselves? Certainly in most of those cases cricket, indirectly at least, was a contributory cause.

Like few other sports of the field, cricket is played very much with the mind. Only the unimaginative player escapes the tensions. Many, whatever their seeming unconcern, retreat into caverns of introspection. I long ago discovered that for the professional cricketers, particularly the sensitive ones, the match-winning cheers and bar-room bonhomie are outweighed by collective self-doubt and dressing room silences. Harold Gimblett knew all about that.

From *Harold Gimblett – Tormented Genius of Cricket* by David Foot
(Heinemann, London, 1982).

None of the problems I faced in life, marital or otherwise, ever affected my performance on the field. When I walked to the end of my run-up there was only ever one thing on my mind – how to remove the opposition as quickly as possible.

In a phrase, I suppose I was determined to bloody well show them all. And the more the MCC put me down, the harder I tried.

F.S.T.

Strangely Qualified

R. C. Robertson-Glasgow

R. C. Robertson-Glasgow played cricket for Oxford University, a good match for the counties in the twenties, and also for Somerset. He was strangely qualified for the latter – a Ciderman by remote adoption.

F.S.T.

After Middlesex led by 24 of the first innings, we ran up 349 for 8 declared. We won, by 139 runs; but that was nothing to me compared with bowling Hendren when he was well set at 50. It was a snifter, though I say it, bending in very late from the off. I walked on air, and would certainly have missed any catch that had come in my way.

We followed this victory by beating Essex by 239 runs. The match was doubly notable; first, because Douglas Jardine, in a spell of seven overs and 3 balls took 6 for 6, including the mighty P. Perrin, bowled for 0. Douglas, with a pensive and halting run, bowled what purported to be slow leg-breaks. Secondly, I acquired a nickname which has stuck ever since. Charlie McGahey and A. C. Russell had put on some 50 runs at the start of their second innings when I bowled McGahey with a full pitcher which he later referred to as a yorker. In the bowels of the pavilion, Johnny Douglas, the Essex captain, asked him how he was out, and McGahey answered: 'I was bowled by an old —— I thought was dead two thousand years ago, called Robinson Crusoe.' ...

On Wednesday, June 2, 1920, I first met John Daniell [the Somerset Captain] and next day he asked me to play a few matches for Somerset. This was an unorthodox request, as I had no qualification for Somerset, having been born in Edinburgh and living wherever the family, or parts of it, happened to be. Technically, I was qualified for Scotland, but the Scottish selectors have always been rather stuffy about Anglo-Scots, and I was never asked to play for the land of my birth. Not that it matters.

My connection with Somerset was our cousins, the Foxcroft family, of Hinton Charterhouse, of whom Charlie was Member of Parliament for Bath and a High Tory of the utmost spirit and pugnacity. But John Daniell reckoned that this would be good enough. At least I was in the position that no other county could claim me, even supposing they wanted my services. Herein was the mistake made by my friend Leonard Crawley. Being qualified for Durham, he went off to play for Worcestershire, and Durham objected. This little difference led, finally, to a quarrel between George,

Lord Harris, Hon. Treasurer to MCC, and Lord Deerhurst, the High Panjandrum of Worcestershire. They met, it was reported, on the pavilion steps at Lord's, and Lord Deerhurst swept off his grey top-hat and offered Lord Harris a short speech of congratulation on his alleged mismanagement of cricket. Stormy tea-cups long ago.

From *Crusoe on Cricket* by R. C. Robertson-Glasgow
(Pavilion Books, London, 1985).

Farmer Jack White

R. C. Robertson-Glasgow

John Cornish White relied on flight and accuracy rather than spin. From 1919 onwards he regularly took 100 wickets a season for Somerset and twice did the 'double' (1,000 runs and 100 wickets) in 1929 and 1930. He took 2,361 wickets for 18.58 runs each. He played in fifteen matches for England and the high point was the tour of Australia in 1928–9, as vice-captain under A. P. F. Chapman when his economical bowling made him, in the the words of M. A. Noble, the former Australian captain, 'the only man who truly and actually won the Ashes'.

F.S.T.

Let us here consider one of the great figures in English cricket, farmer John Cornish White. His father, in a comfortable silence that was presumed to represent approval, used to watch him trundling away his slow left-handers at Taunton. Jack inherited his father's tranquility. I never saw him excited, though sometimes he would go a little redder when an important catch was missed off his bowling, and he would mutter: 'The trouble about that cock is that he's fast asleep.' Most cricketers were 'cocks' to Jack, and he would say of some new batsman who had not troubled the scorer: 'I didn't think *that* cock would last long, Glasgy; he had one of those fancy caps on.'

Jack came from Stogumber when he first played for Somerset in 1909, at the age of sixteen. His beginnings were negligible. He took 1 wicket for 90 runs in three innings. Next year, he did little better, and for the next three summers, Somerset, oscillating around bankruptcy and the bottom of the Championship, did without him. But in 1914 he returned to head their bowling averages with 93 wickets. In 1919 he began that run of uninterrupted success which placed him among the few unquestioned greats. In 1921, against Worcestershire at Worcester, he took all 10 wickets in an innings.

He differed from other famous slow left-handers in that he relied very little on spin. Varied flight, guile, persistence, liveliness from the pitch, these were his secrets. He also had the gift of making the ball bounce unusually high for a slow bowler, and he took many wickets by causing the batsmen to play the ball too high on the bat to silly-point, where John Daniell awaited the prey. Many times I stood to White at short slip, and I never saw a bowler who so harassed and teased the batsmen. He would peg down the most aggressive, till by sheer desperation they were driven to their doom. Frank Woolley, being left-handed, was usually White's master; but the most accomplished right-handers, such as Hobbs, Hendren, and Hammond, did not attack him. He bowled, and they played. Hendren used to say that no bowler made him so tired.

White was turned thirty-seven when he first went to Australia, and his fair hair was greying at the temples. Few could have prophesied that he was going out to his triumph. From the first, the Australian batsmen could not decide whether to play him back or forward. Young Archie Jackson, that beautiful player who was to die four years later at the age of twenty-three, solved the problem; but for the most part the batsmen were driven into the crease. The climax came in the Fourth Test, at Adelaide, when, in stifling heat, White bowled 124 overs for 13 wickets and 256 runs, an historic feat of combined endurance and skill. England won by 12 runs. White had to leave the field to change his shirt twice during one afternoon, and, at the same time, to take in a draught of the right stuff. Hendren tells how, when the last Australian batsman, Don Blackie, came in to face White, he, that guileful Patsy, standing close to the wicket, said: 'My word; I wouldn't be in *your* shoes for all the money in the world.' 'I shall never forget,' said Hendren, 'the look of pitiable horror that came over Blackie's face when I said this.' Bravely Blackie defended for a few balls, then was caught by Larwood at deep mid-wicket.

White was a grand fielder to his own bowling, and a good slip-fielder to anyone else's. He was less effective farther from the wicket, as he could throw but little. As a batsman, he had begun, and looked like finishing, close above the extras; but, by industry and imitation, he made himself into a counting player. He used his pads more than most, and I have a fancy that the umpires whose decisions Jack, as a bowler, accepted with such equanimity gave him the benefits of many doubts. I never saw him throw his wicket away. He had the husbandman's dislike of waste. Apart from cricket, he was no games-player, but he was a cunning cardsman, and one of the best poker-players in Somerset. He migrated from Stogumber to Combe Florey.

No other county knows so well how to name its places. I used to drive with Guy Earle on summer evenings after the cricket from Taunton to Minehead, through Bishop's Lydeard, Combe Florey, and Crowcombe. Guy was a mighty hitter, the highest and farthest of his day, with arms like a grown man's thigh. At Bristol, in 1923, he hit 111 off Gloucestershire in the August Bank Holiday match, scoring his first 76 in half an hour and lifting Charles Parker four times clean over the track that encircled the ground.

But it was the Kent bowlers who most suited his designs, and 'Tich' Freeman most of all. 'Tich' would arrive at Taunton on his way to his annual 200 wickets and Guy would hit him over the river or into the timber-yard. The supposed variety of the legbreak and googly lost all relevance. Guy put his left leg down the pitch and clapped the ball an awful blow. He regarded all bowlers as so much sawdust and any success on their part as a personal insult. Returning to the pavilion after being caught at third-man while trying a six to square-leg, he would cast down his bat with a resounding boom and say: 'I'll wring his ... little neck.' Within three minutes the thunder-cloud had almost passed, returning in little puffs when Guy would say, as he gazed at the cricket: 'I can't think how anyone ever gets out to that bandy-legged ...'

From *Crusoe on Cricket* by R. C. Robertson-Glasgow
(Pavilion Books, London, 1985).

'*Is the test match exciting, dear?*'

A. W. Wellard – Hitter of Sixes

Gerald Brodribb

The world of first-class cricket has never seen a more consistent hitter of sixes than Arthur Wellard of Somerset. In the course of a county career lasting from 1929 to 1949 he scored over 11,000 runs, of which over a quarter came from his 500 sixes. This is a greater quantity of over-the-boundary hits than ever achieved by any other players, with the possible exception of Jessop, whose number of such hits can never be known. Wellard's aggregate of sixes is even more impressive when particular seasons are considered. In each of four seasons he reached a total of over 50 sixes:

> 72 in 1935
> 57 in 1936
> 57 in 1938
> 51 in 1933

No other batsman has ever reached as many as 50 sixes in a season, and only a dozen or so batsmen have recorded as many as 30.

These figures are so overwhelming that it is not easy to know where to start in any survey of Wellard's hitting feats. But since we have broached the subject of 'records', we might first deal with the two occasions when Wellard hit 5 consecutive balls for six. Several batsmen have hit 4 consecutive sixes, but Wellard is the only one to go one better by hitting 5*, and he did this twice. The first occasion was in the match Somerset *v.* Derbyshire at Wells in 1936. Wanting 174 runs to win the match on an uneasy wicket, Somerset seemed beaten when their fifth wicket fell at 143. At this point Wellard came in, and was promptly dropped in the deep off Armstrong, a slow left-hander. But in that same over he drove 2 consecutive balls over the screen and out of the ground for six. Armstrong was then taken off, but soon came back again, much to Wellard's delight. The first ball he played quietly to leg; the second and third he sent over the heads of the spectators into the car park, the fourth went straight out of the ground and was lost, and the fifth and sixth were also driven high and straight right out of the ground. When Townsend caught him off Copson, Wellard had scored 86 out of 102 in sixty-two minutes, the game had been pulled round, and Somerset eventually won a great match by one wicket. Wellard's score was composed thus: 1 4 6 6 1 1 1 4 1 4 4 1 2 6 6 6 6 3 4 1 4 4 4. All 7 sixes came off two consecutive overs bowled by Armstrong – 0 4 6 6 1 0 0 6 6 6 6 6 – but, as has been explained, the

---

* A feat since beaten by Garry Sobers' 6 sixes in an over off Malcolm Nash of Glamorgan.

first of these overs ended one spell of bowling, and the other began another spell. Despite that gap, the fact remains that 10 consecutive balls which Armstrong bowled to Wellard cost him 47 runs, one of the most devastating onslaughts a bowler has ever suffered.

The ground at Wells is a small one, and two years later, against Kent, Wellard again made the most of it, this time at the expense of F. E. Woolley, then playing in his last season. Wellard had already hit 2 sixes out of the ground off Lewis when Woolley was brought on to see what he could do. Wellard swept his first 5 balls for six – 4 of them right out of the ground – and 3 were lost in the gardens. This led to a shortage of balls, and no sooner had the Secretary produced a replacement than another one was needed. The last ball of the over Wellard attempted to despatch like the rest (he himself thinks Woolley sent him an easy one on purpose), but he failed quite to get hold of it and it fell in the neighbourhood of the screen, where the fielder got a hand to it, but dropped it, and a single was taken. Wellard says that if the fielder had not touched it at all it would have carried over the line for another six. So Woolley's over ended up with 31 runs – 6 6 6 6 6 1 – to surpass by one run Wellard's previous best of 30 runs in an over. When out, Wellard had scored 57 runs, including 7 sixes, and in the second innings he scored 37, with 4 more sixes, making 11 sixes in the match, an extraordinary proportion for a match aggregate of 94.

On two later occasions Wellard hit 3 sixes off consecutive balls: off D. V. P. Wright, when he scored 21 against Kent at Maidstone in 1939, and off E. Hollies, when he scored 34 *v.* Warwickshire at Birmingham in 1949. No other batsman has appeared as frequently as four times on the list of those who have hit 3 (or more) consecutive sixes. It is at the best of times a difficult fear against an experienced bowler, but Wellard hit the ball with that controlled power which made such feats possible. He stood 6 feet 2 inches, possessed very strong hands (he sometimes used a bat weighing 2 lb. 11 oz) and increased experience enabled him, unlike many other natural hitters, to develop from a crude slogger into a scientific driver of extreme consistency. Anything pitched up he drove, with the knowledge that if he really got hold of the ball it would safely carry to the boundary. All round the country there are recollections of his hitting. ...

It would seem that the longest hit he ever made was one at Brabourne Stadium, Bombay, during Lord Tennyson's tour of India in 1937–8. In the fifth unofficial Test he scored 33, and his hit was made off the bowling of Amar Singh. He had just sent a six off Mankad into the Club House, and then, batting at the opposite end, he drove Amar Singh towards the North Stand and out of the ground. W. J. Edrich in his book *Cricket Heritage* describes the hit:

'Wellard straight drove Amar Singh sky high over the sight screens, over the top of the stand behind it, and out of sight. I was sitting with Lord Tennyson at the other end of the ground, and I said, 'Good heavens, that one's gone right over the top!' Lord Tennyson said, 'Don't be a damn fool; no one could do it.' This was interesting because Tennyson himself was a tremendous hitter. I confirmed my statement, and Tennyson said, 'I'll lay you a pound you're wrong.' I took his bet and his money. It was 97 yards when we measured the distance from the wicket to the edge of the turf where the sight screen stood; then there was a cinder track, then a series of terraces, then the stand, over 60 feet high. The ball had skied over the whole lot into the blue Indian distance.'

Wellard himself considers that hit the biggest he ever made, and both N. W. D. Yardley and Alf Gover rank it as the biggest hit they ever saw. Gover recalls it as a low, skimming hit which made the umpire duck, and then went on and on and on, until it finally rose to clear the stand and vanish for ever. It was obviously one of the greatest hits in the history of the game.

From *Hit for Six* by Gerald Brodribb
(Heinemann, London, 1960).

The Catch That Never Came Down

R. C. Robertson-Glasgow

From the inimitable 'Crusoe' a very tall story indeed

F.S.T.

What you tell me is very interesting,' said Drayson; 'but did I ever tell you the story of the catch that never came down?'

I stirred uneasily. Distant rumours of this – well – story had reached me some years before. There was a ruminative wildness in Drayson's eye. He helped himself to a cigarette, settled into his chair, and said: 'You don't believe it, of course. No one wants to believe it. It doesn't suit them. It cracks science from top to bottom. It wrecks Newton and Einstein; Jeans and Horstflobbler and that bunch would have to think again. But I know. You see, I was the bowler.'

'What and where was the match?'

'I'll leave you to guess, and just tell you what happened.'

'Ah.'

'We were sworn to secrecy. You see, it would have been awkward for the Club, if it had got around. Either everyone would have wanted to come and play here, to see if it would happen again, or else no one would have consented to play on a ground where a ball might disappear upwards for good. Nervous cricketers could never have stood the suspense. Any moment it might have come. A casual jerk from third-man; gone for good. A promising leg-break; switched away into eternity. Cummings, the treasurer, foresaw the implications; and already he had to answer to the committee for the unaccountable absence of a new ball. But it never happened again; and now the ground is built over.'

There was a short silence.

'It was in the second over that it happened, on the first ball. Curlew, our fast man, had opened in a very erratic manner. His first two balls went full pitch to Wilkinson, the wicket-keeper, nearly vertical wides. The next two were long-hops, which the batsman hooked for four each; then two more full-pitchers. The second of these was immensely, almost inhumanly, fast; and it nearly decapitated Wilkinson, I remember it bounced back an unusual distance from the screen. I asked Curlew at the end of the over what he was up to. He was puzzled, and said the ball was very slippery; dangerously slippery, he thought, and it didn't feel quite like an ordinary ball. It was warm, he said, to the touch. He was right. There was an unearthly warmth about that ball.'

Drayson sat up straight in his chair. He spoke more slowly, and in a lower tone. 'I recall the start of my over,' he went on, 'as if it was yesterday. Two women had begun to settle in front on the screen with a picnic-basket and a small dog. It took some time to move them, also to shift Gandars, a minor poet, who was lost to the world at square-leg when he should have been at mid-on. I was itching to bowl; for the ball was getting warmer. It had reached the temperature of an unsatisfactory hot-bath. You know my style; slow tempters, with a bogus twirl of the hand to indicate leg-break. I tossed it up. The batsman mistook it for a half-volley, as so many have done to their cost. The upward sweep of his bat caught the ball on the rise, and it soared into the air.

'A light breeze seemed to be wafting it towards Wilkinson at the wicket. I called his name, and he began to revolve, in his clumsy manner, underneath it. Gandars, for no apparent reason, shouted 'Mine!' and teetered in on his toes from mid-on. Cover-point began to interest himself; and I stood half-way down the pitch, in an alert posture. Then I noticed something. The ball was not coming down. It went on up; slowly, slowly, getting smaller and smaller. Ganders, who is short-sighted, was the first to give up. He shouted 'It's gone. Holy mushrooms. That's done it!' and put his hands in his pockets. The batsmen, after running three, stopped, and both stared into the sky. The ball was now only just visible, about the size of a moderate spider, some 150 feet up. There, for a space, it stopped, hovering in miraculous indecision. If it didn't, well . . . It didn't.

'One spectator thought we were being funny, shouted something about 'horse-play', and left the ground. Cartwright, the groundsman, walked out to the pitch, looked steadily up at the ball, then at me. 'Who done that?' he asked, unanswerable; then felt he was a fool; which he is; and began to laugh stupidly. Then the batting side came out, mostly running. Wilkinson wanted to send for a gun. 'Extreme range,' he explained, 'but it's worth trying.' Suddenly the ball shot up again, and in a second was lost to view. It just went, I tell you, slap into the void – empyrean, if you like.'

'Did you get another?' I asked.

'Oh, yes,' said Drayson, 'We got another; and we finished the game, though I can remember next to nothing of it. It fell pretty flat, you see. At tea we arranged to keep the affair a secret, and the spectators, just a handful, agreed. But now, of course, it doesn't matter who knows.'

'I wonder if it ever came down anywhere, Drayson.'

'I should doubt it. In fact, I hope not. I prefer to think that for one instant in the world's history the laws of gravity were suspended.'

From *Crusoe on Cricket* by R. C. Robertson – Glasgow
(Pavilion, London, 1985).

The Croucher

Neville Cardus

He was the most remarkable hitter the game has produced. 'The most consistently fastest scorer I have seen. Gilbert Jessop drew the crowds even more than Bradman I should say,' declared Sir Jack Hobbs. He once hit 101 out of 118 in forty minutes against Yorkshire at Harrogate. Among 53 centuries there were five double centuries including 233 out of 318 in 150 minutes for an England XI v Yorkshire at Lord's in 1901. The following year he was to earn undying fame at the famous Oval Test, hitting 104 in 65 minutes, to enable England to win by one wicket.

F.S.T.

It does not always rain at Old Trafford. The ghost of a happy small boy walks there, to this day. Old Trafford was bombed by the Germans. I might have thought it was being bombed, except that the possibility of bombs on cricket fields had not yet occurred to us, when first I saw Gloucestershire playing at Old Trafford round about 1899. Towards lunch-time I left my seat to buy a bottle of ginger-beer before the crowd swarmed into the refreshment-room. I was placing my money on the counter, standing on tiptoe to reach, when suddenly there was a terrible noise and crash. Broken bottles and splinters of glass flew about everywhere, and I thought that the end of the world has come and that Professor Falb had been right after all. A man in the bar soothed my fears. 'It's all reight,' he said, in a strong and honest Lancashire speech, 'it's all reight, sonny – it's only Jessop just coom in to bat.'

After Ranjitsinhji and Victor Trumper, Jessop was the most incredible cricketer that ever lived. Nowadays when a slogger hits sixes, you will hear people call him 'a regular Jessop'. It is a libel. Jessop was not a crude slogger; he did not heave his bat about from a fast-footed position, rooted to the earth. A good bowler can get a slogger caught in next to no time by sending him an outswinger just a little short. Jessop scored thousands of runs at a great speed against some of the greatest bowlers in the history of cricket. Rapid scoring is not possible unless a batsman can cut. It is the presence of the cut that compels a bowler to avoid bowling that just-two-short-of-a-length ball which cannot be driven. Jessop had a flexible wrist, and his square-cutting was as terrible as his hooking. And so the bowler was obliged to pitch the ball up to Jessop's bat – and then he sprang upon it like a tiger. He was a small compact, sturdy man, with a square chin, and he walked to the wicket ferociously, then bent low over his hat. They called him the 'Croucher' ...

> the human catapult
> Who wrecks the roofs of distant towns
> When set in his assault.

At Kennington Oval in 1902, Jessop played the most wonderful innings in all the annals of Test matches. On a bad wicket England were trapped; they needed 263 to win. Three men were out for 10, and five for 48 – the cream of English batsmanship; Maclaren, Palairet, J. T. Tyldesley, Hayward and Braund. Nothing apparently could be done against the Australian attack on the vicious turf. F. S. Jackson played a watchful game while the pitch was at its worst; but in the circumstances science was out of the question. For science demands some foundation of logic and order; and how was it possible for mortal batsman to apply known principles to bowling which on an insane wicket performed illogicalities of spin, and behaved like something in a Walt Disney film? Jessop came forth, and he at once took the game out of the prison of cause and effect; he plunged it into the realms of melodrama, where virtue is always triumphant. Before he came to the wicket on this lurid afternoon, the Australian team had been a ruthless machine – the unplayable ball and the clutching hand in the slips. In a short period this same Australian team was reduced to a rabble. Jessop scored 50 in 55 minutes; and then another 54 in ten minutes; that is, he made 104 in 65 minutes, in a Test match, on a bowler's pitch, after his team had lost five wickets for 48. Kennington Oval that day went crazy. People had been leaving the ground in thousands. Jessop caused delirium; perfect strangers embraced. The ball was a dangerous missile all over the ground and out of it. Fieldsmen went in danger of decapitation. The windows of Kennington were threatened, and the neighbouring streets were noisy with an excited mob who could hear, if they could not see, what was going on inside the Oval.

From *Autobiography* by Neville Cardus
(Hamish Hamilton, London, 1984).

Over the Pavilion at Lords

Sir P. F. 'Plum' Warner

Oxford University and captain of Middlesex and England, one of the game's greatest servants, chairman of Test selectors, and manager of touring teams, 'Plum' Warner was knighted Sir Pelham in 1937, and became MCC President in 1950. Founder of *The Cricketer*. He recovered the Ashes in Australia in 1904 and his own ashes were scattered at Lords in 1963.

F.S.T

Sir, It was in the MCC *v*. Australia match at Lord's at the end of July 1899, that Trott drove Mr M. A. Noble, the Australian, clean over the pavilion. I was playing in the match and was sitting in the second row of the pavilion seats just behind Mr C. I. Thorton, a giant hitter himself, and I remember it as if it were but yesterday. Just to find the range, as it were, Trott has previously driven the ball twice into the pavilion, and then came this mighty blow – a straight drive – the ball landing in the garden of Philip Need, the dressing-room attendant, and one of the nicest, best, and most faithful servants MCC ever had. I can see 'Alberto', as Trott was called, leaning on his bat as he gazed upward as this sixer climbed the sky.

Earlier in the same year Trott had only just failed to clear the pavilion, an on-drive off F. W. Tate, the father of the present Sussex bowler, hitting the iron scroll work with 'MCC' engraved on it on the top of the South Tower, the ball bouncing back into the pavilion seats below the Committee Room.

Without wishing in any way to lay down the law, I am ready to lay long odds that the only occasion on which a ball has been hit over the pavilion at Lord's was by Trott on the occasion named. Mr F. T. Mann nearly succeeded in so doing, driving Rhodes three times in the course of one over on to the top of the pavilion. That was, I fancy, in the year 1928, and the match Middlesex *v*. Yorkshire.

Trott's historic hit ruined his batting, for ever afterwards he went about armed with a 3 lb 'club' trying to 'carry' pavilions. He was a great all-round cricketer, but, as Mr G. J. V. Weigall would put it, he had 'sawdust in his brain!'

I am, &c.
P. F. WARNER

In recent times Mike Lewellyn, of Glamorgan, and Kim Hughes, of Australia, have reached the top deck of the pavilion. The old pavilion was a good deal lower than its successor, which was opened in 1900 and stands today.

From *The Way to Lord 's – Cricketing Letters to the Times*
(Willow Books, London, 1983).

Death of A. E. Trott

It is said that Trott became obsessional in his attempts to repeat his feat. In time it so preyed on his mind that his entire game – and life – were upset by it.

F.S.T.

Famous cricketer found shot

31 July 1914. The death is announced of Albert Edward Trott, the well-known Australian and Middlesex cricketer. He was found dead in bed yesterday by his landlady at his residence in Denhigh Road, Harlesden. Trott had a wound in the temple and a Browning pistol was found beside him. The police and a doctor were summoned, but death was practically instantaneous.

For some considerable time Trott had been an in-patient at St Mary's Hospital and only left that institution recently. He was 42 years old, and had lived for nearly $3\frac{1}{2}$ years at Harlesden.

Trott was a very great cricketer and a man who, in spite of faults, was quick to win affection. The modern professional is very different – and in many ways superior – to his predecessor, but in older days there were many more of the class that may be called 'characters,' and Trott was essentially one of these.

The feat, probably, that his name will always be remembered by is that of being the first, and at present the only man who has ever hit a ball over the present pavilion at Lord's. Possibly there may have been bigger hits on the ground. Long did Trott persevere in his ambition to make this feat, and at last he achieved it. He used the most enormously heavy bat in his efforts – it is rumoured that it was over 3 lb – and his batting powers suffered probably in his many attempts. Trott was essentially an all-round cricketer, a very great, and in some ways unique, bowler, a good hard-hitting batsman, and a glorious field, particularly in the slips.

A younger brother of Harry Trott, the famous Australian captain, he had made his mark in Australian cricket before he came to England and was engaged as a member of the M.C.C. staff, and qualified for Middlesex, for whom he did great service in the late '90's and the early years of this century. His great years were 1899 and 1920, when he achieved the feat of getting over 200 wickets and making 1,000 runs, which so few cricketers have accomplished. For a number of seasons afterwards he was one of the mainstays of the Middlesex side, but his batting deteriorated and then, after a time, his bowling. He was comparatively quite young when he retired from first-class cricket and should have had many more years of cricket in him. He was, of course, a member of the Middlesex team that won the Championship in 1903.

Another 'record' that stands to his name is that of doing the 'hat trick' twice in a single innings (in one instance taking four wickets in four balls). This was accomplished in his benefit match against Somerset at Lord's in 1907.

His claim to greatness as a cricketer will rest chiefly on his bowling. He was essentially one of all paces and all kinds of balls, and was never afraid to try experiments, even at the cost of runs, to get a man out. His fast 'surprise' yorker was as good a ball probably as any bowler of normally medium pace could spring upon the batsman. There was no apparent change of run or action, and then down it would come as fast as anything the fastest bowlers could do. For all batsmen Trott at his best had terrors, and the best admitted that he was most interesting to play, because one never knew what was coming next.

From *Double Century – Cricket in The Times, Volume One, 1785–1934*,
ed Marcus Williams
(Willow Books, London, 1983).

When a Fiver Fixed a First-Class Game

Bill Andrews

'Shake the hand that bowled Bradman' was a traditional greeting from Bill Andrews, the cheerful Somerset all-rounder (he twice did the 'double' of 1,000 runs and 100 wickets). He never ceased to love Somerset cricket – despite being sacked by the county four times – and was chief instigator, after his retirement, in bringing Brian Close from Yorkshire to captain Somerset, which then became a county to be reckoned with. Life was hard for professional cricketers in the thirties as Bill describes in the second of these pieces. He also reveals that even first-class cricket was sometimes fixed – though nothing compared to the football bribery scandals. It took only £5 in 1936. And yes, he did bowl Bradman – for 202.

F.S.T.

The last match of the 1936 season, home to Lancashire at Taunton, holds amusing memories for me. R. J. O. Meyer had passed his century in the second innings and it was clear that we had saved the game. Suddenly R.J.O. turned to George Duckworth behind the stumps: 'If I make 200, I'll subscribe £5 towards Jack Iddon's benefit.' It apparently appealed to Lancashire. None of the regular Lancashire bowlers went on again – Phillipson, Sibbles, Nutter, Pollard, Hapwood and Iddon.

The marvellously eccentric and mischievous Meyer reached 202 not out and the following non-bowlers turned their arm over: Washbrook, 4–0–15–0; Paynter, 3–0–6–0; Duckworth, 6–0–37–0; Oldfield, 2–0–21–0; W. H. Lister, 1–0–11–0. Yes, Duckworth even took the pads off. An expensive switch it seems.

It's incredible that such an incident could have happened in first-class cricket. But remember it was the last match of the season.

There was a sequel. After the game, Duckworth came into the professionals' dressing room and said Mr Meyer had gone home. The promised fiver for their beneficiary hadn't been paid. The pros managed to scrape the money between them. And, of course, they were quickly repaid.

R.J.O., later to become founder headmaster of Millfield School at Street in Somerset, was a surprisingly fine all-rounder. As a bowler, like George Geary, Jack Mercer and Alec Kennedy, he could serve up every seamer in the book – and perhaps go a little further than the others because he had a leg-spinner and googly up his sleeve as well. The trouble was that it was never easy to place a field to his bowling because he tried the lot on a good wicket. As a batsman, he had all the strokes and it was a pity for Somerset that he could not find time to play more in the late thirties.

Mention of a bowler-batsman 'deal' reminds me of a kind of arrangement that I had with my good friend Joe Hardstaff at Weston-super-Mare back in 1935. After this great batsman reached his century, he whispered to me: 'Keep the ball up, Bill, and I'll give you my wicket.'

The next ball I bowled him was a charitable half-volley. It came back with tremendous power, skimmed my fingers and nearly went for six.

'O.K. Joe,' I shouted, 'Just play your natural game. I don't want any more of those caught-and-bowled ...'

I bowled the immaculate Hardstaff at 128. I can't remember if he gave me his wicket. Knowing Joe, I expect he did.

Three In a Bed

On Jubilee Day, 1936. Somerset had travelled up to London overnight for a match at the Oval. The amateurs were all booked into an expensive hotel. Harold Gimblett, Horace Hazell, our twelfth man Herbert Hunt and myself were all looking for somewhere to stay.

At last we found a modest boarding house near Paddington. We were told the charge was 3*s* 6*d* for bed and breakfast – and that was about our price. All the landlady had available, however, was one single bed and a three-quarter-size one, in the same room. Over the years we had learned to rough it as cricket professionals but this was the worst yet. We also had to tick our names off on a slate as we came in at night.

There was only one answer. Harold Gimblett was the man who should be scoring some runs at the Oval, so we gave him the single bed. The rest of us tried to squeeze into the three-quarters-size one. And it was one of the hottest nights of the year in London.

Just when the three of us were on the point of getting some sleep, about 3 am there was a movement in the room. Harold was walking about. He suddenly threw the window open. 'I can't sleep. The concentration is too much and I'm making too many runs.' In fairness to Harold he had made 93 and 160 not out in the previous match against Lancashire.

You can imagine what Horace Hazell and myself thought about this. Our figures at Old Trafford had just been 5 for 201 and 2 for 115 respectively. The prospect of Surrey batting first at the Oval was too much for us. They did. But Gimblett didn't let us down. He stroked a delightful half-century.

Often Arthur Wellard and myself used to share a double bed on away games to save expenses. I had a fright in the early hours of one Sunday morning when I felt something like a pin sticking into me. I turned on the light and gingerly felt half-way down the bed. It was Arthur's set of false teeth – they must have slipped out during the night. We always used to have an extra pint on a Saturday night.

In 1938 the Australians visited Taunton in late July. They took a look at the perfect strip and again none of their star batsmen wanted to stand down. We batted first and were all out for 110. The Australians replied with 464, declared and then they had us all out for 138, to win by an innings and 218 runs.

Traditionally, we never seem to get the Australians on a 'green 'un' or on a day when there were rain clouds or enough atmosphere to make the ball swing. This time, Bill O'Reilly and Fleetwood-Smith were the bowlers on form. C. L. Badcock (110) and Don Bradman (202) piled on the runs.

By the time Bradman got to the wicket the shine had long been taken off the ball and there was little swing left. But I was determined to keep the ball up to him. I was surprised to find him playing me defensively on the front foot. I thought, 'Here should be a chance for the leg-trap.'

His first two scoring shots, off the edge of the bat, went in the air between my close leg-side fielders. Both would have been catches if they had gone fine to Arthur Wellard or forward to 'Bunty' Longrigg. Instead they went squarish and I won't name the other two fielders in my leg trap. The ball went for 2 runs each time and Bradman muttered something like 'Bad luck, son' when he came down to my crease, running between the wickets.

There was no more playing forward after this. He hit me all over the field and I finished with 2 for 108. Generously he gave me his wicket in the end. To reinforce my claim that I had Don in trouble early on, there is confirmation both in *Wisden* and in A. G. Moyes's book on Bradman.

From *The Hand That Bowled Bradman* by Bill Andrews
(Macdonald, London, 1973).

Sad Lament For Sorry Cidermen

Jack Fingleton

From 1952–5, to the distress of all good Cidermen, Somerset were seventeenth out of seventeen in the championship, a record of failure only exceeded by Northants in the thirties. There was even talk of Somerset losing it's first-class status. Perhaps it never did because of dedicated work by supporters and because of the rustic charm described here by Jack Fingleton.

F.S.T.

August 22 1953, London down to Taunton: Somerset were wooden-spooners last summer and will be so again. It is sad to see a county fall upon such evil days and when that club, as Somerset does, serves the first-class cricket outlet for Devon, Cornwall and Wiltshire as well. The county had some great players over the years – the fabulous Sammy Woods, Australian born, of both rugby and cricket distinction whose outlook on life is shown by the jaunty pose he has on the donkey in the photograph in the pavilion – the Palairets – Jack White, whose slow to almost stationary left-handers twiddled Australians out in 1928–9 – Arthur Wellard, a most attractive all-rounder – and Gimblett, another dasher who was thrice in the running to come to Australia but never came.

The Taunton ground is full. Across the road in a sheep and cattle sale farmers with leggings and odd hats prod and survey the beasts. In the distance are the pretty Quantock Hills. On the ground mingle all manner of delightful characters. One with long side-beavers carries a crook like Mary. Oi be in Zummerset, Oi be, listening to a throaty gargling accent. And London is only three hours away in the train!

A little Somerset piece recurs: –

> *When be yon blackbird to?*
> *Us know where he be.*
> *Underneath yon wurzle bush,*
> *And us be after he,*
> *He be chasing we all day,*
> *Us be chasing he.*

But it must be said by a Somerset man.

Hassett and McDonald put on a century stand but it is early obvious why Somerset 'be where she be'. The bowling, apart from Hall, a hard-trying fast bowler, is all over the ship and at least three of the fieldsmen could do with a range-finder as they return the ball yards wide of the keeper. I counted four full-tosses in one over.

Len Hutton is resting from the Yorkshire team today. Hassett would be justified in doing the same but he hits up a sparkling 148. It is his fourth century of the tour and, from the viewpoint of strokes, his best. Davidson hits his first first-class century and he and Lindwall add 100 in 45 minutes. The Somerset crowd be very appreciative, they be, and Ring delights them more by opening with a 6. So Lindwall hits another. Hassett and Davidson have also hit a 6 apiece so de Courcy follows suit. He bats brilliantly. Only Craig and Hole miss the scoring bus. Craig pads up and is out lbw for the third successive innings. Hole skies one and two Somerset fieldsmen attempt the catch together, one emerging with the ball and the other with a bung eye.

Another good day of hitting but a veil is best drawn over the Somerset out-cricket. Hall, who had copied Lindwall in some things, never stops trying but the best of the rest are Kamah Saeed, a young Pakistani, and Wight, of British Guiana, who apparently has seen Ramadhin bowl. A few of the young professionals are mighty noisy in the pavilion as I yarn with J. C. White who, strangely, has no position in the Club. Not much is achieved in cricket without discipline.

From *The Ashes Over the Years* by Jack Fingleton
(Pavilion, London, 1986).

A Breathless Close in the Hush Tonight

Peter Grosvenor

In 1972 the sports editor of the *Daily Express* asked specialists on the paper to write about their favourite sport. I chose cricket and then we invited readers to say what they liked about the sport. Sender of the best card got seats to Lord's for the 1973 Test against the West Indies. It was quite a day. Play was interrupted by a bomb scare and Garry Sobers' swashbuckling 150 not out was interrupted by an attack of stomach pains due to a sleepless night on the tiles (see the piece on Sobers under All-Rounders, page 97).

P.G.

Lord Mancroft once said: 'The English not being a spiritual race have had to invent cricket in order to give themselves some conception of eternity.'

Even as a devotee, I have to admit that there are times when the game unfolds a little too slowly.

But that makes the electrifying moment all the more memorable.

For me the most incredible was that celebrated 1963 Test at Lord's against the West Indians when a draw, tie or victory for either side was possible right up to the last ball.

Heroic Brian Close was actually charging down the wicket to Wes Hall at his fastest and getting knock after knock on his body which he never even bothered to rub.

The Finale – with an injured Colin Cowdrey coming in to bat one-handed either to save the match or win it – was pure Henry Newbolt as in that famous poem: 'There's a breathless hush in the close tonight.'

Someone remarked: 'There's a breathless Close in the hush tonight.' He was bruised all over. It was a draw more exciting than any win.

The West Indians, captained by the late Sir Frank Worrell, were real cricketing ambassadors on that tour.

I rank tustles with the old enemy – the Aussies – as more blood feud than entertainment.

Provided the news is good, I actually enjoy getting up at 6 a.m. on a freezing winter morning, running a nice hot bath, and listening on the transistor to the latest score from sunny Sydney.

Remembering the way Bradman's Aussies humiliated us in 1948. I shall always rejoice at whatever margin we beat Australia by – preferably a repeat performance of the Oval, 1938, when we smashed them by an innings and 579 runs.

This episode also burnt a hole in Bradman's psyche. When the Aussies lashed up 721 in a day against Essex in 1948. Keith Miller kept urging Bradders to declare. The little man just shook his head dourly and said: 'Remember the Oval in 1938.'

It was a fine moment when Colin Milburn collared the Aussie attack at Lord's in 1968, making the cream of their Test bowlers look like village trundlers.

Milburn's mighty frame flexed the bat like a piece of matchwood while the bowlers were running up. Twelve 4's and two 6's in a pre-lunch 83. Something to celebrate and that's what I did.

Cider boy

Only one other man in recent times could equal Milburn for cultured hitting and that was farmer's boy Harold Gimblett from my own county of Somerset.

I've seen Harold crack the first ball of the first innings for a 6 against Sussex at Frome, which was also the scene of his memorable debut for the county when he smashed Essex for a century in only 63 minutes. (I was two years old at the time, but I've heard about it so often it seems as if I was there.)

I've supported my cider boys through thick and thin since 1946 when Somerset skittled the Indian touring team for 64 before lunch on a green wicket at Taunton. It's been a bit thin at times, but we've always enjoyed our cricket.

No one could hit sixes like Arthur Wellard, a 6 ft 2 in bowler with massive forearms. What a meal he'd have made of Gillette and John Player League cricket. More than a quarter of his 11,000 runs in first-class cricket came from 6's, a higher proportion than anyone else.

The moment Arthur came to the crease, the field retreated automatically as if running for cover. Then wham, wham, wham. It was good scientific slogging down the line of the ball.

Once, at Weston-super-Mare, Arthur hit a 6 which landed on the head of a man asleep outside the beer tent and knocked his hat off. He woke up looking very angry. They told him what had happened. He smiled beautifully. 'Good old Arthur,' he said, put his hat back on and went back to sleep.

From the days of Sammy Woods, Somerset have always welcomed the foreign import. To me, ageless Aussie Bill Alley was the greatest. In 1961, he scored 3,000 runs in a season. No one has done it since and now no one will.

Things are looking up again for Somerset with Brian Close as our skipper. I'll be back in the beer tent at Bath and Weston next summer – not just hoping for great things but expecting them.

From the *Daily Express* 1972

13

IT'S A FUNNY GAME
When Fred Hi-jacked the Bowling

Colin Cowdrey

Colin Cowdrey was right in the piece which follows when he said I wanted my 300th test wicket badly, and that, if you like, is why I hi-jacked the bowling by taking the ball from skipper Ted Dexter's hand at The Oval against the Australians in 1964. Mind you, I might have got the wicket a bit sooner in the game if I'd been allowed to operate off my shorter run which I'd been using for as much as four years – and it's not easy to switch a run-up off and on like a tap.

   But Ted wanted me on my long 'international' run which I had been less used to and that is why I had trouble finding my rhythm to begin with. Then came two wickets with two successive balls after I had 'hi-jacked' the bowling, and when I walked off at lunch time on a hat-trick for my 300th wicket I never felt more determined in my life. I only had a cup of tea and a ham sandwich. When play resumed I still had to finish the over with Neil Hawke facing, for my hat-trick. I wanted to pitch the ball on the off stump, but it was just outside and Hawke let it go. We had taken the new ball before I finally got Hawke, c. Cowdrey b. Trueman.

F.S.T.

Trueman, in that summer of 1964, was just beginning to run out of steam. He had been a world-class bowler for some twelve years. Now the old theatrical gestures were intact but some of the fire had gone. Indeed the only real luck he had was to be relieved from bowling on the Manchester wicket where fast-bowlers looked like galley slaves. Poor Fred Rumsey was given this task and was duly dropped for the final Test. Trueman, who had been experimenting with a shorter run for Yorkshire, was recalled to the England team. To say he was pleased was probably the understatement of the season for he had never been indifferent to records, and at that point in his career he had 297 Test wickets to his credit. He realized that he had not much longer to go and I think we all felt that this was to be his last appearance for England.

He had reason to be disappointed when England won the toss and batted, for the pitch on that opening morning was grassy and would certainly have given him real assistance. Instead it improved steadily during our innings and by the time Trueman came to bowl on it with trumpets blaring and great flourish, back now on his long 'international' run, it was clear there would be no immediate sensations. By the Saturday morning he was understandably tense and visibly nervous. He could not find his rhythm. He knew that he was bowling badly. To add to his depression Australia were rapidly running out of batsmen to bowl at, but none of them had fallen victims to Trueman.

The more anxious he became the worse he got until, in the end, Ted Dexter had to take him off. The words must have sounded like a life-sentence to Trueman. His jaw sank down on his chest as he walked from short-leg at one end to short-leg at the other, cursing his luck and visibly ageing.

It was at this point that England got stuck. We had begun the morning well but in the half hour before lunch we were bogged down again and Dexter was beginning to look as desperate as Trueman. He came in from the covers at the end of an over, tossing the ball from hand to hand, and as we met in the middle of the pitch he simply said, 'We must try something different, any ideas?' Whatever plans he had in his mind, only one thing was certain. None of them included bringing back Trueman.

For once, however, Dexter was over-ruled. Before I had time to answer his question a frantic voice just behind me said: 'I'm going to bowl.' It was Freddie Trueman about to prove that possession is ten-tenths of the law. For as Dexter said, 'Wait a moment Freddie,' Trueman snatched the ball from his captain's hand and began striding away towards the sight screen to begin his run. Short of actually starting a punch-up in the very centre of a Test pitch, Dexter was nonplussed. He chuckled away, walked out to cover point and accepted the situation for the next six balls. It may not have been orthodox captaincy but in this instance it proved to be wise. After all, if your leading bowler, a great one at that, wants to bowl, why stop him.

Trueman's first three deliveries could only be described as wildly inaccurate. But with the last two he saved himself. They were just enough on target to earn him another over, the last before lunch, without any real argument. And it was in that over that he knocked out Redpath's middle stump and then, with the very next ball, had McKenzie flashing a catch which I held at slip. So Trueman walked off to lunch not only just one Test wicket short of his 300 but also on a hat trick. The Oval was buzzing with excitement.

No luncheon interval can ever have been longer for us or Freddie, or shorter for the spectators. Trueman never left the dressing room. He ate and drank nothing, merely sat down, stood up, prowled around and then sat down before going through the whole meaningless routine again. He was rarely a man to show nerves but that day he could not conceal his agitation. He wanted that 300th wicket more than anything in the world. Equally, no spectator intended to miss that first ball. Waitresses rushed to and fro in the Oval dining rooms and cleared away cups of untouched coffee. There was no lingering over brandy or cigars as everyone jostled back to their seats while we filed down from the pavilion and into the field again. The tension was acute, not only for Trueman himself but for Neil Hawke, the new Australian batsman, and for the English fielders who must all, like me, have been fighting down the nightmare of how awful it would be at this moment to drop a catch.

At least there was to be no further delay. Trueman's over before lunch had not been completed so he had to bowl immediately. He ran up to the wicket in total silence, bowled – and Hawke, gently pressed forward and kept the ball out of his stumps. There was to be no hat trick and Hawke, with a tone of genuine sympathy called down the wicket: 'Bad luck, Fred. Well bowled.'

Yet happily the greater prize was eventually to come Trueman's way. For the next fifteen minutes or so he bowled with real inspiration. He was not perhaps quite so fast as he had been at the peak of his career, but all the skill and fire came flooding back and he was a wonderful sight to watch. It was as though he felt that this was his final act in Test cricket and he was determined to leave an indelible memory of his prowess. Ironically the wicket took some time in coming, but this time Trueman kept a firm control on his frustration and at last Hawke nicked a catch to me at slip. It was straightforward, but sharp, coming firmly at a good height just to my right, and I took it comfortably. But easy or not it was several minutes before my heart resumed its normal pace. It would have been on my conscience for the rest of my days had I dropped that catch on the day Fred Trueman hi-jacked the England bowling.

As it happened, of course, Trueman *was* chosen for the first two Test matches against New Zealand the following summer and, in the end, raised his haul of Test wickets to 307. But we were not to know that at the time. At the moment when he grabbed the ball from Dexter on that Saturday morning at the Oval he looked a spent force and I think it quite possible that, had he not overheard the captain's remark to me and reacted mutinously as he did, he might never have bowled in a Test match again. On such small turns of fate do great things happen.

From *MCC – The Autobiography of a Cricketer* by Colin Cowdrey
(Hodder and Stoughton, London, 1976).

The Wit and Wisdom of F.S.T.

I always said that if you were a cricket genius and came from the North you might play for England, but if you were good and came from the South it was a certainty. Many players picked for England in my time just weren't good enough to make the Yorkshire side.

I calculate that I missed at least thirty Tests because the MCC never stopped looking for an excuse to drop me.

My stock reply to any fielder apologizing for dropping a catch was, 'Don't worry, son – you didn't drop it very far. About eighteen inches, I'd say.'

Occasionally I was moved to a little sarcasm if a man kept on missing chances off my bowling, like the Reverend David Sheppard in Australia. I did tell him once to pretend it was Sunday and keep his hands together. And there was another, more celebrated occasion when a well-known England player not only dropped a vital catch off a batsman I'd been trying unsuccessfully to remove all day but let the ball go through his open legs for a four. When he apologized, adding that it wouldn't have been as bad if only he had kept his legs together, I made a crack which can only be repeated at stag nights.

From *Ball of Fire – An Autobiography* by Fred Trueman
(J. M. Dent, London, 1976).

The First Floodlit Cricket – London, August 1952

Andrew Ward

Who'd have thought it – floodlit cricket a quarter of a century before the Packer Circus?

F.S.T.

In the daytime Middlesex were skittled for 77 by Surrey. In the evening, in aid of Jack Young's benefit, they took a team to Highbury football stadium to play a team of Arsenal footballers – at cricket. The novelty of the game was the use of floodlights, used on occasions in the early days of cricket. A crowd of 8,000 turned up, while millions saw the last part of the action on television.

Instead of sight-screens there were goal-posts, while the centre-circle was partly covered by a black matting wicket. The rectangular shape of Highbury's football pitch necessitated short on and off boundaries, but fair-sized straight boundaries. The Bedser twins acted as umpires, the Compton brothers were the two captains, and the crowd knew they were in for a strange, entertaining evening when the Middlesex team of 13 players, having lost the toss, came out of the tunnel kicking footballs.

Taking advantage of the short boundaries, Arsenal rattled up an all-out score of 189, made in little more than an hour. Colin Grimshaw made 65, Freddie Cox scored 21 and big centre-forward Cliff Holton scored more easily than he usually did at Highbury. Les Compton, playing for Arsenal though he had an option on either team, mixed sports easily when he shoulder-charged Bill Edrich, the Middlesex fielder, in order to ensure a safer single.

The Arsenal innings ended in gloomy conditions. When the floodlights were switched on, the crowd cheered. The tannoy announcer then communicated one of the strangest messages heard at a cricket ground: 'Keep your eye on the ball. When you see it coming, keep low. The batsmen will try to keep it down, but they can't promise.'

To make the spectators' task easier, the ball was white, constantly replaced when the paint chipped off. The cricketers said later that they had no trouble spotting the ball.

Bill Edrich scored 70, but Middlesex collapsed. At 187 for nine, they needed three to win with three wickets to fall, remembering that this was a 13-a-side game. At this critical point, out came Jack Young, the beneficiary, a bowler who would take 137 wickets that season despite a troublesome knee injury. Young came to the wicket wearing a miner's helmet and lamp. Middlesex scored the required runs, and were allowed to bat on until they were all out.

The floodlighting experiment received a good press, but there was little likelihood that it would enjoy the same popularity in cricket as it did in football towards the end of the 1950s. There were various cricketing experiments with luminous stumps in South Africa and lighting for schoolboys in Australia, but it was not until the late 1970s that the idea of floodlit cricket games was resurrected.

ARSENAL 189 all out.

MIDDLESEX 237 all out.

From *Cricket's Strangest Matches* by Andrew Ward
(Robson Books, London, 1990).

When The Umpire Called 'No Apple' and Greg Chappell Bent the Rules

Dennis Lillee

In 1972 against Leicestershire, I came up against my friend and West Australian team-mate Graham McKenzie. As planned beforehand, when 'Garth' came to the crease I gave him a big bouncer and his antics when he ducked for cover got a few laughs from the crowd at Grace Road. But a couple of balls later as I reached the top of my mark I noticed a tennis ball rolling on to the ground from a knock-up game between some kids. I veered out, bent down as if to do up my bootlaces and picked the tennis ball up, then slipped the cricket ball into my pocket and took off to bowl the tennis ball to Garth.

It was reasonably well pitched up, but it took off sharply and ballooned over Garth's head, frightening ten months growth out of him and the wicketkeeper. Way down at fine leg, Bob Massie thought I'd bowled the red cover off the ball and just the white innards went down to the batsman ... at slip John Inverarity thought the ball had gone so fast it had turned white hot! And, by freak coincidence, an amateur photographer at the ground captured the moment and my tennis ball delivery made the national Press. Garth gave a sort of sheepish grin and obviously stored it away in his memory box. A few years later in a double-wicket competition back home in Perth he brought out a tennis ball and gave me some of my own back. It certainly does come as a shock.

I must admit I wasn't beyond having a bit of a lark in some of the County games. A bit later in the tour, when we played Sussex at Hove, I spied a large, shiny red apple on the lunch table and pocketed it. The apple went out with me and I did the switch for the first ball after lunch. It landed on a good line and length, but broke up on hitting the hard turf. One piece hit the stunned Sussex batsman on the pad dead in front, while another careered on to hit the stumps. An international incident was avoided when a sharp-witted umpire threw out his right arm and called 'No apple!'

*   *   *

Greg Chappell was involved in a major incident which did little to cement relationships between Australia and New Zealand. Going into the last over of the game, to be bowled by Trevor Chappell, New Zealand needed 11 runs to win the match. They'd scored 5 off the first 5 balls, so (barring a wide or a no-ball) they had to score a six off the final delivery. I remember thinking, 'Oh well, set them as far and wide as you can, bowl him a yorker and let him try.'

On the wide expanses of the MCG and with a new batsman, tail-ender Brian McKechnie, the odds were thousands to one to win. Then I saw Greg and Trevor talking and I thought. 'That's what he'll be telling his brother to do ... throw it right up in the slot, close to his legs, or something like that.' But next I saw Greg talking to the umpire, then the umpire talking to McKechnie and I wondered what was going on.

All of a sudden I realized as I saw Trevor walk up to the crease that he was going to bowl the final ball underarm. I thought, 'Heck, there's going to be a bit of an uproar about this.' But it was within the rules and I could see why Greg was doing it ... we were very tired and here was a chance to guarantee that the end of the one-day series was one game closer for Australia. If the Kiwis had won that game it would have meant having to go one extra game to win the series before dashing back to Melbourne for the final Test against India. Greg had given so much to the side that summer; batting, bowling and leading the team superbly. I could see what was going through his mind and I felt for him, I really did.

On reflection Greg realized that what he'd done was morally wrong and he took steps to put the matter right. I backed his decision at the time and if he'd asked me to be the one to bowl the ball I would have. Mind you, I would have tried awfully hard to convince him that I could have bowled a ball that couldn't have been hit for six. If he'd still instructed me to bowl underarm, then I would have. Straight after the game there was a real stir brewing and Greg and I decided to slip off up to Sydney that night, rather than wait and go up with the other guys the following day.

Greg said to me, 'Could be a good idea to get out of that hotel ... could be a few bombings tonight!' So off we went with the Sydney-based players, who wanted to have the night at home. One of them was Doug Walters, who was overheard saying to another (just loud enough for Greg to hear), 'You know, pal, there's only one thing that worries me about that game.' Came the reply, 'Yes, what's that?' Said Doug with a smirk, 'When I was a kid I was always told the game's not over until the last ball's *bowled*!'

The media really went to town, calling for Greg's blood, and even the two countries' Prime Ministers had their crack. But it gradually simmered down and by the time the next final game began two days later the crowd were back on Greg's side and there were no real problems. I thought the New Zealand players did their bit in playing it down, too. There were a few banners at the ground – one saying 'Greg ... your underarm stinks!' perhaps summed it all up best – and the game was uneventful as we strolled to victory and won the trophy for the first time. I suppose when it's all boiled down, the rules were to blame for what happened. Now the rules have been changed and there can be no repeat performance of an underarm delivery in an international one-day game.

From *Lillee, My Life in Cricket* by Dennis Lillee
(Methuen, London, 1982).

Famous Cricket Fiascos

Stephen Winkworth

The first streaker

The year 1975 was one of the first of the long hot summers, England were playing Australia, and even in the Long Room at Lord's there was a loosening of ties and removal of jackets. But no one was prepared for the next event – Lord's first streaker. He wore nothing but plimsolls and socks and he streaked towards the grandstand before turning right, then running towards the Nursery End and down the pitch, neatly straddling both steps of stumps. Alan Knott, batting at the time, said it was the first time he had ever seen two balls coming at him down the pitch. Soon after, in December 1975 when Australia were playing the West Indies, another streaker performed the same stump-straddling feat.

Birdie Shots at Cricket

The Lord's cricket museum contains the stuffed remains of a sparrow mounted on the ball which killed it when Cambridge University were playing MCC.

An Adelaide seagull altered cricket records when Keith Stackpole, playing for Australia, glanced a ball to leg which the seagull 'fielded' at the expense of a broken leg and saved two runs. It survived, was treated for the break and then wisely flew off, never to field again.

Gover over and out

Every cricketer who has toured India knows about Indian tummy – but few have shown more spectacular symptoms of it than fast-bowler Alf Gover during a tour under the captaincy of Lord Tennyson.

Alf had a magnificent run-up, arms going like the pistons of some fine old steam engine – but on this occasion he failed to deliver the ball, running past the wicket at his end, past the startled batsman at the other end, on to the boundary, up the pavilion steps and so, as he hoped, to the nearest loo. 'Did you make it Alf?' they asked him when later the ball was prised from his hand. He had not.

The longest ball

In July 1876 while batting for South Versus North at Hull, W. G. Grace hit a ball which landed in a railway truck and was then carried all the way to Leeds, thirty-seven miles away.

From *Famous Sporting Fiascos* by Stephen Winkworth
(Bodley Head, London, 1982).

Perfect Training for Life's Disappointment

Ernest Raymond

Ernest Raymond's First War novel *Tell England* had an astonishing best-seller success in the twenties – but only after an agonizing wait of many months during which it was rejected by thirteen publishers. Raymond, a young curate at Brighton, whiled away the frustrating delay by watching cricket.

P.G.

Hove Cricket Ground was nearer to me than Lord's or the Oval, and I was often there – indeed many clerical collars would be dotted about the Pavilion, such persons being among the few who could steal week-days off – and there were times when I sat there and wondered if watching first-class cricket wasn't the perfect training for accepting disappointment after disappointment, and adjusting thereto, as is so often required of us during our journey through life. One sat there hoping that every next ball would produce an excitement, but it didn't – and again it didn't – and again – and at length one knew, with arms folded and mouth yawning, that one was learning patience and stoicism and all the long littleness of life; *hoping* still of course, but no longer *expecting*. On the contrary, accepting the overwhelming probability that ball after ball would produce only disappointment through the long dreamy afternoon.

From *The Story of My Days* by Ernest Raymond
(Cassells, London, 1968).

T.B.W. – Tight Before Wicket

Neville Cardus

Our Sutcliffe's and Hammonds, with their tailors obviously in Savile Row, have taken us far far beyond the echo of Billy Barnes and his rough horny-handed company of paid cricketers of the 'eighties and 'nineties – savages born too soon to benefit from Mr Arnold Forster's Acts of Education. It was Billy Barnes who turned up late at Lord's when Nottingham were playing Middlesex; he was more than tipsy; but to prevent scandal – for he was a famous man and beloved by the crowds – his captain sent him in as usual, first wicket down. And Billy scored a hundred and more in two hours, banging the ball everywhere, powerful, safe, magnificent. Still, discipline is discipline; behaviour must be seen to, so when the Nottinghamshire captain returned to headquarters at Trent Bridge he felt it was his bounden duty to report Barnes to his Committee, composed mainly of Midland lords, squires and county notables. Barnes was called before them and solemnly reprimanded. He had disgraced Nottinghamshire cricket – at Lord's, too. Billy listened patiently, and when they had finished, he spoke:

'Well, your lordships, Ah can only say Ah'm sorry, reight sorry, that Ah am. But, beggin' your lordships' pardons, it strikes me as bein' like this, beggin' your lordships' pardons – if Ah can go down to Lord's and get drunk and mek a century 'fore lunch, then Ah thinks it ud pay t'Notts Committee to get mi drunk afore every match – beggin' your lordships' pardon, of course.'

The modern professional cricketer does not get drunk at Lord's or often get a century there, or anywhere else, before lunch.

From *Autobiography* by Neville Cardus
(Hamish Hamilton, London, 1984).

Compo l.b.w. – Umpire C. Short.

Brian Johnston is in his 45th season in the commentary box in 1990. After all that practice no one tells a cricketing yarn better than Jonners. First time he saw Compers (Denis Compton to you and me) the then eighteen-year-old was last out l.b.w. for only 14. 'That wasn't out,' said his partner Gubby Allen to umpire Bestwick.

'I know he wasn't Mr Allen,' replied Bestwick, 'but I am dying to have a wee.'

Wales for Gloucester

The only county to have a Princess for a patron is Gloucester – with Princess Diana.

14

THINGS AIN'T WHAT THEY USED TO BE

Lloyds, Lillees – Products of the Permissive Society

John Arlott

Whither cricket in the future? That great sage of the game John Arlott, writing in 1985, had already seen most of the changes to the modern game. Now the West Indies have yet again demonstrated that the routine of unbroken pace is unbeatable, other countries will feel driven to adopt it too. Then the risk is that Test cricket will become a slow, monotonous and certainly dangerous game of short-pitched intimidatory bowling with a deplorable over rate down to twelve or less per hour. So how can we prevent the international game descending to these depths?

'The International Cricket Council will have to legislate against four fast bowlers in a side,' declares Tony Lewis, the former England captain and now chairman of Glamorgan. 'The sight of batsmen being hit, bones being cracked and hands being split no longer has the fascination of a joust between two men. It is more like putting a man against the wall and four others stoning him.'

Robin Marlar said: 'The fact is that batsmen who stay at the wicket longest against short-pitched West Indian bowling are bound to be hurt. That is not a matter of luck but of deliberate policy.'

In my view there must be fines for slow over rates – say 3 runs for every over by which the fielding side falls short of 96 overs in a full six hours play. At least spin will then get a chance to play a role when the over rate has fallen behind the clock. Umpires must enforce law 42 on intimidatory bowling. There is also a case for limiting bouncers to one or two an over. Can it be right that a prime aim is to maim a good player so that he loses the will or the ability to stay in? In other sports (apart from boxing) you get sent off for deliberately trying to hurt a man. No-one should be allowed to bowl bouncers at ill-equipped tail-enders. When I was bowling nobody had to tell me that. Indeed I more than once refused point blank to bowl a bouncer at a tail-ender.

F.S.T.

February 1985. If, at my first Test match, fifty-nine years ago, I could have looked forward to cricket in 1985, I should have been staggered. Now, at seventy-one, looking back on the game then and as it is now, I am not the least bit surprised.

Life changes, the world changes, and, as those who grow near to it understand, cricket is pre-eminently the game of change.

It is not instantly obvious that a print of an eighteenth-century match played on the bare down at Hambledon – with underarm bowling; curved bats, two-stump wickets; players wearing velvet jockey caps, nankeen breeches and buckle shoes – is the same as the game now played in vast stadia by men hurling bouncers at one another with straight bats and three stumps and in helmets and light-weight boots.

Yet the same they are: unmistakably so; and we can trace every phase of the development – steady development – that took the game from that to this.

Cricket, though we do not always realize it in youth, truly reflects the society in which it is played. The reason for this mirroring probably lies in the length of matches: not the hasty hour and a half of a football match, but five or six days; even at club level, five or six hours, so that the players change together, spend their time when not batting or fielding together, eat together and generally drink together afterwards. In other words, cricket fits into their life pattern and, therefore, reflects it.

Not only were those Hambledon players as unmistakably Georgian as their modern counterparts are the product of a permissive society; but the cricket of different countries reflects national characteristics – as is apparent to anyone observing the differences between India and Pakistan at play.

Such ideas, though, were remote from – even beyond – a twelve-year-old boy going to the first Test match of his life, at The Oval in 1926. A Test match then was a rare occasion. Before that England–Australia series began, in June 1926, no country had played a Test since the same two countries met in Sydney in March 1925. After it ended, in August 1926, no country played a representative game until South Africa and England at Johannesburg in December 1927. By way of contrast, between September 1983 and April 1984, twenty-eight Tests were played; and, in its home season of 1979–80, India alone played eighteen home Tests.

Even the 1926 Oval scoreboard would seem strange today; amateurs were accorded the title Mr, but professionals were not; just as, in those days, gentlemen addressed their grooms – as Sir Pelham Warner addressed professional cricketers – by their surnames.

There they were, the cricket idols, their brilliantined short-back-and-sides hair, topped by caps with peaks so narrow that they accorded virtually no protection against the sun. Some of the aristocrats of the game played in trilby hats, like Lord

Hawke (who also affected butterfly collars). Others habitually paraded the ground in straw boaters.

The scorecard reads like a match played on the Elysian Fields: Jack Gregory, Charlie Macartney, Bill Woodfull, Warren Bardsley, Bill Ponsford, Herbie Collins, Arthur Mailey and Clarrie Grimmett were on the Australian side; England had Jack Hobbs, Herbert Sutcliffe, Frank Woolley (completing an unbroken run of fifty-two Tests since 1909), Wilfred Rhodes (recalled at forty-nine), Patsy Hendren, Maurice Tate, Harold Larwood, Bert Strudwick, Percy Chapman.

The match was to be played to a finish to decide the rubber. In the event, although interrupted by rain and slowed by a difficult wicket, it was over in less than four days.

The details are salutary for those accustomed to present day standards. In $21\frac{3}{4}$ hours, two fast, two fast-medium and six slow bowlers sent down 482 overs (about 22 an hour); forty wickets fell and 1143 runs were scored (52 an hour). At the end the decorous, dark-clad crowd (some 20,000) moved in orderly fashion to the front of the pavilion and gave cheers for both sides; the captains uttered a few formal words; the spectators gave another round of cheers and then made their way home.

A few boys lingered for autographs; but did not press for them as the Australians went to their charabanc and the English players – except the amateurs who took taxis – made their way to the underground station or buses. They could not afford motor cars on professional cricketers' wages.

The age of stardom was approaching, but had not yet fully dawned. Jack Hobbs had already recommended a specific make of fountain pen, and advocated teetotalism – 'Alcohol dims the eye' – but when, having beaten W. G. Grace's record of 124 centuries, he was offered several hundred pounds merely to be introduced from the stage of the London Coliseum, he refused in some alarm.

The inter-war period, of course, saw the high points of the careers of three of the greatest of all batsmen, Jack Hobbs, Don Bradman and Walter Hammond (W. G. Grace must have been the other) as well as Patsy Hendren, Philip Mead, Frank Woolley and Herbert Sutcliffe, all of whom made over 140 centuries. It was, too, the high point of batting records, first pointed by Bill Ponsford and then dominated by 'The Don'.

This was transformation. Jack Hobbs, whose ability has never been questioned, was little concerned with records. 'How many hundreds did Jack make?' asked Wilfred Rhodes one day. 'A hundred and ninety seven.' 'Well ah can tell thee, if he hadn't given it away so often when he had made 60 or 70, it could have been 297 – or (with a chuckle) 300.'

There can be no doubt – because it is the pattern of cricket – that this challenge by batsmen led first to the fast leg theory known as 'bodyline' – and then to defensive bowling.

Warwick Armstrong, bowling leg-rollers from round the wicket, had checked fast-scoring batsmen as long before as 1911–12. The regular pattern of unambitious bowling to restrictive fields had yet to come. Bowlers used habitually to attack. Indeed, when, at Headingley in 1930, Australia's score during the Bradman–Kippax stand stood at 400 for two, that fast-medium eternal optimist Maurice Tate was still bowling with two slips, a gully and a short-leg.

England first – at Melbourne in 1932–3 – introduced the pattern of unbroken fast bowling with Harold Larwood, Bill Voce, Gubby Allen, Bill Bowes, plus the fast-medium of Hammond. It remained, though, for the West Indies to introduce a routine of unbroken pace (at a deplorable over-rate). Clive Lloyd explained, blandly enough, that, given such a weapon as his pace posse, a captain would be stupid not to employ it; and that, if it contained an element of intimidation, it was the duty of the umpires to curb it.

Fiery pace had already proved the decisive factor in the wearing of protective helmets by batsmen; and, in many ways, the eclipse of attacking spin – or at least finger-spin bowling. That lately has required qualification. When, in the recent fifth Test at Sydney, the wrist spin of Bob Holland and the orthodox left-arm of Murray Bennett exposed, for the second time, a weakness of West Indian batsmen against the turning ball, the rest of the world must have scented hope. No one anywhere can expect that the magnificent sequence of West Indian pace will dry up. On the other hand, it must be possible that their batsmen will continue to be vulnerable to spin until, perhaps, they once more produce a Ramadhin and a Valentine in sheer defence against another Grimmett and O'Reilly.

Many of the changes in the game have crept up on it almost unnoticed. Gradually bowlers became more pragmatic. The one-day game proved conclusive; in some ways violently so. It began, at county level in England, out of sheer economic necessity. The county game was going broke; it needed to draw in those casual spectators who spent Sunday afternoons watching county benefit matches. Soon came the Nat West knock-out trophy in 1963; the John Player (Sunday) League in 1969; and finally, the Benson and Hedges league/knock-out Cup in 1972. The entry of the Packer organization into the international game meant that the over-limit game had come to stay. That was visibly apparent in the horrid coloured garbs foisted on the players; which argued an acceptance of many new values. The over-limit game, though, produced other effects: valuable financially but, most profoundly, damaging technically on English cricket; least in the West Indian game.

Primarily, and with immense benefit to the world game, as demonstrated first by Lancashire under Jack Bond in the early days of the English knock-out competition, it showed that raised standards of fielding could prove conclusive.

Absolute peaks of catching and, above all, of ground fielding were soon demanded in all quarters. Australian and the best of West Indian fielding had always been of high quality. English fielding had not. Indeed, the giants of the English game – men like Hobbs, Woolley, Mead and Rhodes – could never have continued to play into their fifties if such high fielding standards had been demanded of them. In their day it was possible to 'hide' men in the field; the one-day game ended that.

Standards in the field had already been lifted before, and more rapidly after, the Second World War. As Philip Mead, maker of 153 centuries, remarked, in his blindness, after asking the precise placing of Cliff Gladwin's leg-side field: 'Well, that would have cost me a few hundred runs a year; my old leg-glance wouldn't have been much use.'

The exploitation of close catching, especially by Glamorgan which effectively won the County Championship of 1948 through its ability in that direction, was soon taken up throughout the world game. The furious ground fielding performance, however, was almost purely a product of the over-limit game. During the 1920s, Bertie Oldfield and Bert Strudwick could keep wicket at Test level virtually unruffled. George Duckworth, though, began, and the rest of the world, force put, followed, the salmon-leap take and the catch to lift wicket-keeping to new heights – or perhaps widths is a more fitting word.

Whether the employment of plug-away, short-of-a-length defensive bowling is a gain is questionable. The value of flat, speeded-up 'slow' bowling is even more doubtful. The record, for the English Sunday League, of the permitted eight overs for no runs, is held by Brian Langford, the Somerset off-spinner.

One fact beyond question is that, in England especially, the over-limit game has given rise to bad batting habits: the taking of unorthodox and – by Test standards – uneconomic risks. That has undoubtedly disturbed the foundations of the country's batting at three-day and five-day level. The performance of the Australian, Pakistani and, above all, West Indian Test batting has been less affected.

Apart from the mechanics of the game, the seventy-year-old spectator notes with some grief a steep decline in manners. This is the age of Dennis Lillee and John McEnroe; not only of those two persons, but of those who support them. Sheer human good sense will eventually rectify that. In the politics of the game, the shift of power from the establishment of the game to the players is historic. The Cricketers' Association came coolly and acceptedly to power in England, the formerly militant Players' Association more rapidly, but equally effectively, in Australia, where the board of control was routed by Packer. The scars are slowly – if only superficially – being healed.

Financially, cricketers are more fairly rewarded for their skills and efforts than ever before. Still some leading players earn more from endorsing commercial products than from playing cricket; but that is simply a reflection of the world in which we live. Some of the problems of the future are clear to foresee. If other sports – especially the various football codes – pay more than cricket, they will syphon off much talent from the game. If the staggering proliferation of Test matches and, even more, of international knock-out play continues, the value of both will be debased.

In the past, however, it has not only reflected but always, within itself, resolved the problems of its period.

From *The Essential John Arlott – Forty Years of Classic Writing* ed. David Rayner Allen
(Collins Willow, London, 1989).